MW01087265

Black Linguistics

"This collection is one more step on the road toward the decolonization of Black languages and Black thought."

Ngũgĩ wa Thiong' o, University of California, Irvine, USA

Enslavement, forced migration, wars, and colonization have led to the global dispersal of Black communities and to the fragmentation of common experiences. These sociohistorical forces have impacted on language research and issues in Black communities throughout the world.

This groundbreaking collection reorders the elitist and colonial elements of language studies by drawing together the multiple perspectives of Black language researchers. In so doing, the book recognizes and formalizes the existence of "Black Linguistics" and highlights the contributions of Black language researchers in Africa and the Americas.

Written exclusively by Black scholars on behalf of (and occasionally in collaboration with) local communities, the book looks at commonalities and differences among Black speech communities in Africa and the Diaspora. Topics include:

- linguistic profiling in the US
- language issues in Southern Africa and Francophone West Africa
- the language of the Rastafari in Jamaica
- language and society in Black America and the Caribbean

This is essential reading for anyone with an interest in the linguistic implications of (neo)imperialism and enslavement.

Contributors: Hassana Alidou, H. Samy Alim, Arnetha F. Ball, John Baugh, Awad El Karim M. Ibrahim, Sinfree Makoni, Nkhelebeni Phaswana, Velma Pollard, Zaline M. Roy-Campbell, Donald Winford. Foreword by Ngũgĩ wa Thiong' o.

Editors: **Sinfree Makoni** is Associate Professor in Linguistics and Applied Language Studies at The Pennsylvania State University. **Geneva Smitherman** is University Distinguished Professor of English at Michigan State University. **Arnetha F. Ball** is Associate Professor of Education at Stanford University. **Arthur K. Spears**, a linguist and anthropologist, is Professor and Chair at the City University of New York.

BLACK LINGUISTICS

Language, society, and politics in Africa and the Americas

Edited by Sinfree Makoni, Geneva Smitherman,
Arnetha F. Ball, and Arthur K. Spears

Foreword by Ngũgĩ wa Thiong' o

Routledge
Taylor & Francis Group

LONDON AND NEW YORK

First published 2003
by Routledge
2 Park Square, Milton Park, Abingdon, Oxon, OX14 4RN

Simultaneously published in the USA and Canada
by Routledge
711 Third Ave, New York, NY 10017

Routledge is an imprint of the Taylor & Francis Group

© 2003 Sinfree Makoni, Geneva Smitherman, Arnetha F. Ball,
and Arthur K. Spears for selection and editorial matter; individual
contributors for their contribution

Typeset in Baskerville by The Running Head Limited, Cambridge

British Library Cataloguing in Publication Data
A catalogue record for this book is available from the British Library

Library of Congress Cataloging in Publication Data
A catalog record for this book has been requested

ISBN 0-415-26137-6 (hbk)
ISBN 0-415-26138-4 (pbk)

To our forebearer, Mark Hanna Watkins, Linguistic Anthropologist, and to Uncle I.J. Makoni Sr, for his moral and material support throughout Sinfree's academic career.

Contents

CONTENTS

Figures and table

Foreword

Decolonizing scholarship of Black languages

When scholars and writers in African languages met in Asmara, Eritrea in 2000 at the historic conference *Against All Odds*, they issued the Asmara Declaration in which they called upon African languages to take the duty, the responsibility, and the challenge of speaking for the Continent. This was also a call for Black scholars to take on the duty and the challenge of researching and expanding the possibilities inherent in African languages and the varieties of Black languages they have generated around the globe over the years. Bringing into one volume studies of Black languages by Black speakers, this book is very much in tune with that call, especially in the aim of celebrating and creating space for knowledge about Black languages. Some of these languages bear a variety of names—Ebonics, African American Language, Patwa, Creole, Kreyol, Haitian, Nation Languages—but they clearly have roots in the syntax and rhythm of speech of Continental African languages.

Remarkably, these languages have developed despite all the odds set against them by the historical experience of the plantation, the colony, and the neo-colony. This in itself is a great act of resistance and creative survival. Languages meant to die have simply refused to die. Languages pushed to the periphery have refused to stay on the periphery. But their survival has not been without the trauma of the great divide between the majority of Black people who speak and use the languages to express their everyday needs and conception of the universe, and the Black educated elite who distance themselves from these languages, often taking this distance, consciously or unconsciously, as a measure of their advancement in the modern world. Research by illustrious sons and daughters of the speakers of these languages ends up encased in languages furthest removed from Black languages. The result has been a weakening of the development of Black languages as adequate vehicles for knowledge in the arts, the sciences, and technology. In my book, *Decolonizing the Mind*, I have described this phenomenon as one of creating societies and nations of bodiless heads and headless bodies, and this is what all structures of domination hope to generate among the dominated.

It is not that Black languages are incapable of expressing the modern universe but there have to be workers in ideas who are expanding the possibilities of those languages in that and other directions. The present collection, with its wide-ranging issues from ideology to the practice and politics of language, is an important contribution toward narrowing the divide. Between them, the contributors have already published many papers and books on different aspects of Black speech, and they thus bring to this volume knowledge gained from years of research and reflections from a variety of regional, cultural, and individual vantages. They, to use Smitherman's titles of her other books, are *Talkin' That Talk* to evaluate the status and scholarship of *Black Talk*. The volume should interest both the scholar and the general reader in what Black languages have to offer to the world.

A most significant aspect of this book for the future is the very fact that, in editing and contribution, it is collaborative by Continental and Diasporic Africans. All varieties of Black languages face similar problems and challenges, not the least being that of moving them from the margins of power to claim their space among the other languages of the earth. Collaboration between Black scholars on either side of the Atlantic and beyond is important. The editors readily acknowledge that all the contributions are in English for that is the linguistic means the scholars have in common. This position presents another challenge: the use of Black languages by Black scholars to theorize on Black languages. It also challenges all Black scholars to learn and encourage the learning of at least one Continental African language in addition to what they already have. Translation among Black languages and between Black languages as a whole and other languages will itself become a means of enabling dialogue and conversation among languages. In such a situation, English can be put to better and more creative use: to *enable and not disable*. So, hopefully, future collections like this one will be English translations from Black languages. In this way, decolonizing the use, study, and status of Black languages, which is one of the aims of this collection, becomes possible.

This collection is one more step on the road toward the decolonization of Black languages and Black thought.

Ngũgĩ wa Thiong' o
Director, International Center for Writing and Translation and Distinguished Professor of English and Comparative Literature
University of California, Irvine
July 28, 2002

Introduction

Toward Black Linguistics

This book foregrounds contributions to research on Black languages by Black scholars in Africa and the Americas. It identifies key epistemological and political underpinnings of what we are here calling "Black Linguistics": a postcolonial scholarship that seeks to celebrate and create room for insurgent knowledge about Black languages. Black Linguistics is committed to studies of Black languages by Black speakers and to analyses of the sociopolitical consequences of varying conceptualizations of and research on Black languages. The overall goal of Black Linguistics is to expunge and reorder elitist and colonial elements within language studies. In so doing, Black Linguistic scholarship will contribute to a rethinking of the discipline. By challenging conventional constructs such as multilingualism, indigenous languages, linguistic human rights—and even the term "language" itself—Black Linguistics research will contribute to the formation of a new intellectual climate. Black Linguistics seeks to argue that a notion such as multilingualism, unless handled carefully, becomes a plural variant of monolingualism, that indigenous language is itself a product of colonial language ideology, and that it is unrealistic to imagine that social equality can be realized through linguistic human rights when notions about "language" and "rights" are both open to contestation. In this introductory essay, we examine the effects of a Black Linguistics perspective on the nature and type of research we conduct and the ways we communicate our work to our constituencies in and outside of the Academy.

Although this book is on Black languages, it has not been written in a Black language. As Black scholars from varying ethnolinguistic backgrounds, English is the language we have in common. The use of English in writing and communication between Black scholars is here a counter-hegemonic move: an attempt to challenge the hegemony of English by using English to create an intellectual counter-discourse in language studies (Pennycook 1994, 2001).

Within the study of Black languages by Black scholars, there are, of course multiple perspectives. The aim of this book is to bring these multiple voices together to explore the significance of their work for mainstream theoretical and applied language studies.

Despite the range and different types of Black social and linguistic experiences, numerous scholars, either explicitly or implicitly, speak to the commonalities of these phenomena in their research. Yet, no "Black Linguistics" perspective, *per se*, has emerged from the literature in the way in which Black scholars in other fields—e.g. psychology, sociology, literary criticism—have formulated well-established perspectives and paradigms. This book seeks to create opportunities to demonstrate similarities in the work we do, to relate our common shared experiences as scholars on/in the margins and to reflect on issues that consume Black language and communication scholars.

Most of our examples of Black languages in Africa are drawn from "sub-Saharan Africa." However, we do not subscribe to an elevation to epistemological status of this and other similarly divisive, demeaning, balkanizing categories, such as "Francophone," "Anglophone," or "Lusophone" Africa. While we use such terms for communicative convenience, we insist that these terms be used circumspectly because they are not particularly illuminating as conceptual tools. For example, on the one hand, "Anglophone," "Francophone," and "Luso-phone" Africa have a good deal of language, social practice, and ethnocultural history in common, clearly much more than is implied by the colonial distinctions "Anglophone," "Francophone," and "Lusophone" Africa. On the other hand, these conceptual categories conceal substantial sociolinguistic diversity within these regions of Africa.

The term "Black languages" covers languages of Africa and the Diaspora. In this book, however, we are restricting ourselves to the Western Hemispheric Diaspora. These languages and those in Africa are grouped together because the problems and possibilities associated with these languages are similar. All exist in social contexts of white supremacy and resource expropriation characteristic of neoimperialism and internalized oppression. In the various communities in which these languages are spoken, there exist similar problems and possibilities. The social settings of Black languages are typically different from those of other languages in the so-called "Third World." For example, in comparison to Latin America, Africa has a greater degree of multilingualism, and it is spread over wider areas and in key administrative centers—e.g. capitals, ports, and manufacturing and mining areas. In fact, African multilingualism exists among such a high percentage of the population that Fardon and Furniss suggest that "multilingualism is the African lingua franca" (1994: 4). Further, a majority of the people in Latin America speak some form of the official language—Spanish or Portuguese—and even those who don't have speaking proficiency have at least receptive competence (understanding) in Spanish or Portuguese. By contrast, only a minority of the various creole language populations have spoken proficiency in the official ex-colonial language (although many may have a high degree of receptive competence in the official language, for example English in Jamaica).

"Black languages" are generally construed to include pidgins and creoles in Africa and the Caribbean; African American (Vernacular) English in the US (also known as US Ebonics, African American Language, Black English); standardized and non-standardized African languages; and "vehicular" languages emerging in urban African centers (Childs 1999). The names of the languages which fall under the broad rubric of Black languages may at times be different from the names used by speakers of these languages. For example, speakers of US African American English refer to what they speak as "English"; the creole in Jamaica is referred to as "Patwa" by Jamaican speakers; in Haiti, it is "Kreyol," which is increasingly being replaced with "Haitian"/"Haitian language" (Devonish 1986; Winford, this volume). And in "sub-Saharan Africa," there are speakers who simply refer to what they speak as part of being human, "chivanhu." For example, in Southern Africa those who do not speak Shona are regarded as not speaking "chivanhu," the human language. In SiSwati, it will be said that "abatsefuli sintvu." In Zulu, it will be "abathethi isintu." In all cases what is being asserted is that the person(s) does not speak the human language. Rarely is the name of the language given.

It may come as a surprise to many that some speakers of Black languages do not have a specific name or label for their form of speech. However, languages without names are not an oddity. Naming languages is a type of consciousness, an artifact embedded in the consciousness of Western formal education. Communities with limited or very little formal Western education sometimes do not possess the type of consciousness of which language naming is a component (Romaine 1984). Naming, or more accurately namelessness, is not a criterion for excluding or categorizing a language as a "Black language." What is of central importance in Black Linguistics is that we describe and analyze the ways members of communities relate to their speech, so that we do not rely exclusively on outside analytical categories. Thus, if communities do not have distinct names for their languages, we take into consideration their "folk" terminology, rather than creating and superimposing categories and labels on their behalf, however convenient that might be for us intellectually. Our interest in taking into consideration the categories of language users arises from our concern for local-level perspectives. Further, in Black Linguistics we are acutely aware that even when a given language does have a name shared by linguists and members of the local communities, there may be vast differences in the conceptualizations of that language, in terms of where the linguistic boundaries are situated, the linguistic spaces within that language, and the social constructions of that language by its speakers (LePage and Tabouret-Keller 1985).

The naming and appropriation of languages is of crucial significance because of the conceptual complexity in the way in which language, ethnicity, and culture are compounded. The conceptual clustering of language, ethnicity, and culture has vast political significance. The injunction early on, by anthropological linguist Franz Boas, against incorrectly conflating language, culture, and race is important in dealing with Black languages. For example, the South African apartheid regime clustered the relationships between language, ethnicity, and culture in a very specific way such that the languages used by different groups

3

became "metonyms" (Cook 2002) for their rights, status, and privileges (or lack of privileges for the vast majority of the speakers).

There are two key themes in the languages we are analyzing. Irrespective of whether the languages are drawn from "sub-Saharan Africa," the Americas, the Caribbean, or elsewhere in the Diaspora, all are spoken and used largely by communities that were institutionally disadvantaged, at one time or another, by colonization, imperialism, and white supremacy. Indeed the formation of some of these languages was an active reaction to colonization and extreme forms of domination. Black languages in some of these contexts are a product of post-liberation whereby "new" urban speakers attempt to forge new identities, with their new languages functioning as anti- or counter-languages (LePage and Tabouret-Keller 1985). A very recent example is the adoption of US African American English by Sudanese youth in Canada who are imagined and have begun to construct themselves as "Black" in North America (see Ibrahim, this volume).

A book of this nature is now possible because of the substantial number of Black critical scholars working on Black languages, both as trained professional linguists and as native speakers in the Black communities where they are working *in, for*, and *with* Black languages. Several challenges relating to epistemological frameworks confront these scholars. The problem is well articulated by Skinner who writes:

> One of the major problems facing scholars and lay people of African origin is to be able to develop and use paradigms that are based on their experience. They must insist that if the paradigms are to be useful to them, they must be filtered through the African experience before being judged truly universal and not simply hegemonic.
>
> (Skinner 1999: 450)

Because of the increasing presence of Black scholars in language scholarship, language study can no longer be read as if it were a "whites only" preserve. This volume explores the implications and consequences of the "darkening" of language studies. It should be seen as the naming of a strand of language research, done by Black scholars on Black languages and written either fully or in part by these scholars.

The roots of Black Linguistics can be traced to a few monumental but institutionally marginalized works by scholars such as Devonish (1986), whose book is appropriately entitled *Language and Liberation*, and Williams (1975), whose edited volume *Ebonics: The True Language of Black Folks*, represented an interdisciplinary effort by Black scholars to treat Black language from a Black perspective. The emergence of a strand of Black language scholarship is not an anomaly. As mentioned above, there is a relatively robust tradition of Black research in areas such as psychology and anthropology (Harrison 1991a). What is different about language scholarship is that debates about the desirability of and necessity for such an approach have not (yet) emerged. One of the objectives of this volume is to generate such a debate, to force the issue onto the language scholarship agenda.

Because Black languages are used by people who have historically been colonized and who are socially disadvantaged, their languages have been and are often used as a source of discrimination against them (see Ball, Baugh, this volume). Black Linguistics has had to confront the legacy of colonization and continued oppression manifest in several forms in the social lives of Black people—notably, limited access to resources, power, and education through a race-based hierarchy.

To the extent that we can talk at present about a Black Linguistics, it involves four main principles:

1   membership in or life experience with the communities whose languages we research and analyze;
2   use of an ideological orientation designed to analyze and expose the workings of ideology in research *on*, *about*, and *for* Black languages;
3   race as a defining feature of our linguistic autobiographies as Black language scholars;
4   analysis of language as social practice with a keen eye/ear attuned to its sociohistory, changes and continuities in the "categories of thought," and the historiography of linguistic analyses of Black languages at different historical periods.

Membership/sociological affiliation

As Black scholars we are anthropologically members of or sociologically affiliated with the communities we are working in. Our research as Black scholars is on behalf of and in collaboration and consultation with local communities. We are seeking to impact positively on speakers of Black languages in these communities. We are therefore very much concerned about the relevance and application of our work. "The socially responsible researcher acknowledges his or her responsibility to individual participants and to his or her community. Social responsibility also precludes short sighted, self-aggrandizing research that does little more than imitate or perpetuate negative stereotypes" (Harris 1996: 30).

The impact of our work might range from raising awareness about the language basis of discriminatory practices and the disempowering nature of descriptions of language in mother tongue education in Africa, to the ways language abilities are used to exclude people. Our insider status impacts on different facets of what we do, ranging from the selection of topics to be investigated and our preferred methodologies to the analysis and dissemination of results. The selection of research topics originates in the proposition that Black Linguistics must contribute toward an understanding of the nature of oppression and strategies for conquering it, or at the very least for containing it. The selection of topics of intellectual inquiry in Black Linguistics is not a mere academic exercise. Rather, it is motivated by what the communities themselves feel is the key problem confronting them. The research topics are defined in collaboration between linguists, as "organic intellectuals" (Gramsci 1971, quoted in Dombrosky 1989: 330), and those directly affected by the "problem." For example, research on language and health in late life has traditionally focused on dementia and Alzheimer's disease. However, after conducting a series of focus group discussions with older persons from Black communities, it was clear to us that the concern of older African Americans was not dementia or Alzheimer's, but diabetes and its effect on language and cognition. The shift in focus from a preoccupation with Alzheimer's disease to diabetes research in older African Americans is an example of how our research agenda shifted to accommodate the perspectives of the communities. The shifts demonstrate the extent of our social sensitivity arising from feelings of social responsibility. Social sensitivity is also an excellent basis for good science. For example, it is increasingly being shown that a large majority of older people within ethnic minorities who subsequently get dementia have diabetes; thus diabetes is a high-risk factor for dementia.

Not only is the research topic defined in collaboration with the speakers directly affected, but also the research results are validated through the participation of the community. For example, in a research project on communication and health among speakers of African American (Vernacular) English, we ran a series of workshops and presented the data and results to the community as part of a postexperimental debriefing procedure. This has proven to be a powerful way of exploring the extent to which research interpretation resonates with the experiences of members of the communities in which the research was conducted.

Working within the paradigm of Black Linguistics, our role is clear: we are both professional linguists and members of the speech communities we work in. We are creole speakers, or speakers of Venda (a South African language), or African American Language speakers, and/or speakers of other Black languages. Because of our sense of social responsibility, we seek to bring our analytical expertise together with the social experiences of our communities. Our analysis benefits from and draws on our expertise as linguists and our insights as members of local speech communities. This dual role enables us metaphorically (to) "see out of more than one eye" (Harrison 1991b: 91), or to see more out of each eye, a welcome intellectual double vision.

Applying the notion of "double consciousness" (DuBois 1903), we argue in Black Linguistics that our double, or more accurately "multiple," consciousness arises from our professional membership in Western-dominated areas of study and anthropological membership in communities with histories and remnants of oppression. Multiple consciousness plays a key role in our struggle to develop a decolonized science of humankind in which language and communication sciences play a significant role. Concurring with Worsley (1984: 36–7), Harrison states:

> Multiple consciousness and vision are rooted in some combination and interpenetration of national, racial, sexual, or class oppression. This form of critical consciousness emerges from the tension between, on the one hand, membership in a Western society, a Western dominated profession, or a relatively privileged class or social category, and, on the other hand, belonging to or having an organic relationship with an oppressed social category or people . . . the conjuncture of multiple subaltern statuses and bases of Otherness, combined with the apparent irreconcilability between them and the ideals and normative expectations of the "free world" of capitalism, the American dream, or middle class privilege, may heighten and intensify our counter-hegemonic sensibilities, vision and understanding.
>
> (Harrison 1991b: 90)

Our double vision or multiple consciousness enables us to metaphorically code-switch into the living and lived experiences of our communities, hence providing us with access to particular forms of data which might be difficult for outsiders to access. Examples in this volume include Alim's research on the language of Hip Hop artists, Pollard's analysis of the language of Rasta music, and Ball's analysis of the voices of Black teachers in the US and South Africa. Because we can metaphorically code-switch into the lived and living experiences of the communities, we are "best positioned to provide insights that may escape scholars unfamiliar with the intricacies of local contexts" (Roy-Campbell, this volume). This metaphoric code-switching creates conditions for fruitful lines of communication between Black linguists and members of local communities, as illustrated, for example, in Baugh's research on linguistic profiling (see Baugh, this volume), in Spears's (1999a) work treating language within the larger framework of race and ideology, and in Smitherman's language activist work, e.g. in *King* (the 1977–9 "Black English" Federal court case, in which Black parents filed a lawsuit against the Ann Arbor School District for using the children's language as a basis for denying them their right to an equal education).

The advocacy work we are trying to describe here is not without potential problems, particularly when the positions we want to advocate conflict with deeply held views of our local community. Under such circumstances, if we cannot change the views and practices of the community to share our professional positions, our strategy should be to follow the lead of the community and to mitigate the potentially negative effects that may emanate from the community's decision. A striking example of a context in which a language policy position held by language activists conflicts with the community's position on language can be cited from South Africa, where language activists are experiencing resistance from local communities about the use of African languages as media of instruction for schoolchildren. The linguists are well aware of the long-established, voluminous research from around the globe about the advantages of mother tongue education. However, these South African communities have expressed an explicit preference for English as the language of education.

This "pressurizing for English" (as South Africans refer to it) is exerted perhaps more intensely in South Africa's Western Cape than in any of the country's other eight provinces. According to Pluddemann, the "pressurizing" has already begun by first grade (2000: 40). In some schools, even teachers may exert such pressure (although it is well documented that teachers encounter severe pedagogical difficulties when teaching through English, primarily because they are not fully proficient in English themselves). The pressurizing for English is not a "love" for English *per se*. Rather it reflects a sharp sensitivity to the social and economic disparities between schools. English-language schools receive more and better resources, and they have a higher level of professionally qualified teachers than African-language schools. Owing to the disparity in educational quality between African-language and English-medium schools, most advocates of African-language schools do not send their children to these schools! Because we are unlikely to change the deeply entrenched position of the communities on language in education, we should thus focus our attention on improving current teaching practices with English as the medium of instruction and on ways of reducing the educational disadvantage of students being taught in a foreign medium (Ferguson 2000). When there is a difference between our professional position on a language issue and the position of the community we work in, our strategy should be based on a "critical engagement with the wishes of the communities, their desires and histories, that is, a way of thinking that pushes one to question rather than to pontificate" (Pennycook 1998: 343).

That Black Linguistics cannot merely be an "academic" language exercise is neatly captured by Gordon when he writes:

> Intellectual production which is not instrumentalized through praxis has no liberating effect. The knowledge and truths unveiled by critical intellectuals in conjunction with the community must be assimilated by the people, turned into concrete strategies and ultimately into activities which move the collectivity towards liberation.
>
> (Gordon 1991: 155)

He further notes that activism moves the decolonizing of anthropology to an anthropology of liberation. Whether the issue is addressed explicitly or implicitly, liberation is foremost in the thinking and intellectual practices of Black Linguistics. It serves and promotes the interests of the oppressed (Gordon 1991) and seeks to contribute toward social liberation.

In the course of promoting the interests of the communities of Black-language speakers, Black Linguistics has the potential for advancing and enhancing the field of language studies. In our efforts to take the linguistic affairs of our own people into our own hands, we as intellectual activists, trained in the methods and theories of the human sciences, may also uncover, discover, recover concepts that end up generally advancing knowledge in the field. For example, Alim's research in Hip Hop has implications for notions about language variation and code-switching (see Alim, this volume). Vaughn-Cooke's (1987) theorizing about the need for time-depth studies of African American English as a counter to notions about its postmodern "divergence" from white varieties of American English resurrected theories about longitudinal data collection research. The work of linguists in the "Ebonics Movement," dating back to 1973, and the coining of the term "Ebonics" by Black psychologist Robert Williams, has led to a reexamination of the whole notion of what constitutes a "language" (see e.g. Blackshire-Belay1996; Smith 1998; Fasold 1999; Nehusi 2001; Palacas 2001). Similarly, in South Africa, the recent emergence of urban vehicular African languages is raising fundamental issues about the conceptualization of language (Cook 2002; Makoni, this volume).

Ideological orientation in Black Linguistics

Any intellectual enterprise is ideological (Joseph and Taylor 1990; Cameron *et al.* 1992; Blommaert 1999). Black Linguistics is, therefore, ideological. The fruitful line of inquiry to pursue in Black Linguistics is not whether Black Linguistics is ideological or not—that is taken for granted—but what type of ideological orientation is a useful line to pursue in Black Linguistics. Our preoccupation is with the conditions and purpose of the production of knowledge about Black languages. Interest in an analysis of the conditions under which knowledge of Black languages is produced is justifiable because of the wide range of scholars working on Black languages and the historiography of intellectual thought in the production of knowledge about these languages. For example, historically knowledge production within Creole Studies occurred during an era when speakers of the language were considered less than human. The early work on African languages was, by and large, carried out by white missionaries and linguists with limited expertise in the languages they were describing and inventing as part of empire building. Because of the less than ideal conditions under which some of the work on Black languages began, it is logical to raise questions about the current nature of the conditions under which knowledge of these languages is being produced.

Because of our ideological orientation, our analysis of language and language varieties becomes inseparable from the sociohistories which created them. For example, an analysis of the emergence of vehicular languages in urban Africa requires an understanding of the emergence of urban youth identities. The youth seek to deliberately distance themselves from rural identities seen as "backward," and to forge a new identity and create new languages which best define them.

An important aspect of the ideological orientation of Black Linguistics is its global and comparative perspective, unlike the tendency of much of the work done on Black languages which has been to focus on the social and linguistic phenomena of individual Black communities to the exclusion of Black experiences outside a given community—for example, work on US Ebonics that ignores creoles and African languages. Because of enslavement, slavery, wars, colonization, and the continuing migration *en masse* of Continental Africans to North America, there has been a global dispersal of Black communities. Black researchers have emerged from these communities with perspectives growing out of circumstances experienced in many societies around the world. These circumstances have led to the development of a research perspective that looks at local phenomena with global vision. The comparative thrust in Black Linguistics is consonant with that in other social science research which deals with aspects of Blackness in the Diaspora (Fredrickson 1999; also comparisons of the political and economic histories of Blacks in South Africa and the US, e.g. Walters 1993; Fredrickson 2001). Winford (this volume) provides such a linguistic perspective in his analysis of African American (Vernacular) English and Caribbean creoles. Other examples are analyses of language policies and provisions for higher education for Blacks in South Africa and the US (Smitherman 2000; Ball, this volume).

Race as a defining feature of Black Linguists

That race is not a scientific concept but socially constructed is well known. What is less well known is how this non-scientific construct impacts on our scientific work as Black researchers of Black languages. Current research by Ibrahim (1999, this volume) illustrates that even areas of linguistics such as language learning, which some scholars might feel is psychologically oriented, are not color blind. We work in communities in which color, and indeed variations in color, are perceived and endowed with social meanings (Harrison 1991c).

In Black Linguistics we explore the intellectual consequences that our identities, including those which we select and those which select us (those attributed to us), have on our academic research. We seek to examine the various ways in which our identities as scholars are implicated in our epistemologies, in the work we do, and in the research orientations we adopt. The central issue which we address in Black Linguistics is what *being Black*, or *becoming Black*, means in language scholarship. One critical thing that it means, as this volume demonstrates, is that the Black Linguistics perspective asks "fundamental-liberation oriented" questions and candidly seeks to provide language solutions to problems. In Africa and the Caribbean, particularly, language issues are central in the social lives of Black communities. More so than in the US and other "developed" countries, language in African and Caribbean communities is an integral part of the nature of statecraft and governance (Devonish 1986). Solutions to language problems in these communities vary depending on the nature and magnitude of the problem. For example, in some cases we argue for the appropriacy of linguae francae as media for education, while in other cases we call for extended use of standard languages and the establishment of common orthographies as possible solutions to the language-in-education problem.

Language as social practice

The general thrust in Black Linguistics is to conceive of language as social and communicative practice, conceptualized within a wider framework than formalistic theories of language. Contrary to Chomskyan linguistics, which treats grammar as neutral (e.g. Newmeyer 1986), in Black Linguistics language is conceived of as socially embedded. Grammatical patterns have to be deconstructed and understood within the social and political contexts in which they are used.

From the vantage point of Black language as social practice, our analyses of language and language varieties become inseparable from the communities and the sociohistories which created these languages and varieties. This mandates a perspective and an analytical framework that go beyond the now common methodologies and scholarly practices of quantitative sociolinguistics, which, like Chomskyan linguistics, tends to dichotomize language and speaker and to focus on the former, rather than both the former and the latter. Black Linguistics is keenly attuned to the fact that we are producing knowledge about both the creation (language) and the creator (Black people). It is thus imperative that our scholarship reflects the histories, social circumstances, political economies, aspirations—and voices—of the people whose language we study.

We bring this discussion to a close by stating that Black Linguistics is concerned not only with analysis but with why the analysts are doing the analysis; concerned not only with results, but with the impact of the dissemination of the results on audiences both in and outside of the Academy.

Overview of chapters

The chapters in this volume are divided into three main sections: ideological practices in research on Black languages; conceptualization and status of Black languages; and inclusion and exclusion through language.

Ideological practices in research on Black languages

The volume begins with Winford's chapter which analyzes the political and ideological thinking that shapes linguistic debates about African American (Vernacular) English (AAVE) and links AAVE to Caribbean creoles and African languages. One of the recurring and controversial debates about AAVE is its status. In some analyses of this particular Black language, it is conceptualized as a distinct language system with its own unique structural patterns, discourse, and rhetorical style. In other analyses, it is viewed as subordinate to Mainstream (White) American English. The debate about the status of AAVE, Winford argues, is not a purely linguistic one. In a mode consistent with the ideological orientation of Black Linguistics, Winford demonstrates that the debate is about history and the role of African Americans in shaping their own lives and destiny.

The chapters by Alim and Pollard might be said to demonstrate the operations of linguistic ideology in Black musical culture in the US and the Caribbean. Alim focuses on an analysis of Hip Hop language while Pollard analyzes the language of Rastafari and Reggae. Both scholars demonstrate the extent to which ordinary speakers are consciously in control of their language and manipulate its variability to achieve specific social and ideological goals.

Alim shows how Hip Hop artists consciously manipulate AAVE and the US language of wider communication ("standard English"). A central factor in his work is his contribution to our understanding of the relationship between identity, ideology, and Black languages. Although he presents descriptions of the linguistic characteristics of AAVE found in Hip Hop music, Alim's main focus is to illuminate how "street speech culture breathes" through an analysis of the linguistic sophistication of Hip Hop artists. His results demonstrate that these artists carefully manipulate the variability of linguistic forms as part of their identity and ideological bonding with the African American community in the US.

Using the specific situation of the language and history of Rastafari culture in Jamaica, Pollard focuses on "Dread Talk," also known as "I-ance," "I-yaric" and " Rasta Talk." It is a specific type of code, carefully crafted from the raw materials of English, the "principal lexifier of all language in Jamaica," to serve the objectives of the Rastafari as a cultural–religious group. The Rastafari regarded themselves as responsible for their own liberation, as articulated in the words of their visionary musical artist, the renowned Bob Marley: "Emancipate yourself from mental slavery/None but ourselves can free our minds" (1980). This emancipation was the chief objective of Dread Talk, a language created as a challenge to white domination which has now spread beyond Jamaica to the global community. Pollard analyzes the linguistic creativity characteristic of I-yaric and shows how semantic license and creativity are part of the Rastafari strategy of liberation and empowerment. Her work is important for demonstrating how speakers' sense of control over language manifests itself in the way speakers invent and invest new meanings in language.

Conceptualization and status of Black languages

Roy-Campbell's chapter draws on work that is largely, though not exclusively, by African scholars to demonstrate the legacy of colonial thinking in shaping language-in-education policies in East Africa. She shows how the continuing use of "ex-colonial" languages as media of instruction in education hinders learning and is also, to a large extent, a waste of resources—which resource-weakened African countries can ill afford. She illustrates that the continued use of "ex-colonial" languages in postcolonial societies benefits social classes who have greater access to these languages—therein perpetuating existing social and economic inequality. Some Southern African countries, notably Zimbabwe and South Africa, have made serious attempts to "develop" indigenous African languages so they can be effectively utilized as media of instruction. However, as Roy-Campbell demonstrates, the massive investment in the development of dictionaries and grammar books is not improving the literacy level of local populations. The important lesson we learn from Roy-Campbell's contribution is that language development as a strategy does not necessarily achieve people development. Her work has implications for issues about the conceptualization of speaker equality. Indeed linguistic equality is one thing, but social and economic equality is another.

Hassana Alidou analyzes language-in-education policies in three "ex"-French colonies, Niger, Mali, and Burkina Fasso, and shows how conceptualizations about language in education have evolved since the 1980s. According to Alidou, the continued use of French as medium of instruction in West African schools accentuates class differences between the urban middle and upper classes and the rural poor who constitute the majority in West African countries and who have a dramatic failure rate on national examinations. In foregrounding the social-class consequences of the medium of instruction in postcolonial societies, Alidou makes an important contribution because media of instruction debates have been silent on the social and economic impact of media of instruction. Significantly also, she raises the issue of teaching learning through indigenous language materials which have not been constructed with uniform orthographies and which do not speak to the local experiences of most West African language learners. Alidou outlines how models of language learning which are historically sensitive and contextually relevant might be constructed and argues against blindly following models from outside the African context.

Following Roy-Campbell's and Alidou's analyses of East and West Africa, the chapters by Phaswana and Makoni adopt divergent perspectives on language issues in Southern Africa, specifically South Africa with its Constitutional policy of eleven official languages. Phaswana's chapter investigates the extent to which South Africa's language policy is being affirmed by the South African national government. His research involves an analysis of data collected in a wide variety of ways—e.g. Parliamentary reports and other published documents, interviews with key elected officials, and systematic observation of Parliamentary sessions and subcommittee meetings. Phaswana concludes that:

1   in spite of the eleven-official-languages policy enshrined in the South African Constitution, English is the preferred language of the South African national government;
2   the government's doctrine of language equality is a disingenuous rhetorical move;
3   for the future of freedom and democracy in South Africa, Black linguists must help politicians rethink language issues in line with Black empowerment.

13

The chapter by Makoni argues that, paradoxically, the problems with the implementation of the South African eleven-official-languages policy should be welcomed instead of being perceived as the national government's unwillingness or inability to abide by its Constitutional obligation. The problem of implementability forces us to examine the conceptualizations of language underlying the national language policy. He contends that the policy is linguistically unimplementable because it constructs languages as bounded discrete entities, conceptualizations inconsistent with the social experiences of most users. Furthermore, Makoni argues, implementation of such a policy would only result in entrenching existing social and ethnic divisions inherited from the apartheid era, a situation which the current South African national government is seeking to reverse. In other words, the government cannot change South Africa's social, class, and ethnic landscape by using the very ways of conceptualizing social relationships which apartheid utilized in the first place. Makoni concludes that in order for societies in transition to contain history and effect change, they need to imagine new ways of conceptualizing problems rather than trying to solve problems using the very same conceptual apparatus which created the problems.

Inclusion and exclusion through language

This section is made up of chapters by Baugh, Ibrahim, and Ball. Each takes a different perspective and setting to address issues about social and economic access and exclusion. Baugh addresses issues about access and exclusion from the perspective of access to housing, Ibrahim confronts the issue from the perspective of identity politics in language learning, and Ball addresses the phenomenon from the perspective of discourse in education.

Developing the concept of "linguistic profiling," Baugh's work demonstrates how speech cues over the telephone can lead to racial identification and influence a person's access to apartment and housing rentals. In the US, sounding "Black" or "Latino" often results in denial, i.e. the applicant is told on the telephone that there are no vacancies. However, sounding "white" opens the housing "gate." The US national government and most local governments have laws making housing discrimination illegal, but the case has to be proven empirically. Reflecting the scholarly activism that is a tenet of Black Linguistics, Baugh makes his research and expertise available to fair housing organizations who utilize legal venues to assist Black and Latino victims of linguistic profiling and exclusion from access to housing.

Ibrahim's chapter describes the social and political processes involved in the learning of AAVE by African student refugees in Canada, who were learning English as a second language. His research involved observations, interviews, and social interaction with the students, most of them Sudanese, both in and outside of school. He demonstrates how the selection of (US) African American Language was central to these Sudanese youths' objective of learning to be

14

Black, an identity which they became aware of only after entering the North American discursive space. They became Black through language learning. For these Francophone African youth, living in Southwestern Ontario, Canada, Hip Hop was the dominant source for learning AAVE. At the same time, they held on to their African languages which, according to Ibrahim's research, were fundamental to the youths' articulation of a sense of nationality and to the "creation of safe spaces of comfort, bonding, and familiarity."

Ball's chapter focuses on language attitudes and classroom practices of teachers in the US and South Africa. A substantial number of Ball's teacher groups over the three-year period of her study were students of color who have historically struggled for access to quality education. Within this context, educational institutions have served as linguistic gate-keepers, guarding the routes to social mobility in countries around the globe. Ball shows that this practice is particularly evident in official and unofficial language policies embedded in classroom practices in the US and South Africa. Teachers operate with a body of assumptions and beliefs, which constitute a language ideology that reflects—or resists—the national language policy. Ball examines how teachers' ideologies can be changed through an innovative educational program. The notion of ethically responsible intervention is always important in Black Linguistics because of our overwhelming sense of social responsibility to the communities in which we work.

Taken as a whole, the chapters in this book, including this introductory chapter, reaffirm our call for an international conversation that will lead toward Black Linguistics.

References

Blackshire-Belay, C.A. (1996) "The location of Ebonics within the framework of the Africological paradigm," *Journal of Black Studies*, 27 (1): 5–23.

Blommaert, J. (ed.) (1999) *Language Ideological Debates*, Berlin: Mouton de Gruyter.

Cameron, D., Frazer, E., Harvey, P., Rampton, B., and Richardson, K. (1992) *Researching Language: Issues of Power and Method*, London: Routledge.

Childs, G. Tucker (1999) "The status of Isicamatho, a Nguni based urban variety of Soweto," in A. Spears and D. Winford (eds) *The Structure and Status of Pidgins and Creoles*, Amsterdam and Philadelphia, PA: John Benjamins, 341–70.

Cook, S. (2002) "Urban language in a rural setting: the case of Phokeng, South Africa," in G. Gmelch and W. Zenner (eds) *Urban Life Readings in the Anthropology of the City*, Prospect Heights, IL: Waveland Press, 106–13.

Devonish, H. (1986) *Language and Liberation: Creole Language Politics in the Caribbean*, London: Karia Press.

Dombrosky, R.S. (1989) *Antonio Gramsci*, Twayne Publishers.

DuBois, W.E.B. (1903) *The Souls of Black Folk*, New York: Dover.

Fardon, R. and Furniss, G. (1994) *African Languages, Development and the State*, London: Routledge.

Fasold, R.W. (2001) "Ebonic need not be English," in J.E. Alatis and A. Tan (eds)

Language in our Time: Bilingual Education and Official English, Ebonics and Standard English Immigration and the Unz Initiative (Georgetown University Round Table on Languages and Linguistics 1999), Washington, DC: Georgetown University Press, 262–80.

Ferguson, G. (2000) "The medium of instruction in African education: the role of the applied linguist," in S. Makoni and Nkonko Kamwangamalu (eds) *Language and Institutions in Africa*, Cape Town: Centre for Advanced Studies of African Society, 95–111.

Fredrickson, G. (1999) "Reform and revolution in America and South Africa freedom struggles," in D.C. Hine and J. McCleod (eds) *Crossing Boundaries*, Bloomington, IN: Indiana University Press, 71–87.

Gordon, E. (1991) "Anthropology as liberation," in F.V. Harrison (ed.) *Decolonizing Anthropology: Moving Further toward an Anthropology for Liberation*, Washington, DC: American Anthropological Association, 149–68.

Harris, J. (1996) "Issues in recruiting African American participants for research," in G.K. Alan, K.E. Pollock, and L. Joyce (eds) *Communication Disorders in African American Children: Research Assessment and Intervention*, London: Paul Brookes Publishing Company, 19–36.

Harrison, F.V. (1991a) "Anthropology as an agent of transformation. Introductory comments and queries," in F.V. Harrison (ed.) *Decolonizing Anthropology*, Washington, DC: American Anthropological Association, 1–15.

—— (ed.) (1991b) *Decolonizing Anthropology: Moving Further Toward an Anthropology for Liberation*, Washington, DC: American Anthropological Association.

—— (1999c) "Ethnography as politics," in F.V. Harrison (ed.) *Decolonizing Anthropology: Moving Further Toward an Anthropology for Liberation*, Washington, DC: Association of Black Anthropologists/American Anthropological Association, 88–110.

Ibrahim, A. (1999) "Becoming Black: Rap and Hip Hop, race, gender, identity and the politics of ESL," *TESOL Quarterly*, 33: 349–65.

Joseph, J.E. and Taylor, T.J. (1990) *Ideologies of Language*, New York: Routledge.

LePage and Tabouret-Keller, A. (1985) *Acts of Identity*, Cambridge: Cambridge University Press.

Marley, B. (1980) "Redemption Song," Bob Marley Music Ltd B.V.

Nehusi, Kimani S. (2001) "From Medew Netjer to Ebonics," in C. Crawford (ed.) *Ebonics and Language Education of African Ancestry Students*, New York: Sankofa World Publishers, 56–122.

Newmeyer, F. (1986) *The Politics of Linguistics*, Chicago: University of Chicago Press, 13/20.

Palacas, A. (2001) "Liberating American Ebonics from Euro-English," *College English*, 63 (3): 326–52.

Pennycook, A. (1994) *The Cultural Politics of English as an International Language*, London: Longman.

—— (1998) *English and the Discourses of Colonialism*, London: Routledge.

—— (2001) *Critical Applied Linguistics*, Mahwah, NJ: Lawrence Erlbaum.

Pluddemann, P. (2000) "Education with multilingualism in South Africa: an overview," in E. Ridge, S.B. Makoni and S. G. Ridge (eds) *Freedom and Discipline: Essays in Applied Linguistics*, New Delhi: Bhari.

Romaine, S. (1984) *The Language of Children and Adolescents: The Acquisition of Communicative Competence*, Oxford: Blackwell.

Skinner, E. (1999) "Hegemonic paradigms and the African world: striving to be free," in C. Hine and J. McLeod (eds) *Crossing Boundaries*, Bloomington, IN: Indiana University Press, 45–71.

Smith, E. (1998) "What is Black English? What is Ebonics?," in T. Perry and Lisa Delpit (eds) *The Real Ebonics Debate: Power, Language, and the Education of African American Children*, Boston, MA: Beacon Press, 49–58.

Smitherman, G. (2000) "Language and democracy in the United States of America and South Africa," in S. Makoni and Nkonko Kamwangamalu (eds) *Language and Institutions in Africa*, Cape Town: Centre for Advanced Studies of African Society, 65–90.

Spears, A.K. (1999a) "Introduction," in A.K. Spears (ed.) *Race and Ideology: Language, Symbolism and Popular Culture*, Detroit, IL: Wayne State University Press, 11–58.

—— (ed.) (1999b) *Race and Ideology: Language, Symbolism and Popular Culture*, Detroit, MI: Wayne State University Press.

Vaughn-Cooke, F. (1987) "Are Black and White vernaculars diverging?," *American Speech*, 62: 12–32.

Walters, R.W. (1993) *Pan Africanism in the African Diaspora*, Detroit, IL: Wayne State University Press.

Williams, R.L. (1975) *Ebonics: The True Language of Black Folks*, St. Louis, MO: Institute for Black Studies.

Worsley, P. (1984) *The Three Worlds: Culture and World Development*, Chicago: University of Chicago Press.

Part 1

IDEOLOGICAL PRACTICES IN RESEARCH ON BLACK LANGUAGES

1

Ideologies of language and socially realistic linguistics

Donald Winford

Like so many of my Caribbean and African American colleagues, I have devoted my entire career to the study of the languages of the New World Black Diaspora. For the most part, these languages are associated with the socially disadvantaged, though their use is not exclusive to such groups, and they are often perceived as corruptions or deviations, lacking expressive power and rules of grammar. These languages were created by Africans across the Diaspora, as they came into contact with speakers of European languages under conditions of forced relocation and enslavement. They include the languages that linguists refer to as "Creoles," spoken in Africa, the Caribbean, in areas along the Indian Ocean, and in parts of the US.

The speakers of these languages often refer to them by other names, e.g. Patwa in Jamaica, Papiamentu in Aruba and Curaçao, Sranan Tongo in Suriname. Sometimes the popular names match those used by linguists, for instance Kweyol in St. Lucia, Kreyòl in Haiti, Creolese in Guyana, and Creole in Belize. All of these languages display varying linguistic continuities from English and other European languages, though they have been restructured to different degrees as a result of creative learning by Africans. My own scholarly interests lie in the varieties of English that were created by Africans in the Caribbean and the US during the seventeenth and eighteenth centuries, which I refer to as "New World Black Englishes." In the US, they include the language linguists refer to as African American Vernacular English, recently popularized as "Ebonics" (although the term was coined in 1973), as well as Gullah, the creole that emerged in the coastal areas and on the islands of South Carolina and Georgia. In the Caribbean, English-lexicon creoles are the primary vernaculars of the vast majority of the population in Anglophone countries. The latter include Antigua, Barbados, Belize, Jamaica, St. Kitts, and various other former British colonies. Among them is Trinidad, my home country, where I learned my own native language, Trinidadian Creole, which we call "Trini." In Trinidad, as in the other Anglophone Caribbean countries, the Creole vernacular exists in a diglossic relationship with Standard English, the official language

(Winford 1985)—a situation that applies equally well to African American Vernacular English (AAVE).

Since I have written extensively on the sociolinguistic situation in Caribbean English Creole communities (e.g. Winford 1985, 1988, 1994), I will say little about them here. Instead, I wish to focus my attention on AAVE and examine some aspects of its history, status, and use from my perspective as a Caribbean creolist.

AAVE is part of a spectrum of varieties that can collectively be assumed under the label "African American English" (AAE). The spectrum includes Standard English as spoken by Blacks (cf. Spears's 1988 "Standard Black English"), as well as various regional (both rural and urban) and socially based varieties of African American Vernacular English. AAVE itself is not monolithic, displaying differences related to region, age, class, and gender. Moreover, there is some overlap between AAVE and more standard varieties of AAE, particularly in the usage of middle-class and educated Blacks. On the whole, however, varieties of AAVE across both urban and rural communities share a set of linguistic features that distinguish this vernacular from others in the US (Wolfram 2002). The urban varieties in particular are the focus of this chapter.

It is evident to all linguists that AAVE and other varieties of New World Black English are legitimate, rule-governed systems of communication—true manifestations of the human faculty of language. But it is equally clear that they are subject to extreme forms of linguistic prejudice, rooted in ideologies and belief systems, which have no basis in linguistic fact, or arise from one-sided interpretations of the facts. The main focus of this chapter is the continuing struggle between ideology and fact in the way these languages are perceived and written or spoken about.

Following Wolfram (1998), I interpret "language ideology" to mean an often subconscious, deeply rooted set of beliefs about the way language is and is supposed to be. Like all ideologies about the world, language ideology is a part of, and derives from, what Bourdieu (1977) refers to as the *habitus*. The concept refers to a "set of dispositions which incline agents to act and react in certain ways. The dispositions generate practices, perceptions, and attitudes which are regular without being consciously coordinated or governed by any 'rule'" (Thompson 1991: 12). These dispositions affect every aspect of social life, and inculcate in individuals a set of expectations and attitudes about the world and how to act in it. Like any other social practice, a language (the social practice *par excellence*) "only exists as a linguistic habitus, to be understood as recurrent and habitual systems of dispositions and expectations" (Duranti 1997: 45).

It isn't just non-linguists that have such expectations and beliefs. Linguists themselves operate with a certain body of assumptions—a "paradigm" which itself constitutes a form of language ideology. And not all linguists share the same set of beliefs. Among scholars, there are two radically different approaches to the nature of language. On the one hand, language is viewed as an abstract system of rules for the combination of sounds into meaningful units known as morphemes, which are further combined to yield more complex units such as phrases and sentences. In other words, language is viewed as pure code, a set of sentences generated by a set of grammatical rules. On the other hand, language is viewed as a set of culturally transmitted behavior patterns shared by a community of speakers. In other words, language is seen as a form of social behavior, an inextricable part of cultural practice. Linguists emphasize this dichotomy in various ways.

Adherents of the first approach claim a clear boundary between "competence" and "performance," between *langue* (the internalized knowledge of grammar) and *parole* (the actual use of language). In their view, the goal of linguistic theory is to describe an abstract construct—a discrete system of grammatical knowledge divorced from the sociocultural contexts of language use. Chomsky (1986) refers to this abstraction as "Internalized" language or "I-language," and distinguishes it from "Externalized" language or "E-language," language in actual use. He further questions whether the latter can become an object of serious study. If such linguists are asked how abstract grammatical rules relate to the behavior of actual human beings, they would say that the rules are meant to account for the behavior of ideal speakers living in ideal, uniform speech communities. But exactly how do these idealizations relate to what we in fact observe in actual communities?

This problem has been explored by LePage (1989), who examines four senses in which the term "a language" is used, and how the different interpretations reflect powerful social stereotypes. First, there is the individual's perception of what his or her language is. Second, there is the community's perception of and consensus about its own variety of language. Third, there is the set of data that makes up actual language performance, the behavior we observe in everyday life. Finally, there is the linguist's description of a grammar, an abstraction based on the kinds of data the linguist chooses to use, often based on his or her intuition. Each of these is a product of some kind of ideology. An individual's or community's perception of its own language often runs counter to beliefs that deny status to it as a legitimate or autonomous variety. A particularly insidious form of this kind of belief is what some refer to as "standard language ideology" (discussed below). The notion of linguistic homogeneity that many linguists operate with is also itself a product of ideology, rooted in the idea that the variability of language behavior is not an ideal basis for a theory of grammar. Indeed, Chomsky (1986: 17) specifically says this about the variable language behavior characteristic of bilingual speech communities (and by extension, the variability common in every language).

The crucial problem here is to reconcile the data of performance with the linguist's construct of the grammar and to reconcile each with the community's conception of its own and others' linguistic practices. It is seldom the case that the linguist's notion of grammatical system is equivalent to the folk notion of language. The two concepts reflect different ways of abstracting from communicative behavior. This in part explains the frequent clashes that occur between linguists and non-linguists in their perception and evaluation of language behaviors.

Sociolinguists, who view language primarily as a sociocultural construct, attempt to bridge the ideological gap between these two ways of looking at language. We see language not just as a set of rules, but as a way of behaving, a way of belonging, a way of creating social identities and relationships. It should come as no surprise, then, that this perspective on language is often at odds with the linguist's attempt to abstract systems of rules from the data of performance. Nowhere is the conflict more apparent than in the treatment of the vernacular of African Americans. I once witnessed an impassioned attack by a noted sociolinguist on a formal analysis of the AAVE auxiliary system that was based on the analyst's own intuitive judgments. Apparently, the sociolinguist saw this as a departure from empirical accountability. But there is, in fact, no real incompatibility between the two approaches. The formal analyses of AAVE grammar done, for example, by Green (1997, 2000) provide invaluable insight into the competence shared by users of this variety. On the other hand, the sociolinguistic approaches of scholars like Mitchell-Kernan (1972), Morgan (1994a), Smitherman (2000), and others provide insight into how this grammatical competence is linked to communicative competence and translates into skilled performance. It is high time we reassert the complementary relationship between studies of I-language and studies of E-language, rather than treating them as polar opposites.

Unfortunately, as the controversy over AAVE stirred up in the Ebonics debate has shown, linguists continue to make little headway in their attempt to demonstrate to the public the richness of AAVE grammar and the competence of its speakers. Indeed, the scholarly treatment of this language variety has itself sometimes (not always intentionally) contributed to the negative popular stereotypes of it. I will first consider two areas in which (the potential for) such bias exists—the study of AAVE's history and the variationist approach to its relationship with Standard English (SE). I will then consider the social contexts of inequality and discrimination that reinforce the negative bias toward the linguistic practices of African Americans.

Ideology and historicity

Historicity—the notion of continuity and tradition, of a distinct lineage and genealogy in the development of a language—is a vital part of the ideology that assigns legitimacy to any language. But because the languages of the African Diaspora were for the most part creations of Africans, this aspect of their history has been either denied or used as grounds for defamation. Thus, G.P. Krapp asserts the following about AAVE: "The Negroes indeed in acquiring English have done their work so thoroughly that they have retained not a trace of any African speech. Neither have they transferred anything of importance from their native tongues to the general language" (1924: 190). This view conveys the impression that AAVE is an exact replica of some unspecified English dialect, and that there is nothing distinctive about its grammar. While no one would deny the strong connections between AAVE and the settler dialects introduced to the American South in the colonial period, it is equally clear that there was a great deal of creative innovation that gave a distinctive stamp to the character of this vernacular. The influence of African languages on the structure of AAVE is admittedly not as strong as in the case of Gullah or the Creoles of the Caribbean. But it is not entirely absent. There is evidence of it in phonology and in some of the vocabulary, as many scholars have noted. And above all, traces of African influence persist in the communicative styles and modes of interacting of African Americans, in the counterlanguage of signifying (Morgan 1993), in boasting and loud talking (Mitchell-Kernan 1972; Smitherman 1986), and perhaps today in Hip Hop. Rickford and Rickford (2000: 13–88) provide a more extensive survey of how African Americans exploit the richness of their linguistic heritage in areas such as preaching, comedy, singing—several of which show evidence of continuities from Africa.

Sometimes the African influence is camouflaged in English guise. In AAVE as in New World Black English generally, we find expressions like *bad-mouth* "to speak ill of" (cf. Mandingo *da-jugu*, Hausa *mugum-baki* "bad-mouth"), *suck-teeth* "a disapproving sound" (multiple West African sources), and *cut-eye* "a scornful look" (Rickford and Rickford 2000: 95). These expressions are as familiar to African Americans as to their cousins in the Caribbean. They represent loan translations of African expressions, disguised in English words.

The idea that African Americans played no creative role in the development of their vernacular is very much alive in the scholarly literature today. One instance of this is the recent anthology, edited by Poplack (2000), with the title *The English History of African American English*. Its main thesis is that "the grammatical core of contemporary AAVE developed from an English base," and that features peculiar to AAVE are recent developments resulting from a process of "divergence" brought about by racial segregation in the post-Civil War era. Examples of the "grammatical core" treated in this volume include the copula, plural marking, negation, *was/were* alternation, auxiliary inversion in questions, and relativization strategies. It is argued that in almost every one of these cases, quantitative variationist methodology has shown the system governing their use to be that attested in older forms of English. One notable exception is (variable) copula absence, "perhaps the only variant studied in this volume which cannot be identified as a legacy of English, except perhaps as an additional strategy, complementary to contraction, for reducing prosodic complexity" (Poplack 2000: 20). What this means is totally unclear to me. There is no independent evidence that prosodic demands trigger "deletion" of any other sounds in AAVE. The fact is we have a quite reasonable explanation for copula absence in AAVE as the result of simplification and regularization strategies used by Africans in the acquisition of early settler English. Such strategies are well known from many other cases of the restructuring of English under conditions of contact.

No objective scholar would deny that most of the features listed above, and indeed many others, can be traced back to one or another (British) English source. There is no question that several of these features are thoroughly English dialectal in character, as Schneider (1989) and Winford (1998) have argued. Hence, in these cases, it is not surprising to find patterns of use and variability that reflect those in other dialects of English (with the exception of the copula pattern). To focus entirely on uncontested British dialectal continuities in AAVE, however, conveniently ignores other distinctive features of AAVE grammar that are not so easily explained. The features treated in Poplack's anthology (Poplack 2000) include none of the tense/aspect auxiliaries and other grammatical features that make AAVE unique among American English dialects. The precise origins of these features are not explained. All we are told is that "many of the features stereotypically associated with [urban AAVE] . . . would have emerged and/or spread since the last quarter of the nineteenth century" (Poplack 2000: 25). The details of this emergence, however, remain a mystery. No explanation or motivation is offered for the "divergence" that supposedly reshaped the grammar of AAVE. There is no hint as to how or why AAVE speakers, in the course of a few generations, proliferated the use of zero copula (e.g. *She tall*), while oddly increasing use of plural marking, and developed a whole range of tense/aspect markers that had never been part of the vernacular before.

Approaches like these to the history of AAVE are selective and one-sided, conveniently ignoring those aspects of AAVE grammar that do not fit the historical scenario (first proposed by Krapp) that "AAVE originated as English" (Poplack 2000: 27). Also one-sided is the comparison of AAVE with the contemporary descendants of varieties of earlier African American English transported to Samaná and Nova Scotia. No attention is paid to evidence from places like Liberia (Singler 1991a, 1991b) to which African Americans also migrated in large numbers in the later nineteenth century. For example, Singler (1998) has shown that many of the AAVE features that supporters of Krapp claim to be recent developments can, in fact, be found in Liberian Settler English, thus indicating that they must have been present in late nineteenth-century AAVE. Such features include preterite *ain't* (= "didn't"), the auxiliary combination *be done*, the adverb *steady* expressing habituality, and habitual auxiliary *be*. Thousands of loyalist slaves and freemen from the US migrated to the Bahamas after 1783 (Saunders 1983; Hackert 2001); hence some varieties of Bahamian English may provide insight into earlier AAVE. Holm and Hackert (in press) suggest that most of the new arrivals from the US came from South Carolina and Georgia, and thus probably spoke Gullah rather than AAVE. But research still needs to be done to determine whether some varieties of Bahamian English preserve features of earlier AAVE. Wolfram and Thomas (2002), using evidence from intergenerational differences in language use among African Americans in Hyde County, North Carolina, conclude that the roots of AAVE were established early on in the history of the vernacular and that many AAVE features were present in Hyde County at least by mid-nineteenth century.

All of this is evidence that Africans played an active and creative role in shaping their vernacular in its earlier stages of development. The view that they slavishly imitated the English dialects around them goes against all we know about creative learning and restructuring under conditions of language contact. Denying this creativity and ignoring the African continuities in oral tradition and communicative strategies is denying a key aspect of the distinctive lineage and historicity of AAVE. Apart from the communicative styles of indirectness (signifying), loud talking, and boasting mentioned above, there are other continuities of African modes of speech that have been explored by Abrahams (1970, 1983). These include "toasts," that is, narrative poems such as "The Signifying Monkey," which can be used to display the verbal talent of the performer, as well as to celebrate his prowess and manhood. Though some of these older traditions are not as widespread today, they survive in newer forms of verbal performance such as Hip Hop. (Rickford and Rickford [2000: 84ff] explore these connections in more detail.) Similar kinds of oral performance exaggerating manhood and strength can be found in the Caribbean, for instance in the so-called "Robber Talk" of Trinidad. Abrahams (1970) also explores continuities in narrative folklore. There appear to be many other parallels (see Abrahams 1983).

Ideology and autonomy

One of the most vexing issues in both scholarly and public discussions of AAVE (and other minority vernaculars) is the question of their autonomy *vis-à-vis* other varieties. A prime example of this is the problem of naming—the labels we use to refer to vernaculars. This is an area of frequent conflict that reflects, once more, deep-seated differences between linguists and non-linguists in their perception and evaluation of language behaviors. Many linguists (including myself) refer to the vernacular of African Americans as "AAVE." More recently the term "Ebonics" has gained popularity, at least in the media, for whom it has become an object more of derision than of objective discussion. African Americans in general use neither of these labels, preferring to say that they speak English, while recognizing that they have a distinct way of using the English that they speak. If pressed, like Trinidadians, some might say they speak "bad" English" or "street talk" or "slang," none of which is a linguistically valid label. So what's in a name, then, as Smitherman, herself a "ghetto lady turned critical linguist," asks. And she replies: "Everything, as we acknowledge that names are not merely words but concepts which suggest implications, values, history, and consequences beyond the word or mere 'name' itself" (1986: 42).

Morgan tells us that "The scholarly debate over what to call African American English reflects the debate over the role of African Americans in the history and culture of America" (1994b: 327). In simple terms, she explains, the issue is whether African Americans form a culturally distinct group. And of course, language is always a badge of separate cultural identity. That there is still resistance

27

to the idea of a distinct African American culture is reflected in the fact that, even among some African Americans, AAVE is, in the words of Geoff Pullum, "a language that dare not speak its name" (Pullum 1997: 321).

From a purely linguistic perspective, the question of the autonomy of AAVE poses the same difficulties that concepts like "language" and "dialect" have always posed. Put briefly, the issue is primarily not a linguistic but a sociocultural one. Dialects and languages are sociocultural constructs, and the boundaries between them are not definable in purely linguistic terms. Despite this, linguists have attempted to write grammars of AAVE from two very distinct perspectives, that of the generative theorist who assumes homogeneity in the grammar, and that of the variationist who assumes that variability is part of the system of rules. Neither has resolved the question of AAVE autonomy in a satisfactory way.

The theorist seeking homogeneity abstracts away from the data of performance a set of invariant rules that aim at capturing speakers' own intuitions about how their grammar works. For instance, most speakers of AAVE would accept structures like *She at home* or *You trippin'* as well as *I BIN had this* as perfectly grammatical and normal productions. Grammars of the verb complex (e.g. Green 1997) try to represent this kind of internalized grammatical competence. The problem with this approach, however, is that it ignores other aspects of speakers' ability—the "polylectal" or "varilingual" competence that allows them to vary production by switching or mixing AAVE and SE features. One of the main thrusts of variationist sociolinguistics has been to develop models of this kind of variable behavior. Ironically, this approach seems to have created idealizations of language behavior akin to those created by theoretical models of language as an abstract system of rules. Studies within the variationist paradigm assume that the patterns of variation typical of African American speech can be translated into "variable rules" (Labov 1969; see Alim, this volume, for analysis of this language use by Hip Hop artists). In other words, this approach treats much of the variation as "inherent" or belonging to a single grammatical system. Moreover, it is assumed that the underlying categories and forms that serve as input to these rules are those of SE. For instance, it has been claimed that copula *is* and *are* are "underlyingly present" in AAVE, but that speakers "contract" and "delete" such forms subject to certain linguistic constraints (Labov 1969). These rules of "contraction" and "deletion" strike one as an artifact of this particular model of variability, rather than as an accurate account of the AAVE speaker's actual competence. It suggests that learners "begin" with full forms of the copula, which they contract and delete according to the constraints mentioned above. This seems somewhat counterintuitive, when one considers the development of AAVE either from a historical perspective or from the point of view of individual acquisition. Children who acquire AAVE as a first language in fact display a pattern of copula variability similar to that of adult users, but if anything their use of full copulas is less frequent (Wyatt 1996). Moreover, they use zero copula more often at the age of three than they do at ages five to seven (Kovac 1980). It is only in the later stages of acquisition, as they learn to code-switch and vary choices between the vernacular and the standard, that they incorporate more overt forms into their production. Arguably the same pattern of partial replacement of zero copula by overt forms characterized the historical development of AAVE. This scenario is certainly true of Caribbean English vernaculars like Bajan and Trinidadian Creole (Winford 1992).

At any rate, the variationist approach encourages an ideological position that sees AAVE as a derivative, if not a deviant, form of SE, when in fact there is neither historical nor synchronic evidence for it. This approach has led some to propose that AAVE is made up of "co-existent systems" (Labov 1998). The idea is that, on the one hand, AAVE shares most of its grammar, the General English (GE) component, with other American dialects. But, on the other hand, it also has a "distinct" African American (AA) component. The latter contains grammatical features and rules peculiar to AAVE, such as tense/aspect auxiliaries and their combinations, "absence" of 3rd sing. /−s/, etc. Labov argues that the GE component is "a fairly complete set of syntactic, morphological and phonological structures which can function independently" (Labov 1998: 118). By contrast, he claims, "the AA component is not a complete grammar, but a subset of grammatical and lexical forms that are used in combination with much but not all of the grammatical inventory of GE" (Labov 1998: 118).

There is a curious kind of linguistic bias in this view of AAVE. It is as if the so-called AA component is a superfluous appendage, subservient to the GE component, rather than being fully integrated with it into a single coherent whole. This is perhaps an inevitable consequence of viewing AAVE through the filter of SE or other American dialects (OAD) rather than as a communicative system in its own right. Such an approach overlooks the wealth of lexical and structural features that distinguish AAVE from OAD, some of which, like aspectual adverb *steady* (Baugh 1983, 1984) and semi-auxiliary *come* (Spears 1982), have only recently been unearthed, while others no doubt remain undiscovered or unreported. This approach also overlooks the creativity of AAVE, as evidenced in continuing internal change (e.g. the spread of habitual *be*) and its exploitation of prosody and rhythm, about which so little has been done. Not least, the tendency to view AAVE from the perspective of SE belittles perhaps its most vibrant feature, the richness of its lexical innovations, usually dismissed as "slang," as though it were not legitimate lexical knowledge and creativity.

The fact that many AAVE rules overlap with those of OAD is neither here nor there. What matters is the fact that AAVE is as systematic and rule-governed as any other dialect of English. Structural overlap between varieties is quite irrelevant to their sociocultural status as distinct forms of communication associated with distinct speech communities. Again we must avoid confusing language varieties as sociocultural constructs with the grammar that linguists attempt to abstract from the behavior of the community. Both AAVE and SE are constructs of this kind, the former associated with the culture and social practice of the African American community, the latter with some ideology of what "correct" linguistic behavior should be. The ideological clash between

29

these two perspectives lies at the heart of the problem of the status and autonomy of AAVE.

Ideology and prestige

As Sidnell (1997: 299) reminds us, ideologies of language have the power not only to shape the way people talk and interact generally, but also to naturalize relations of power and privilege. Unfortunately, correlational sociolinguistic studies have tended, perhaps quite unintentionally, to foster this sense of the privileged status of certain ways of speaking over others. Such studies explore patterns of social differentiation in language (related to categories such as class, gender, and age) as well as patterns of style differentiation (related to informal vs. formal situations). This tradition of research has led to a conception of speech communities as characterized by "shared norms of usage and evaluation," despite substantial differences in the linguistic practices of different social classes. In other words, it is claimed that all social groups alternate between standard and non-standard forms in the same way, associating superiority with the former and stigma and inferiority with the latter—hence the curious idea that the social classes of the community are united in their common evaluation of the very differences that set them apart.

This assumption, when applied to the African American speech community, would mean that African Americans uniformly judge Standard English to be "prestigious" and AAVE to be stigmatized. Yet several attitudinal studies (Hoover 1978; Speicher 1992; Ogbu 1999) have revealed a much more complex pattern of evaluation than that. These studies demonstrate that African Americans, while well aware of the social advantages of SE in the linguistic marketplace, also value their vernacular as a badge of their identity and a symbol of resistance to their assimilation to the dominant "white" culture, as indeed other minority groups do (Lippi-Green 1997).

There is a clear distinction between the "status-oriented " norms of evaluation that favor use of SE, and the community-oriented norms that place value on AAVE. Morgan (1994a: 121) quite justifiably chastises variationist approaches to African American speech for failing to unveil the true values that underlie language choices within this community. Like other sociolinguists, she rightly rejects the assumption that the standard variety always has privileged status as the "norm" against which vernacular usage must be judged. Far from being stigmatized and lacking in social value, AAVE functions as an expression of community membership and solidarity across class lines. This aspect of the language has unfortunately been neglected in the past by variationist studies. In short, the focus on class differentiation in variationist approaches to African American English failed to accurately reflect the dynamics and dialectic of the community, which is characterized by conflicting norms of usage and conflicting loyalties to vernacular and "standard" varieties. The fact is that most of the earlier variationist sociolinguistic research on the African American community failed to elucidate our understanding of the social meanings and values it attaches to its distinctive ways of speaking.

The shortcomings of these earlier approaches are being remedied now by studies that examine the role of social networks (Labov and Harris 1986) and ethnic identity (Ogbu 1999) in African American Language behavior. Drawing on language data collected in a Black Philadelphia community, Labov and Harris point to a strong relationship between language use on the one hand and speakers' life history and network structures on the other. Ogbu (1999: 154) suggests that the speech behavior of African Americans is related to their construction of a collective identity that is oppositional to White American collective identity. According to Ogbu, "Accommodating White American ways of talking seems to threaten [African Americans'] sense of dialect identity" (p. 155).

But such research is still in its infancy, and there is still need to elaborate a more sophisticated framework within which to examine the effects of network structure and choice of identity on language use (see Hecht *et al.* 1993). Such a framework must draw more fully on social network theory (Boissevain 1974) as well as ethnic identity theory (Tajfel and Turner 1979). The latter has been conceptualized within a broader theoretical framework known as communication accommodation theory (Giles *et al.* 1991), insights from which have been applied only in a cursory manner to African American patterns of language use. Another promising approach is that based on social practice theory (Bourdieu 1977, 1990) and its derivative concept "the community of practice" (Wenger 1998), which has been applied to the study of language and gender (Holmes and Meyerhoff 1999). The question of how to place variability within a theory of social identity so as to explain its social meanings remains a challenge for future scholars of AAVE.

The struggle between the "covert" prestige attached to non-standard speech and the "overt" prestige associated with the standard variety is common to many speech communities throughout the world, particularly those in the Black Diaspora. The everyday vernaculars of these communities have long existed in the shadow of the standard varieties that serve as official languages in domains such as education, government, and the media. These institutions carefully promote the myth that the standard variety is superior to non-standard ones, and is the only "correct" form of the language. This "standard language ideology" (Milroy and Milroy 1985) promotes a linguistic value system that reinforces the unequal distribution of power and privilege in these communities. As Milroy and Milroy note, standardization is motivated primarily by social, political, and commercial considerations. It is deliberately promoted via education, codification, legislation, and other means. It is intolerant of any kind of difference or "deviation." Hence it discriminates against non-standard varieties and rejects the social values of their speakers. This bias is related to the idea that a single uniform national language should be associated with a single national identity—an ideology that accompanied the emergence of modern European states. A radical revision of the traditional sociolinguistic approach in favor of a more socially realistic description of Black ways of speech can help offset this long-standing ideological prejudice.

The emphasis on class-based differentiation of language and the narrow conception of "style" typical of earlier variationist approaches also led to an unfortunate neglect of the "rules of speaking" within the AAE community. One consequence of this is our poor understanding of the cultural norms of inter-action and interpretation and of the culturally based values African Americans associate with flexible choices of communicative strategies in interaction. It comes as a shock that no comprehensive sociolinguistic study of any African American community has been done since Wolfram's (1969) study of a small sample of Detroit residents. Even more shocking is the fact that this study focused only on social class differences, paying no attention to stylistic variation. The study of styles and genres of talk should in fact be the central focus of a socially realistic linguistics. In its broadest interpretation, style subsumes all lin-guistic choices, whatever their motivation. Such choices operate in three dimensions: the social, having to do with choices of social identity and group membership; the situational, having to do with characteristics of settings, domains, topics, etc.; and the transactional, having to do with the manipulation of linguistic resources to achieve different goals. In the future, far more attention must be paid to situated language use, genres of talk, and communicative strate-gies within the African American community.

Fortunately, some research has been done, going back to the work of Abra-hams (1972), Mitchell-Kernan (1972), Kochman (1972, 1981), and others. This tradition continues today in the work of scholars like Smitherman (1986, 2000), Morgan (1998, 2001), Spears (1998, 2001), and others. Some of this was dis-cussed earlier, in connection with African continuities in Black rules of speaking. More of this kind of research is needed if we are to understand the vital role that vernacular forms of speech play in the social and cultural life of the African American community.

Ideology and social control

Like other ideologies based on race, class or similar differences, standard lan-guage ideology helps to promote the interests of a dominant group or class at the expense of less powerful groups. This is accomplished in two ways: first, by means of misinformation and misrepresentation of the disadvantaged group; and second, by denying such groups access to positions of power and privilege. The mass media have been the chief instrument by which the former goal has been achieved. The latter is the province of the educational system, backed by various forms of legislation.

The linguistic prejudice against AAVE is reflected in the pervasiveness of stereotypes of this dialect which have little basis in linguistic reality. Typical of this are jokes about habitual *be*, hundreds of which appeared in the mass media and on the internet during the debate over Ebonics initiated by the Oakland

School Board's proposal to revise its approach to the teaching of Black children. Here's a typical joke:

Q. Do you know what Toys R Us is called in Harlem?
A. We be toys.

Rickford and Rickford (2000: 208) quote the following piece from *Washington Post* columnist William Raspberry, himself an African American. He begins a patronizing and biased article opposing the use of Ebonics in school with the following made-up dialogue, meant to illustrate his own inability to comprehend the AAVE spoken to him by a cab-driver.

"Sup?" the cabbie said.

"No thanks," I said. I was trying to cut back on my caloric intake. "Besides," I pointed out, "it looks to me like you've only got half a fillet of fish and what's left of a small order of fries."

"What you be talking 'bout, my man?" he said. "I don't be offering you my grub; I be saying hello. You know, like *what's up?*"
                                        (*Knoxville News-Sentinel*, December 26, 1996)

Any AAVE speaker would recognize right away that all of the above uses of habitual "be" are ungrammatical. But of course, stereotyping has little time for grammatical accuracy. As Rickford and Rickford (2000) note, these misrepresentations reinforce the myth that "Ebonics is formed willy-nilly, that it is a language without discernible rules or restrictions." Condescending drivel such as this would be bad enough (though maybe more understandable) coming from a white columnist. But Raspberry apparently belongs to that subset of African Americans who profess or pretend ignorance of a variety that they despise for no other reason than that they subscribe to mainstream ideologies about its inferior status. Those who hold that position can hardly be persuaded that AAVE is as rule-governed as Standard English, and that it is just as possible to err grammatically in the former as in the latter.

The other general arena in which AAVE speakers are discriminated against is the school system, about which so much has already been said and written. As Foucault reminds us: "Any system of education is a political way of maintaining or modifying the appropriation of discourses, along with the knowledges and powers which they carry" (Foucault 1984: 123, cited in Lippi-Green 1997: 65).

The continuing failure of the school system to provide an adequate education for the vast majority of African American children in the inner cities reflects, at the very least, a grave indifference to their needs and aspirations. There is no need to repeat the horrendous stories of failure here. Everyone knows that the failure rates and low educational achievement of Black children are nothing short of scandalous. These facts are reported in cycles in the mass media, year after year, each time as if they were a new and startling discovery. Thus we were informed on the national news on March 3, 2001 that African American children end up in special education classes (the euphemism for classes for those diagnosed as educationally "subnormal") three times more often than Whites. Using 1997 Education Department data, studies commissioned by the Civil Rights Project at Harvard University revealed that Black students nationwide were 2.9 times more likely than whites to be identified as mentally retarded. They were 1.9 times as likely to be identified as having an emotional problem and 1.3 times as likely to be identified as having a learning disability (*Columbus Dispatch*, Saturday, March 4, 2001, A1–2). No reference was made to the numerous other times when the same facts were reported.

The cycle has repeated itself for decades, from Ann Arbor in 1979, to Oakland in 1996, until now. So everyone knows that the methods currently being used to teach reading, writing, and language arts to African American children are an abysmal failure. The hardest-hit children are those of the working or poorer classes, whose first language is AAVE. Can there be any doubt about the relevance of language to this pattern of failure? While various other factors are involved, there is no doubt that the vernacular grammar and styles of communication used by many Black children play a crucial role in limiting their scholastic success. Teachers' negative and prejudicial attitudes toward AAVE and Black communicative styles, and their inability or unwillingness to take it into account when teaching language skills, are also part of the problem (Rickford 1999).

Calls for reform such as that made by the Oakland School Board are met with hostile and impassioned resistance from those who control the budgets for education. Indeed, AAVE has the dubious distinction of being perhaps the only minority language ever targeted by legislation specifically designed to exclude it from any kind of use in the school curriculum. Senate Bill 205, introduced by Senator Raymond Haynes (Republican, Riverside) in the California Senate in March 1997, was intended to "eliminate specified funding sources for all non-standard English instruction." Non-standard English was defined as "any vernacular dialect of English," especially "Ebonics, Black English, Black language or African American Vernacular English." It quite clearly repudiated any attempt to train teachers or administrative staff in schools to do any of the following:

- incorporate non-standard English into their lesson plans;
- legitimize, accept, or embrace non-standard English;
- teach that non-standard English is a situationally correct alternative to English in some or all situations.

The list of prohibitions reads like a linguistic wish-list of all that is needed in the school system. The recommendations of linguists are treated as anathema, as a devious threat to the supremacy of "correct" English. This is standard language ideology with a lot of political bite, fed by a dangerous blend of arrogance and ignorance. The only way to counter it is for Black linguists to stand up and fight it with determination and vigor.

Many sociolinguists, both Black and white, are now at the forefront of efforts to devise and apply alternative methods and curricula designed to meet the special needs of AAVE-dominant children (see Baugh 1999, 2001; Labov 2001; Wyatt 2001). Researchers in the field of child language are also making important contributions to our understanding of language development in African American children (see studies in Kamhi *et al.* 1996). The only thing that prevents such efforts from being more widely acted upon is the institutionalized prejudice that exists against Black people, their culture, and their language. Linguists, despite their expertise in these matters, have been relatively powerless to effect changes in social or educational policy for African Americans. But at least they have expressed unanimous support for the principled stand taken by the Oakland School Board, and for the validity and legitimacy of AAVE, as stated in the Linguistic Society of America's resolution on the matter.

The words of linguists, by and large, have fallen on deaf ears. The reason is simple. Languages are not merely systems of rules, as linguists emphasize; they are also vehicles of social interaction and badges of social identity. They are shaped by sociocultural forces, and our perception of them is conditioned by social practice, social relationships, and attendant ideologies. Linguistic prejudice, as we all know, is simply race or class or ethnic prejudice in a subtle guise. A socially realistic linguistics simply acknowledges that fact. Until we persuade the general public, the teachers, the politicians, and the policy makers of that fact, languages like AAVE will continue to be languages that dare not speak their names.

References

Abrahams, R.D. (1970) *Positively Black*, Englewood Cliffs, NJ: Prentice-Hall.
—— (1972) "The training of the man of words in talking sweet," *Language in Society*, 1: 15–29.
—— (1976) *Talking Black*, Rowley, MA: Newbury House.
—— (1983) *The Man-of-Words in the West Indies: Performance and the Emergence of Creole Culture*, Baltimore, MD: Johns Hopkins University Press.
Baugh, J. (1983) *Black Street Speech: Its History, Origin, and Structure*, Austin, TX: University of Texas Press.
—— (1984) "*Steady*: progressive aspect in Black English," *American Speech*, 50: 3–12.
—— (1999) *Out of the Mouths of Slaves: African American Language and Educational Malpractice*, Austin, TX: University of Texas Press.
—— (2001) "Applying linguistic knowledge of African American English to help students learn and teachers teach," in S.L. Lanehart (ed.) (2001) *Sociocultural and Historical Contexts of African American English*, Varieties of English around the world G 27, Amsterdam and Philadelphia, PA: John Benjamins, 319–30.
Boissevain, J. (1974) *Friends of Friends: Networks, Manipulators and Coalitions*, Oxford: Blackwell.

Bourdieu, P. (1977) *Outline of a Theory of Practice*, trans. Richard Nice, Cambridge: Cambridge University Press.

—— (1990) *The Logic of Practice*, trans. Richard Nice, Stanford, NJ: Stanford University Press.

Chomsky, N. (1986) *Knowledge of Language: Its Nature, Origin and Use*, New York: Praeger.

Duranti, A. (1997) *Linguistic Anthropology*, Cambridge: Cambridge University Press.

Foucault, M. (1984) "The order of discourse," in M. Shapiro (ed.) *Language and Politics*, New York: New York University Press, 108–38.

Giles, H., Coupland, N., and Coupland, J. (1991) "Accommodation theory: communication, context and consequence," in H. Giles, J. Coupland, and N. Coupland (eds) *Contexts of Accommodation: Developments in Applied Sociolinguistics*, Cambridge: Cambridge University Press, 1–68.

Green, L. (1997) "Aspect and predicate phrases in African-American vernacular English," in S.S. Mufwene, J.R. Rickford, G. Bailey, and J. Baugh (eds) *African American English: Structure, History and Use*, New York: Routledge, 37–68.

Green, L. (2000) "Aspectual *be*-type constructions and coercion in African American English," *Natural Language Semantics*, 8: 1–25.

Hackert, S. (2001) "'I did done gone' typological, sociolinguistic and discourse-pragmatic perspectives on past temporal reference in urban bahamian Creole English," PhD dissertation: Ruprecht-Karls Universitaet, Heidelberg.

Hecht, M.L., Collier, M.J., and Ribeau, S.A. (1993) *African American Communication: Ethnic Identity and Cultural Interpretation*, Newbury Park, CA: Sage.

Holm, J. (1983) "On the relationship of Gullah and Bahamian," *American Speech*, 58, 4: 303–18.

Holm, J. and Hackert, S. (forthcoming) "Southern Bahamian: transported AAVE or transported Gullah?" in John Lipski (ed.) *African American English and its Congenors*, Amsterdam: John Benjamins.

Holmes, J. and Meyerhoff, M. (1999) "The community of practice: theories and methodologies in language and gender research," *Language in Society*, 28: 173–83.

Hoover, M.R. (1978) "Community attitudes toward Black English," *Language in Society*, 7: 65–87.

Kamhi, A.G, Pollock, K.E., and Harris, J.L. (eds) (1996) *Communication Development and Disorders in African American Children: Research, Assessment and Intervention*, Baltimore, MD: Paul H. Brookes Publishing Co.

Kochman, T. (ed.) (1972) *Rappin' and Stylin' out: Communication in Urban Black America*, Chicago, IL: University of Illinois Press.

Kochman, T. (1981) *Black and White Styles in Conflict*, Chicago, IL: University of Chicago Press.

Kovac, C. (1980) "Children's acquisition of variable features," unpublished PhD dissertation, Georgetown University, Dissertation Abstracts International 42: 2, 687A.

Krapp, G. (1924) "The English of the Negro," *American Mercury* 2: 190–5.

Labov, W. (1969) "Contraction, deletion and inherent variability of the English copula," *Language*, 45: 715–59.

—— (1998) "Co-existent systems in African American Vernacular English," in S. Mufwene, J.R. Rickford, G. Bailey, and J. Baugh (eds) *African American English: Structure, History and Use*, New York: Routledge, 85–109.

—— (2001) "Applying our knowledge of African American English to the problem of raising reading levels in inner-city schools," in S.L. Lanehart (ed.) (2001) *Sociocultural and Historical Contexts of African American English*, Varieties of English around the world G 27, Amsterdam and Philadelphia, PA: John Benjamins, 299–317.

Labov, W. and Harris, W.A. (1986) "De facto segregation of White and Black vernaculars," in D. Sankoff (ed.) *Diversity and Diachrony*, Amsterdam and Philadelphia, PA: John Benjamins, 1–24.

LePage, R.B. (1989) "What is a language?" *York Papers in Linguistics*, 13: 9–24.

Lippi-Green, R. (1997) *English with an Accent: Language, Ideology and Discrimination in the United States*, London: Routledge.

Milroy, J. and Milroy, L. (1985) *Authority in Language: Investigating Language Prescription and Standardisation*, London: Routledge and Kegan Paul.

Milroy, L. (1999) "Standard English and language ideology in Britain and the United States," in Tony Bex and Richard Watts (eds) *Standard English: The Widening Debate*, London and New York: Routledge, 173–206.

Mitchell-Kernan, C. (1972) "Signifying, loud talking and marking," in T. Kochman (ed.) (1981) *Black and White Styles in Conflict*, Chicago, IL: University of Chicago Press, 315–35.

Morgan, M. (1993) "The Africanness of counterlanguage among Afro-Americans," in S. Mufwene (ed.) *Africanisms in Afro-American Language Varieties*, Athens, GA: The University of Georgia Press, 423–35.

—— (1994a) "The African-American speech community: reality and sociolinguistics," in M. Morgan (ed.) *Language and the Social Construction of Identity in Creole Situations*, Los Angeles, CA: UCLA Center for Afro-American Studies, 121–48.

—— (1994b) "Theories and politics in African American English," *Annual Review of Anthropology* 23: 325–45.

—— (1998) "More than a mood or attitude: discourse and verbal genres in African American culture," in S. Mufwene, J.R. Rickford, G. Bailey, and J. Baugh (eds) *African American English: Structure, History and Use*, London: Routledge, 251–81.

—— (2001) "Nuthin' but a G thang: grammar and language ideology in Hip Hop identity," in S.L. Lanehart (ed.) (2001) *Sociocultural and Historical Contexts of African American English*, Varieties of English around the world G 27, Amsterdam and Philadelphia, PA: John Benjamins, 187–209.

Ogbu, J.U. (1999) "Beyond language: Ebonics, proper English, and identity in a Black-American speech community," *American Educational Research Journal* 36, 2: 147–84.

Poplack, S. (2000) "Introduction," in S. Poplack (ed.) *The English History of African American English*, Oxford: Blackwell, 1–32.

Pullum, G. (1997) "Language that dare not speak its name," *Nature*, 386: 321–2.

Rickford, J.R. (1999) "Attitudes towards AAVE, and classroom implications and strategies," in J.R. Rickford *African American Vernacular English: Features, Evolution, Educational Implications*, Oxford: Blackwell, 283–9.

Rickford, J.R and Rickford, R.J. (2000) *Spoken Soul: The Story of Black English*, New York: John Wiley and Sons.

Saunders, G. (1983) *Bahamian Loyalists and Their Slaves*, London: Macmillan.

Schneider, E.W. (1989) *American Earlier Black English*, Tuscaloosa, AL: University of Alabama Press.

Sidnell, J. (1997) "Gender, space and linguistic practice in an Indo-Guyanese village," unpublished PhD dissertation, University of Toronto.

Singler, J.V. (1991a) "Liberian Settler English and the ex-slave recordings: a comparative study," in G. Bailey, N. Maynor, and P. Cukor-Avila (eds) *The Emergence of Black English*, Amsterdam and Philadelphia, PA: John Benjamins, 249–74.

—— (1991b) "Copula variation in Liberian Settler English," in W. Edwards and D. Winford (eds) *Verb Phrase Patterns in Black English and Creoles*, Detroit, MI: Wayne State University Press, 121–64.

—— (1998) "What's not new in AAVE," *American Speech*, 27, 227–56.

Smitherman, G. (1986) *Talkin and Testifyin: The Language of Black America*, Detroit, MI: Wayne State University Press.

—— (2000) *Talkin That Talk: Language, Culture and Education in African America*, London and New York: Routledge.

Spears, A.K. (1982) "The Black English semi-auxiliary *come*," *Language*, 58: 850–72.

—— (1988) "Black American English," in Johnetta B. Cole (ed.) *Anthropology for the Nineties: Introductory Readings*, New York: The Free Press, 96–113.

—— (1998) "African-American language use: ideology and so-called obscenity," in S. Mufwene, J.R. Rickford, G. Bailey, and J. Baugh (eds) *Africanisms in Afro-American Language Varieties*, New York: Routledge, 226–50.

—— (2001) "Directness in the use of African American English," in S.L. Lanehart (ed.) *Sociocultural and Historical Contexts of African American English*, Varieties of English around the world G 27, Amsterdam and Philadelphia, PA: John Benjamins, 239–59.

Speicher, B. (1992) "Some African-American perspectives on Black English Vernacular," *Language in Society*, 21: 383–407.

Tajfel, H. and Turner, J.C. (1979) "An integrative theory of inter-group conflict," in W.G. Austin and S. Worchel (eds) *The Social Psychology of Intergroup Relations*, Monterey, CA: Brooks/Cole, 33–47.

Thompson, J. (1991) "Editor's Introduction," in P. Bourdieu *Language and Symbolic Power*, Cambridge, MA: Harvard University Press, 1–31.

Wenger, E. (1998) *Communities of Practice*, Cambridge and New York: Cambridge University Press.

Winford, D. (1985) "The concept of diglossia in Caribbean Creole situations," *Language in Society*, 14 (3): 345–56.

—— (1988) "The Creole continuum and the notion of the community as locus of language," *International Journal of the Sociology of Language*, 71: 91–105.

—— (1992) "Another look at the copula in Black English and Caribbean Creoles," *American Speech*, 67: 21–60.

—— (1994) "Sociolinguistic approaches to language use in the Anglophone Caribbean," in M. Morgan (ed.) *Language and the Social Construction of Identity in Creole Situations*, Los Angeles, CA: UCLA Center for Afro-American Studies, 43–62.

—— (1998) "On the origins of African American English: Part II, Linguistic features," *Diachronica* 15 (1): 99–154.

Wolfram, W. (1969) *A Sociolinguistic Description of Detroit Negro Speech*, Washington, DC: Center for Applied Linguistics.

—— (1998) "Language ideology and dialect," *Journal of English Linguistics* 26 (2): 108–21.

—— and Thomas, E.R. (2002) *The Development of African American English*, Malden, MA: Blackwell.

Wyatt, T.A. (1996) "Acquisition of the African American English copula," in A.G. Kamhi, K.E. Pollock, and J.L. Harris (eds) (1996) *Communication Development and Disorders in African American Children: Research, Assessment and Intervention*, Baltimore: Paul H. Brookes Publishing Co., 95–115.

—— (2001) "The role of family, community, and school in children's acquisition and maintenance of African American English," in S.L. Lanehart (ed.) (2001) *Sociocultural and Historical Contexts of African American English*, Varieties of English around the world G 27, Amsterdam and Philadelphia, PA: John Benjamins, 261–80.

2

"We are the streets": African American Language and the strategic construction of a street conscious identity[1]

H. Samy Alim

African American Language (AAL)—sometimes referred to in the literature as Ebonics, Black English, African American English, and African American Vernacular English—has commanded more attention on the American socio-linguistic scene than any other language variety in the United States. The topic of AAL is often passionately debated by scholars because of the complex and intricate relationship between language, race, culture, class, and education in America. Language in African America is viewed by many as a direct indicator of one's background, political ideology, social standing, and level of educational attainment. Or as some African Americans might say, to speak is to "put yo business all out in the street."

Black linguists have made and continue to make important contributions to the study of AAL. Two decades ago, one of the pioneering researchers of AAL stated: "Black scholars now define the role that their white allies can play in advancing the study of Black English . . . Members of an oppressed people have entered an academic field, taken up the tools of linguistic research, and used them for the advancement of their nation" (Labov 1982: 186, cited in Smitherman and Baugh 2002). Many Black linguists approach the study of AAL as more than an academic pursuit. In fact, linguistics is often seen as a direct means of quantifying and reversing the myriad social injustices facing Africans in America, including educational, economic, and political subordination.

Linguistics for liberation

Since language permeates all aspects of our lives, for Black scholars, the scientific study of language provides one way to make a way outta no way in the wilderness of North America. Black scholars have been at the forefront of educational, cultural, historical, and legal debates involving language, culture, race, and

40

racism. Recent sociolinguistic scholarship (Baugh, this volume, also 2000a) has examined the relationship between racial profiling and "linguistic profiling"— the racial identification and discrimination of an individual or group of people based on their speech. This research seeks to address the very real problem of landlords rejecting prospective Black tenants (or other linguistic minorities) on the basis of their speech and to provide a basis for legal redress for minorities who have been linguistically profiled. Recognizing a Black voice on the opposite end of the phone, such landlords falsely claim that there are no apartments available for rent. This research is a quintessential example of how the scientific study of language can be utilized to create social change.

Black linguists have long been concerned with issues of social justice and social change. Long before the "Ebonics controversy"[2] caught the public's attention, Black linguists (e.g. Bailey 1969; Smitherman 1981; Taylor 1985; Rickford and Rickford 1995) were already committed to the educational welfare of African American students. They have joined forces with many African American educational researchers who view AAL as a resource to be utilized, rather than a problem to be eradicated (e.g. Lee 1993; Ball 1995; Perry and Delpit 1998; LeMoine 1999). These researchers support policy and pedagogy that both acknowledge the linguistic resources of African American students and further their development of "standard" English proficiency.

Black linguists have also provided numerous insights into the dynamic nature of AAL structure and use. From detailed descriptions and analyses of language use within the African American community (e.g. Mitchell-Kernan 1971; Smitherman 1977; Morgan 1991) to the identification and quantification of several "new" linguistic features (e.g. Baugh 1979; Spears 1982), Black linguists continue to enhance our understanding of the evolving nature of African American speech.

Working toward linguistic liberation, Black linguists have been instrumental in shattering the myth of the *linguistic tabula rasa*, i.e. the myth that the African Holocaust completely eradicated any trace of African linguistic heritage in African Americans. Many Black linguists and scholars (Turner 1949; Bailey 1965; Williams 1975; Rickford 1977; Alleyne 1980; Baugh 1983; Asante 1990; DeBose and Faraclas 1993; Smith 1998) have demonstrated the linguistic connection between AAL and Creole languages (as well as African languages) in an effort to provide an accurate historical account of AAL. Early researchers were responding to the white supremacist view that African Americans were intellectually inferior and, therefore, could not produce the white man's English. Later, many researchers became involved in producing a historical reconstruction of AAL that recognized the linguistic contributions of both Anglican *and* African sources (see Winford, this volume, also 2000).

Research efforts to describe AAL with the highest level of accuracy have been conducted primarily within what is known as the "variationist paradigm" (explained below). The present study utilizes this paradigm to examine the conscious stylistic variation of African American Hip Hop[3] artists in a strategic effort to construct a street conscious identity. Before proceeding to a discussion of the present study, we turn to previous variationist research.

Stylistic variation in
African American Language

The "variationist paradigm" focuses on the statistical analysis and comparison of the distribution and relative frequencies of linguistic variables.[4] Sociolinguistic researchers have outlined three major domains of linguistic variation: linguistic, social, and stylistic (Labov 1972a; Bell 1984; Rickford and McNair-Knox 1994). Much attention has been given to interspeaker variation ("social"—factors include class, age, social networks) and systematic variation within a system ("linguistic"—factors include phonology, morphology, syntax). In addition, sociolinguists are beginning to pay an increasing amount of attention to the way an individual speaker's speech varies across situations ("stylistic"—factors include race, familiarity, setting, topic; see Eckert and Rickford 2001).

Early studies of AAL (Labov *et al.* 1968; Wolfram 1969; Fasold 1972) utilized the quantitative methodology of variation theory to present the systematicity of AAL, that is, to prove statistically that AAL was rule-governed in nature and not a "random" set of "errors" based on "white English." These studies also demonstrated the relationship between linguistic variables and social class: AAL features tended to appear more frequently in the speech of working-class African Americans.

The development of a sociolinguistic theory of stylistic variation begins with Labov's isolation of contextual styles (1966, 1972b), a unidimensional approach focusing on "attention paid to speech" as the main factor influencing speaker style. While Labov's analysis has been criticized for being unidimensional, it is useful here as an introduction to the early work on stylistic variation. Labov was working during a period when most linguists ignored stylistic variation. Furthermore, they considered the techniques of linguistics inadequate to handle stylistic variation, although they knew it was occurring. Labov's aim was to develop a methodology sufficient to measure the extent of regularity in stylistic variation.

Labov studied five linguistic variables as they appeared in five different contextual styles (1972b: 79–85):

> Context A: casual speech
> Context B: the interview situation (careful speech)
> Context C: reading style
> Context D: word lists
> Context E: minimal pairs (i.e. words that have a single differentiating e.g. "singer" and "finger").

These contexts are listed in order of increasing formality, with "casual speech" being the least formal and "minimal pairs" being the most formal. The (in)-

formality of the context is based on the amount of attention paid to speech. Labov believed that speakers paid little or no attention to their own speech when engaged in casual speech, and increasingly more attention to speech as they moved down the list. Labov's studies revealed that, indeed, most speakers used more "non-standard" or stigmatized forms in their casual speech, and that these forms decreased in the same person's speech as they engaged in more formal situations. Importantly, Labov's isolation of contextual styles demonstrated that stylistic variation is context based and follows a certain amount of regularity. However, Labov was aware that the results he obtained might have been artifacts of the procedure, and several scholars have since built upon his unidimensional approach to variation.

Building upon the work of Labov, Baugh's study of what he labeled "Black street speech" (1979, 1983) was a quantitative variation study of language in *situational* contexts. Baugh, a member of the African American Speech Community, witnessed in his childhood what he would later come to describe as the "chameleon" quality of Black speakers. He was describing the ability to shift through a range of speech styles—as he often saw his mother do on the telephone. (He was able to discern the race of the speaker to whom his mother was talking by "analyzing" her speech style.) Thus, rather than controlling for the language content and context of the linguistic interview, Baugh's research led him straight "to the people" in all types of social circumstances. He was attempting to tackle the daunting task of obtaining the casual speech of his informants in various settings. Word lists and minimal pairs were abandoned for "ethnosensitive" interviews in an attempt to describe the informant's speech in various social contexts. Baugh recognized this work as tedious, from an analytical point of view, but felt that it was "the responsibility of black scholars to establish the standards for this kind of research" (1983: 25).

In establishing the standards, Baugh developed a grid for the analysis of speech in four different situational contexts (see Figure 2.1; Baugh 1983: 25–6). Two key factors came into play: whether or not the speakers were familiar with each other, and whether or not the speakers were members of the Black street culture.

Figure 2.1 Baugh's speech event subdivisions

Familiar (*frequent contact*)	Unfamiliar (*occasional contact*)	
Type 1 Familiar exchange	Type 2 Intracommunity contact	*Members of Black street culture*
Type 3 Intercommunity exchange	Type 4 Outsider contact	*Outsiders to Black street culture*

Type 1 depicts speech events that have familiar participants, all of whom are natives of the Black vernacular culture. They also share long-term relationships, which tend to be close-knit and self-supporting.

Type 2 represents speech events where participants are not well acquainted but are members of the Black vernacular culture.

Type 3 indicates speech events where participants are well acquainted but Black street speech is not shared; solidarity may or may not exist between any two or more individuals.

Type 4 corresponds to speech events where participants are not familiar nor is Black street speech common to all.

Baugh had originally expected race to be the major factor in influencing the style-shifting of African Americans, but his results were far more complicated than that. For example, he noted that the frequency of contact between individuals (familiarity) also played a key role.

Rickford and McNair-Knox (1994) built upon Baugh's work on style-shifting in the African American community. They examined two interviews with the same eighteen-year-old African American female informant, one interview done by a forty-one-year-old African American woman with whom the informant was familiar and the other by a twenty-five-year-old European American woman with whom she was unfamiliar. They also discovered that race and familiarity were important variables (although they could not distinguish between the two since the variables were conflated).

Conscious stylistic variation

The present study, while drawing upon variationist methodology, explores variation in AAL with the additional perspective of linguistic anthropology, which views language as cultural practice and as a tool for constructing one's identity. This chapter challenges sociolinguists (particularly scholars of AAL) to go beyond the mere quantifying of linguistic variables to problematize the perceived passivity of linguistic variation and change. Speaker agency, the conscious and strategic use of language, must be considered when discussing these processes. At the same time, linguistic anthropologists are urged to embrace quantitative sociolinguistic analyses, which would add tremendously to their already rich descriptions. The complexity of the African American linguistic situation demands a multidisciplinary approach.

As a language scholar and researcher of Hip Hop culture, as well as a member of the Hip Hop Nation Speech Community within the broader African American Speech Community, I will present an analysis of the conscious stylistic variation in the language of African American Hip Hop artists. Recognizing the high degree of linguistic creativity and verbal virtuosity present in the Hip Hop Nation, this research demonstrates how African American youth possess extraordinary linguistic capabilities that make high school English classes seem *hella* boring (producing extreme ennui). Specifically, this chapter will focus on Hip Hop artists' strategic construction of a street conscious identity through language. By consciously varying their language use, these rappers are forging a linguistic-cultural connection with "the streets" (meaning both members of Black street culture and the sets of values, morals, and cultural aesthetics that govern life in the streets).

This study presents an analysis of two Hip Hop artists' lyrics *and* conversational speech (or as close to natural conversation as one can achieve). The natural conversation data come from interviews conducted by the author, as well as those found in a Hip Hop publication that utilizes the interview format exclusively. Although this research is interesting on comparative grounds alone, it also raises some important questions: How much do we know about the conscious control of grammatical features in language use? If there is conscious control of certain features, how does this control serve the speaker? These questions address the strategic nature of language use and tell us about the social forces that influence speakers' linguistic styles.

Analysis of linguistic features in Hip Hop Nation Language

Several scholars have argued that the syntax of Hip Hop Nation Language (HHNL)—language used by the Hip Hop Nation Speech Community (see Alim, in press)—is essentially the same as that of AAL (Remes 1991; Smitherman 1997, 2000; Yasin 1999; Rickford and Rickford 2000; Morgan 2001). There is a general tendency in linguistics, as well as among the general public, however, to claim that slang is the most noteworthy feature of language use within the Hip Hop Nation, and thus little attention is paid to syntax. For example, Edwards (1998) reports that Hip Hop artists do not employ the central grammatical features of AAL in their lyrics, although they do display some tokens. His main conclusions are:

1 slang is the main aspect of language that Hip Hop artists use to "connect" with African Americans;
2 Hip Hop artists employ standard English grammar in an attempt to appeal to whites.

Edwards conducted a preliminary study in which he used forty-one songs from eight artists, an average of five songs per artist. This amounts to approximately fifteen minutes of speech data per artist. Edwards contends that there is a "virtual absence" of central AAL features in Hip Hop artists' lyrics—features such as perfect/completive *done* (which emphasizes the completed nature of an action, e.g. *I done been through it all*), future completive *be done* (which operates like a future perfect, e.g. *By the time he get home, she be done ate the whole damn cake!*), distributive or invariant *be* (which refers to the habitual nature of an action, e.g. *Y'all be rappin to every girl you see*), aspectual *steady* (which indicates intense actions that occur continuously, e.g. *She be steady typin on that computer*). These particular AAL grammatical features, however, appear relatively infrequently in the corpus of African American speech. Therefore, we should expect them to be used less frequently, relative to other features, in Hip Hop lyrics. Further, to say that such features, especially invariant *be*, are absent from Hip Hop lyrics is most likely a function of the narrow corpus and not the general rule.

Smitherman (1997) provides several examples of AAL features as they appear in Hip Hop lyrics. In discussing the communicative practices of the Hip Hop Nation, Smitherman cites five common features of African American syntax and two common features of African American phonology, respectively:

1 Habitual *be*—indicates actions that are continuing or ongoing. Example: "He *be* gettin on my nerves."
2 Copula absence—absence of *is* and *are* in some present tense forms. Example: "We tryin to get all this paper, cousin."
3 Stressed *been*—denotes the remote past. Example: "I *been* had that Jay-Z album" (meaning I had it a long time ago, and I still have it).
4 *Gon*—indicates the future tense. Example: "You better watch him cause he *gon* take credit for the work that you did."
5 *They* for possessive—"*They* schools can't teach us nuthin noway."
6 Postvocalic *-r*—Mother becomes "Mutha" (the *r* after the vowel is absent).
7 *Ank* and *ang*, for "ink" and "ing." Example: "I'ma get me some dr*ank*" and "You wouldn't understand; it's a Black th*ang*" (dr*ank* = drink and th*ang* = thing).

Smitherman's observations can readily be confirmed. Beyond Smitherman's analysis, I argue that one can find every feature of AAL represented in Hip Hop lyrics. (See Rickford [1999] for a "checklist" of AAL features.) Hip Hop artists employ the wide body of features that make up AAL. This leads to other, perhaps more important, questions. These features may very well appear in Hip Hop lyrics, but with what frequency do they occur? Are these rare, isolated incidents, or do they represent a specific language pattern? Do the patterns of these features in Hip Hop lyrics differ from the patterns found in naturally occurring speech? And, if so, what does that mean? In an attempt to answer these questions, this study analyzed the linguistic variable of copula absence in the lyrics *and* speech of two Hip Hop artists—Eve and Juvenile (artists described below).

Copula absence, as seen in the Smitherman example (2) above, refers to the absence of *is* and *are* in some present tense forms. In linguistic jargon, the copula is the linking verb that connects the subject of a sentence with its predicate. In AAL, a speaker can produce sentences like *He is the leader* (full form), *He's the leader* (contracted form) and *He the leader* (absent form), all of which have the same meaning. The AAL copula cannot be absent in some present tense forms. This speech sample is illustrative: "The Black Man on the rise, and the white man, he runnin scared now, because we wide awake today and he know we not just gon lay down and accept things as they are." While the copula can be absent before prepositional phrases (*on the rise*), progressive verbs (*he runnin scared*), adjectives (*we wide awake*), negatives (*we not just gon lay down*), it cannot be absent when it is in sentence-final position (*as they are*). The copula also cannot be absent in the first person singular form. A sentence such as *I the boss* is ungrammatical in AAL; the present tense form must be *Uhm the boss, I'm the boss,* or *I am the boss.*

Rickford *et al.* (1991) refer to the AAL copula as the language variety's "showcase variable." This pattern is one of the most extensively studied sociolinguistic variables, so much so that a linguist once made this joke at a conference: "Let the copula *be!*" (Only funny to linguists, I imagine.) The AAL copula is important for several reasons. First, it is one of the features that gives AAL its distinctiveness, setting it apart from other varieties of American English. Second, the AAL copula has been used to support the notion that AAL is diverging (growing further away) from other varieties of American English. And third, the AAL copula plays a crucial role in heated debates about the historical reconstruction of AAL described in the introduction to this chapter. The feature has been analyzed extensively to draw support for the creole origins of AAL (Bailey 1965; Baugh 1979, 1980; Alleyne 1980; Holm 1984; Rickford 1998). We shall return to this point in the discussion of methodology below.

Methodological considerations

In obtaining data for analysis, I transcribed one full length CD by each artist: Eve's *Let There Be Eve . . . Ruff Ryder's First Lady* (1999) and Juvenile's *Tha G-Code* (1999).[5] In addition, I transcribed interviews with these artists, who were chosen because of the availability of their speech data. I was careful to make sure that I had nearly equal amounts of speech and lyrical data for each artist. I transcribed about one hour of speech from each artist's interview to match the approximate length of their CD recordings. Eve's interview data were compiled from two sources: from an interview in a volume on Hip Hop culture, *Street Conscious Rap* (Spady *et al.* 1999) and from a recent interview I conducted in Philadelphia.

Juvenile's speech data were also obtained from two sources: from an interview I conducted and from an interview by Black Dog Bone and associates in *Murder Dog*, a Hip Hop magazine that specializes in the interview format. The interviewers interact regularly with the Hip Hop Nation and can be considered members of the Hip Hop Nation Speech Community, as well as the larger African American Speech Community. The data were organized into four groups: Juvenile interview, Juvenile lyrics, Eve interview, and Eve lyrics.

As is well known in linguistics (although not widely reported in linguistic studies), there is more than one way to calculate copula variability. Rickford *et al.* (1991) provide an in-depth look at the varying methods of calculation and their underlying theoretical assumptions. The different formulae exist owing to differing hypotheses about the nature and origin of the AAL copula. Some linguists

47

believe that the copula is an underlying form in AAL, while others believe that it is not. On the one hand, Anglicists (linguists who assert the English origin of AAL) believe that the copula, as in older dialects of British English, was always present in AAL (*He is the teacher*), and speakers contract it (*He's the teacher*) and then delete it to its zero form (*He the teacher*). On the other hand, Africanists/Creolists (linguists who assert the African language(s) origin of AAL) believe that the copula has not always been present in AAL, and that it was inserted into AAL as some African Americans gained contact with speakers of American English varieties in which the copula must always be present. In this case, the process is ordered in reverse—*He the teacher* > *He's the teacher* > *He is the teacher*. Thus, as this line of argument goes, the AAL copula, resembling creole language varieties, was initially absent, then inserted as African American speakers acquired the contracted and full forms. (See Romaine 1982 for insightful argumentation on this issue.) Several linguists have shown convincingly that patterns of AAL copula variation connect AAL to creole language varieties.

This study analyzes synchronic data (data in the present time) and does not attempt to make any diachronic (historical) claims. When viewing synchronic data, there need not be a discussion of "deletion before contraction" or "contraction before deletion." What is important to the synchronic analysis of the data is whether or not the copula, in a given utterance, is in the full, contracted, or absent form. This is not to say that the diachronic analysis is unimportant; it is just beyond the purview of this study. Whether an Anglicist or a Creolist (and whether subscribing to the strong or weak interpretations of these positions), the linguistic researcher must recognize that his/her choice of formulae (if working within the variationist paradigm) essentially aligns him or her with a historical position. I have chosen formulae that are in line with the considerable evidence (cited above) supporting the creole origins hypothesis, and can be used for both synchronic and diachronic analyses. This is precisely why we are speaking of copula *absence* rather than *deletion*.

Analysis of the data

In order to provide a clear picture of what and how copula forms were counted in the data analyzed here and to exemplify the type of copula absence found in AAL, an excerpt from the data is given below. It is taken from my interview of Juvenile (Alim 2000). In this excerpt, sentences containing copula patterns are highlighted: full forms are underlined, contracted forms are italicized, and absent forms are in bold. We are focusing only on present tense copula forms—specifically *is* and *are*—because in the past tense the copula is always present in AAL. It is also present in first person singular constructions as well as in *it's*, *that's*, *what's*.

Following Rickford *et al*.'s (1991) notational schema, the examples that I included in the quantitative analysis are labeled [C] for "counts," and the ones that I excluded are labeled [DC] for "don't counts." As stated above, I analyzed copula variation in the speech *and* lyrics of both Hip Hop artists, using the same analytical procedure.

1 A Do you remember the first Rap record you heard at that time or that
2   you bought at that time?
3 J You know, I wasn't allowed to have that.
4 A Oh, yeah?
5 J Yeah. Couldn't bring that in the house!
6 A [Laughter] Who didn't allow that in the house?
7 J My moms, man. My mama didn't want me to rap. Uh-uh. **She all**
8   **with it now** [C]. *She's down with it now* [C]. Because, you know, it
9   wasn't a big thing when I was young. She was like, "You better think
10   of something else!" Back then it was like a one to a million in my
11   chance of becoming a star. And I wanted to be a *star*.
12 A So she was concerned about you.
13 J She wanted me to make sure that I was straight, and that I didn't spend
14   all my time worrying about rap music and forgetting about what I got
15   to do.
16 A What do you think brought her change about?
17 J Because it opened up to where you could make it out a career. You
18   know, when I was young, a lot of cats would make a song, and they
19   ain't make a record *since* then, you know what *I'm* [DC] *saying*? Now
20   you got it to where artists is [C] going out there making money like
21   football players and baseball players, you know what *I'm* [DC] *saying*?
22   [Laughter]. **She** [C] **widdit**! *I ain't* [DC] *doing nothing. I ain't* [DC]
23   *causing no harm to nobody. I'm* [DC] *living*. **She** [C] **widdit**, you know
24   what *I'm* [DC] *saying? I ain't* [DC] *cutting off nobody arms or nothing to get*
25   *it; I'm* [DC] *just doing my thing*. Believe me.
26 A What do you like the best about being with Cash Money?
27 J *It's* [DC] *family*, man. **We** [C] **family**. *We're* [C] *still living*, man. **Every-**
28   **thing** [C] **the same**. Ain't nothing changed since I got here. **We** [C]
29   **still doing the same thangs. We** [C] **paperchasin, cousin. We**
30   [C] **tryin to get all the money, cousin**.
31 A How important is that to have family around you?
32 J If you don't work, you don't eat, man. That's [DC] the importance. It's
33   [DC] real important to have them around me. *Because* with them
34   along with me, I'm [DC] working. That mean a lot, you know what
35   I'm [DC] saying? That's [DC] less amount of work. As long as it's
36   [DC] with the family, it's [DC] all gravy. We get a lot accomplished
37   when we're [C] together, and we're [C] always together. Just family.

If we examine only a portion of this transcript, lines 19–30, there are numerous examples to illustrate the process of counting the various copula forms. The only full form in this section occurs in line 20 (Now you got it to where artists is going out there making money like football players and baseball players, you know what I'm saying?). This is an example of a "count" full form, despite the fact that *are* is rendered as *is*. The absent form occurs seven times in these lines: twice in lines 22 and 23 (**She widdit [with it]**) and five times in lines 27–30 (**We family; Everything the same; We still doing the same thangs; We paperchasin, cousin; We tryin to get all the money, cousin**). The contracted form occurs ten times in lines 19–30. It is important to note that there is only one case that can be counted out of the ten contracted examples. The one example in line 19 (*I'm saying*) and the four examples in lines 21–5 (*I'm living; I'm just doing my thing*, and the two cases of *I'm saying*) are "don't counts" because, as stated above, the AAL copula is never absent in the first person singular. Therefore, those forms are excluded from the analysis. The uses of *ain't* in lines 22 and 24 are also "don't counts" because the AAL copula is never absent in this negative form. The first form in line 27 (*It's family, man*) is also a "don't count" case. As mentioned above, the AAL copula is rarely absent in cases of "it's," "what's," and "that's" (see lines 32–6 for numerous examples of this "don't count" case). Thus, all those forms are also excluded from the analysis. The only "count" case in these lines (19–30) occurs in line 27 (*We're still living, man*) because, in this environment, the AAL copula can appear in the full, contracted, or absent form. Again, the lyrical data were analyzed using the same procedure.

Before proceeding, a brief biographical sketch about each artist might be helpful. Eve, as a member of the Ruff Ryders, is a rapper who represents Philadelphia. She grew up in the Mill Creek Housing Projects in West Philadelphia and moved to Germantown and other areas in recent years. She made a name for herself as a young teen on the Philadelphia talent show circuit, and she was known as the female rapper who would "bust" into any "cipher"—a highly competitive rhyme circle of rappers (Spady *et al.* 1999). Juvenile, as a member of the Hot Boy$ and the Cash Money Millionaires, is a rapper who represents New Orleans. Like Eve, he made a name for himself as a local rapper and began his career as a teenager. As we saw in the conversational discourse above, wasn't nuthin Juvenile's mother could say or do to stop that boy from rappin! Both Eve and Juvenile claim to be "from the streets" and tell tales of street life in their lyrics. They are now enjoying multiplatinum album sales and international acclaim.

In Table 2.1 data from Juvenile interviews are juxtaposed with data from his lyrics. Similarly, Eve's interview data are juxtaposed with data from her lyrics. The data are displayed this way for comparative purposes. The separation of *is* and *are* allows for additional points of comparison. The reader is reminded that what is being compared is the frequency of copula absence between the artists' interview speech and the artists' lyrics.

We see an increase in the frequency of absence—for all three columns and for both artists—when moving from the interview data to the lyrical data. For Juvenile, *is* absence increases from 55.00 to 68.75 percent. *Are* absence increases from 57.58 to 78.85 percent. *Combined* (both *is* and *are*) absence increases from

Table 2.1 Summary of data

	Juvenile interviews			Juvenile lyrics		
	is	*are*	*combined*	*is*	*are*	*combined*
Rate of absence	55.00%	57.58%	56.60%	68.75%	78.85%	75.00%
	Eve interviews			Eve lyrics		
	is	*are*	*combined*	*is*	*are*	*combined*
Rate of absence	3.39%	12.00%	5.95%	28.00%	87.23%	56.70%

56.60 to 75.00 percent. For Eve, *is* absence increases from 3.39 to 28.00 percent. *Are* absence increases from 12.00 to 87.23 percent. *Combined* (both *is* and *are*) absence increases from 5.95 to 56.70 percent. So, in both cases it is clear that the artists display the absent form more frequently in their lyrical than in their interview speech data.

Strategic construction of a street conscious identity

In this study, I viewed copula variation in two different language contexts: Informal Interview and Hip Hop Lyrics. The Informal Interviews were conducted in a conversational manner, but with several goals in mind: to arrive at a better understanding of Juvenile and Eve as artists, rappers, and, most of all, human beings. Some of the topics covered in the interviews include the writing process, the recording process, Hip Hop as an art form, early Hip Hop experiences, school experiences, hometown experiences, and relationships with family and friends. The interviews most closely related to the concept of "casual speech" in Labov's Context A (as indicated by several cues: tempo, pitch, volume, rate of breathing). The lyrics do not fit any of Labov's contexts (see p. 49), but they do benefit from Baugh's social contexts in terms of familiarity and Black street culture membership (see pp. 50–1). As any fan of Eve and Juvenile will tell you, both artists "got love for the streets." Eve proudly raps on her album that the "Philly streets, they raisin her right!" And Juvenile has developed the concept of *Tha G-Code*, something not unlike what sociologist Elijah Anderson has recognized as "The Code of the Street."[6] In an interview, Juvenile accounted for his success: "I stay down to earth and I stay attached to the streets" (Alim 2000).

Juvenile and Eve are not unlike many of their Hip Hop contemporaries. In Hip Hop culture, "Rap artists affirm that one has to come from the streets, or understand the urban Black street tradition, in order to properly interpret and perform Rap music" (Keyes 1991, quoted in Spady *et al.* 1999: xiii). The streets have been and continue to be a driving force in Hip Hop culture. In "Streets Done Raised Us" (2001), rappers Drag-On and Baby Madison affirm the notion that the streets are the center of Hip Hop cultural activity because for many young Black Hip Hop artists the streets are the locus of life itself. As if to make certain of no misunderstanding, the LOX proudly proclaim and titled their CD, *We Are the Streets*—equating self and street (2000).

From the perspective of Baugh's social contexts, when we examine Hip Hop lyrics, we must ask ourselves: Who is the intended audience? In other words, who are the "interlocutors" in this Hip Hop "conversation"? Certainly, both Eve and Juvenile sold hundreds of thousands of records to white consumers; however, their target audience (as with Hip Hop in general) remains African American (Morgan 2001). "It is important to note that not only are the artists directing their lyrics to people of African descent; they are also directing their lyrics to members of the African American street culture in particular." Thus, according to Baugh's speech event grid (see pp. 43–4), the most appropriate context would fall somewhere in between Type 1 (familiar participants, all of whom are natives of the Black Vernacular culture) and Type 2 (participants who are not well acquainted but are members of Black Vernacular culture). Type 2 is not entirely fitting for this situation because there may not even be "occasional contact." Although the familiarity may vary, membership in Black street culture is important. Familiarity in this sense refers to group experientiality (sharing cultural norms, values, aesthetics, and experiences), rather than to the frequency of contact between individuals (as Baugh described it).

I am not only suggesting that the artists target members of the African American street culture as their audience, I am also suggesting that they modify and vary their speech accordingly. Baugh's study demonstrated that African Americans, like many other groups, vary their speech on the basis of the social interactant. Baugh was concerned with naturally occurring everyday speech. In examining Hip Hop lyrics, we cannot assume that they are comparable to naturally occurring everyday speech, and as the data illustrate, there are some distinct differences. For the most part, Hip Hop lyrics are not as spontaneous as free-flowing speech (although some artists come pretty close to this!). Lyrics are sometimes written, rehearsed, performed, and recorded several times before they appear on CD. Hip Hop artists, in general, pay a great amount of attention to their speech. This is key. Labov noted that stylistic variation depended largely on the attention paid to speech. In his case, the more attention the speakers paid to their speech, the more "standard" their speech became. However, in the case of Hip Hop lyrics, the data suggest that the more attention the artists pay to their speech (comparing interviews to lyrics) the more "non-standard" their speech becomes—as indicated by the increase in the frequency of copula absence.

This raises fundamental questions about the conscious control of phonological and grammatical features in speech. Labov was convinced that, at least with low-level phonological variation (for example, consonant cluster reduction when *last* is realized as *lass*, or *test* as *tess*, etc.), variation was independent of conscious control. Baugh, on the other hand, suggested that although street speakers may not necessarily understand the variable nature of speech, they are conscious that changes are taking place. For example, in his examination of the variable fore-stressing of bisyllabic words (as in *PO-lice* for police and *DE-troit* for Detroit),

Baugh discovered that the feature was sensitive to speaking contexts. He concluded that it is possible that adults have elevated this aspect of dialect difference to the level of (comparatively) conscious manipulation. Such data, of course, point to the refined communicative competence of adult street speakers. Although neither Labov nor Baugh discusses the conscious control of grammatical forms, I am proposing that Hip Hop artists are indeed in conscious control of their copula variability.

Cultural consciousness and African American Language

Thus far, we have discussed the conscious control of variables in cognitive terms. However, consciousness can also be viewed in cultural/ideological terms, i.e. Black consciousness may include awareness of a distinct Black identity, culture, and language. Two theories of stylistic variation are important here—Bell's (1984) *audience and referee design* and LePage and Tabouret-Keller's (1985) *acts of identity*. Bell, like others before him, states that a speaker's style depends primarily on the speaker's audience. Although claiming not to do so, Bell's audience design essentially views stylistic variation as a passive phenomenon. Not until he discusses referee design do we see some sense of agency given to the speaker. Interestingly enough, the speaker is given the most agency when responding to an audience that is not present, as is the case in mass communication. This has direct bearing on this study because the Hip Hop artists are responding to an audience that is not immediately present. The members of the African American street culture, to whom the artists are directing their lyrics, are not physically present, yet they are in conversation.

LePage and Tabouret-Keller's framework gives the speaker a greater sense of agency by claiming that speakers can modify their language to match the language of a group with which they wish to identify if, and only if:

1   they can identify the desirable group;
2   they have both adequate access to that group and the ability to analyze their behavior, i.e. their speech patterns;
3   they have a strong enough motivation to "join" the group, and this motivation is either reinforced or rejected by the group;
4   they have the ability to modify their own behavior.

Consider the situation where Hip Hop artists are producing lyrics for the African American street culture:

1   they have identified the desirable group;
2   they have had and still have adequate access to this group;
3   they have a strong motivation to join the group as "street credibility" is key to a rapper's success in Hip Hop culture;

4   they have the ability to modify their own behavior, as this study has demon-
     strated.

Hip Hop artists assert their linguistic acts of identity in order to "represent" the
streets. This may be viewed as a conscious, linguistic maneuver to connect with
the streets as a space of culture, creativity, cognition, and consciousness. If we
view Hip Hop artists as social interactants communicating with members of the
African American street culture, copula variation appears to be conscious—
street conscious (both cognitive and cultural). Hip Hop artists, by the very
nature of their circumstances, are ultraconscious of their speech. As members of
the Hip Hop Nation, they exist in a cultural space where extraordinary attention
is paid to speech. Speech is consciously varied toward the informal end of the
continuum in order to maintain street credibility. "The streets," as rapper
Method Man says, "is where you get your stripes at" (Spady *et al.* 1999: 67).
   The overwhelming majority of Hip Hop artists in the United States, as
African Americans, are subjected to the "double consciousness" that Dubois
spoke of in the early 1900s, and to what Smitherman (1977) refers as a "linguistic push-pull." In discussing linguistic adjustment, Baugh (1983: 121) states:
"The issue is even more complicated for street speakers because of the question
of group loyalty from within and because of social and economic pressures from
without the vernacular black community." The case of Hip Hop artists is complicated by the fact that both pressures operate in the same direction. That is,
both group loyalty from within the Black community (speaking AAL to connect
with their intended audience) and economic pressures from without (speaking
AAL in order to continue selling records and *earn a living* in a highly competitive
capitalistic economy) favor speaking AAL.
   Since Hip Hop artists are members of the larger African American Speech
Community, street conscious copula variation raises questions about the conscious control of copula variation within the broader African American
community. As we have seen in studies by white linguists (Dillard 1972; Labov
1972a), African American adults are sometimes perceived not to be representative speakers of the vernacular. Could it be that adults do not display features
like copula absence and habitual *be* (when in the presence of whites) because
they possess a refined communicative competence and a heightened sense of the
stigmatized forms in their speech, as perceived by white speakers of English?
And couldn't this refined communicative competence allow these same forms to
be used regularly as a sign of solidarity within the African American Speech
Community (Baugh 1999; Smitherman 2000)?
   Can this street conscious copula variation have any impact on the development of AAL? As several scholars have noted, AAL persists in a society that
readily recognizes its linguistic prejudice. Furthermore, AAL persists despite the
belief by many (whether true or not) that mastery of "standard English" will lead
to greater economic opportunity. Can the conscious use of AAL patterns (in Hip
Hop, and in the broader African American Speech Community) help to main-

tain the unique language of African Americans? To paraphrase rappers P. Diddy and the Bad Boy Family, one thing is for certain, AAL ain't goin nowhere—it ain't goin nowhere—and it can't be stopped now!

Conclusion

What I have described in this paper is *street conscious copula variation*—the conscious variation of copula absence in order for the artist to "stay street," or to stay connected to the streets. More research is needed regarding the strategic use of language to construct identity in the African American community. I conclude with a call for African American scholars, particularly those who are members of one or more African American Speech Communities, to uncover the myriad ways that African Americans utilize language to do more than simply communicate information.

In the tradition of Black linguists who have struggled to legitimize AAL, and thus African American people, future research should continue to examine educational and historical issues as well as explore areas heretofore uncharted. The role of identity, ideology, and consciousness (both cognitive and cultural) in the processes of linguistic variation and change needs to be further explored. Not only will this research shed light on the nature of these linguistic processes, it will also provide greater insight about, as rapper DMX says, *who we be*. If the goal of language scholars is to ultimately uncover what it means to be human, to gain insight into humanity and the complex relationships between language, life, and liberation, we must consider the use of language to not only construct our *worlds* but also to construct our very *beings*. To paraphrase rapper Mos Def, linguistics is our hammer—let's bang the world into shape and let it fall—HUH!

Notes

1   I would like to thank Geneva Smitherman for her close reading of the text and for her many excellent suggestions. I would also like to thank John Baugh and James G. Spady for their encouragement and comments on earlier drafts of this manuscript. Peter Sells also made helpful comments on the first draft. This paper has also benefited from the insights of Arthur Spears, John Rickford, Sonja Lanehart, and Elaine Richardson.
2   What has come to be known as the "Ebonics controversy" came to global attention on December 18, 1996. The Oakland, California School Board passed a resolution declaring all 28,000 of their African American students to be speakers of a language other than English. Despite poor and inaccurate media coverage, the School Board's ultimate aim was to improve the "standard English proficiency" of their students, while maintaining and respecting their "home language." See Baugh (2000b) for an in-depth analysis of this historic event in the struggle for Black language rights.
3   Hip Hop culture is sometimes defined as having four major elements: MC'ing (rappin), DJ'ing (spinnin records), breakdancing (also known as "streetdancing," an array of acrobatic dances associated with the Hip Hop cultural domain) and graffiti art (also known as "writing" or "tagging" by its practitioners). To these, pioneering Hip Hop artist KRS-One adds knowledge as a fifth element, and Afrika Bambaataa,

founder of the Hip Hop Cultural Movement, adds overstanding (more than a cursory understanding of something, an ability to read between the lines to arrive at a deeper, sometimes hidden, meaning; used frequently by Rastafarians—see Pollard, this volume). Even with six elements, this definition of Hip Hop culture is quite limited in scope. It is useful to distinguish between the terms "Hip Hop" and "Rap." Rappin, one aspect of Hip Hop culture, consists of the aesthetic placement of verbal rhymes over musical beats. Hip Hop culture refers not only to the various elements listed above, but also to the entire range of cultural activity and modes of being that encompass the Hip Hop culture-world. This is why Bloods (Blacks) be sayin, "Hip Hop ain't just music, it's a whole way of life!"

4   A linguistic variable is a feature that appears with varying frequencies in various linguistic environments. For example, in many varieties of American English, the "ing" at the end of progressive verbs (*running, jumping, rapping*) is sometimes realized as "in" (*runnin, jumpin, rappin*). Variationists measure the frequency of variant forms to arrive at a description of the language pattern of a given speaker.

5   The data in this study can be analyzed in a number of ways. The strategic construction of a street conscious identity is of paramount importance to this study. Though other factors, such as gender, may play a significant role, they are beyond the purview of this chapter. For a recent, in-depth account of the relationship between language and gender, see Bucholtz (in press).

6   According to Anderson (1999: 21), "At the heart of the code is the issue of respect—loosely defined as . . . being granted one's 'props' (or proper due) or the deference one deserves. Manhood on the streets implies physicality and a certain ruthlessness." Listen to the Hot Boys' (of which Juvenile is a member) "Respect My Mind" for a comparison. Also, on GangStarr's (Hip Hop's highly regarded duo of Guru and DJ Premier) song, "Code of the Streets," (from *Hard to Earn (*1994), Guru rhymes: "So keep abreast to the GangStarr conquest/Underground ruffnecks, pounds of respect/I've never been afraid to let loose my speech/My brothas know I kick the code of the streets."

References

Alim, H.S. (2000) Interview with Juvenile.

—— (in press) "Hip Hop Nation Language," in E. Finegan and J. Rickford (eds) *Language in the USA*, Cambridge: Cambridge University Press.

Alleyne, M. (1980) *Comparative Afro-American*, Ann Arbor, MI: Karoma.

Anderson, E. (1999) *Code of the Street: Decency, Violence, and the Moral Life of the Inner City*, New York: W.W. Norton.

Asante, M. (1990) "African elements in African-American English," in J.E. Holloway (ed.) *Africanisms in American Culture*, Bloomington, IN: Indiana University Press, 19–33.

Bailey, B. (1965) "Toward a new perspective in Negro English dialectology," *American Speech*, 40 (3) October: 171–7.

—— (1969) "Language and communicative styles of Afro-American children in the United States," *The Florida FL Reporter, Spring/Summer, Special Anthology Issue: Linguistic-Cultural Differences and American Education*, 46: 153.

Ball, A. (1995) "Text design patterns in the writing of urban African-American students: teaching to the strengths of students in multicultural settings," *Urban Education*, 30: 3.

Baugh, J. (1979) "Linguistic style-shifting in Black English," PhD dissertation, University of Pennsylvania.

—— (1980) "A reexamination of the Black English copula," in W. Labov (ed.) *Locating Language in Space and Time*, New York: Academic Press, 83–106.

—— (1983) *Black Street Speech: Its History, Structure, and Survival*, Austin, TX: University of Texas Press.

—— (1999) *Out of the Mouths of Slaves: African American Language and Educational Malpractice*, Austin, TX: University of Texas Press.

—— (2000a) "Racial identification by speech," *American Speech*, 75: 362–4.

—— (2000b) *Beyond Ebonics: Racial Pride and Linguistic Prejudice*, London: Oxford University Press.

Bell, A. (1984) "Language style as audience design," *Language in Society*, 13: 145–204.

Bucholtz, M. (in press) "Language and gender," in E. Finegan and J. Rickford (eds) *Language in the USA: Perspectives for the 21st century*, Cambridge: Cambridge University Press.

DeBose, C. and Faraclas, N. (1993) "An Africanist approach to the linguistic study of Black English: getting to the roots of the tense-aspect-modality and copula systems in Afro-American," in S. Mufwene (ed.) *Africanisms in Afro-American Language Varieties*, Athens, GA: University of Georgia Press.

Dillard, J.L. (1972) *Black English: Its History and Usage in the United States*, New York: Random House.

Drag-On and Baby Madison (2001) *Live from Lenox Ave.*, Vacant Lot/Priority Records.

Eckert, P. and Rickford, J. (eds) (2001) *Style and Linguistic Variation*, Cambridge: Cambridge University Press.

Edwards, W. (1998) "Sociolinguistic features of Rap lyrics: comparisons with Reggae," in P.G. Christie, *et al.* (eds) *Studies of Caribbean Language 2: Papers from the Ninth Biennial Conference of the Society of Caribbean Linguistics, 1992*, St. Augustine, Trinidad and Tobago: Society for Caribbean Linguistics, 128–46.

Eve (1999) *Let There Be Eve . . . Ruff Ryder's First Lady*, Interscope Records.

Fasold, R. (1972) *Tense Marking in Black English: A Linguistic and Social Analysis*, Washington, DC: Center for Applied Linguistics.

Holm, J. (1984) "Variability of the copula in Black English and its Creole kin," *American Speech*, 59: 291–309.

Juvenile (1999) *Tha G-Code*, Polygram Records.

Keyes, C. (1991) *Rappin' to the Beat: Rap Music as Street Culture among African Americans*, unpublished PhD dissertation, Indiana University.

Labov, W. (1966) *The Social Stratification of English in New York City*, Washington, DC: Center for Applied Linguistics.

—— (1972a) *Language in the Inner City: Studies in the Black English Vernacular*, Philadelphia: University of Pennsylvania Press.

—— (1972b) *Sociolinguistic Patterns*, Philadelphia, PA: University of Pennsylvania Press.

—— (1982) "Objectivity and commitment in linguistic science: the case for the Black English trial in Ann Arbor," *Language in Society*, 11: 165–201.

Labov, W., Cohen, P., Robbins, C., and Lewis, J. (1968) *A Study of the Non-Standard English of Negro and Puerto Rican Speakers in New York City*, Final Report, Cooperative Research Project 3228, I and II, Philadelphia, PA: US Regional Survey.

Lee, C. (1993) *Signifying as a Scaffold for Literary Interpretation: The Pedagogical Implications of an African American Discourse Genre*, Urbana, IL: National Council of Teachers of English.

LeMoine, N. (1999) *English for Your Success: A Language Development Program for African American Children*, Maywood, NJ: The Peoples Publishing Group.

LePage, R. and Tabouret-Keller, A. (1985) *Acts of Identity: Creole-Based Approaches to Language and Ethnicity*, Cambridge: Cambridge University Press.

LOX (2000) *We Are the Streets*, Ruff Ryders Records.

Mitchell-Kernan, C. (1971) *Language Behavior in a Black Urban Community*. Monograph 2, Language Behavior Laboratory, University of California, Berkeley.

Morgan, M. (1991) "Indirectness and interpretation in African American women's discourse," *Pragmatics*, 1 (4): 421–51.

—— (2001) "'Nuthin' but a G Thang': grammar and language ideology in Hip Hop identity," in S. Lanehart (ed.) *Sociocultural and Historical Contexts of African American Vernacular English*, Athens, GA: University of Georgia Press.

Perry, T. and Delpit, L. (eds) (1998) *The Real Ebonics Debate*, Boston, MA: Beacon Press.

Remes, P. (1991) "Rapping: a sociolinguistic study of oral tradition in Black urban communities in the United States," *Journal of the Anthropological Society of Oxford*, 22 (2): 129–49.

Rickford, J. (1977) "The question of prior Creolization in Black English," in A. Valdman (ed.) *Pidgin-Creole Linguistics*, Bloomington, IN: University of Indiana Press, 199–221.

—— (1998) "The Creole origins of African American Vernacular English: evidence from copula absence," in S. Mufwene, J. Rickford, G. Bailey, and J. Baugh (eds) *African American English: Structure, History and Use*, London and New York: Routledge, 154–200.

—— (1999) *African American Vernacular English*, Malden, MA: Blackwell Publishers.

Rickford, J., Ball, A., Blake, R., Jackson, R. and Martin, N. (1991) "Rappin on the copula coffin: Theoretical and methodological issues in the analysis of copula variation in African American Vernacular English," *Language Variation and Change*, 3: 10–32.

Rickford, J. and McNair-Knox, F. (1994) "Addressee- and topic-influenced style shift: a quantitative sociolinguistic study," in D. Biber and E. Finegan (eds) *Perspectives on Register: Situating Register Variation within Sociolinguistics*, New York and Oxford: Oxford University Press, 235–76.

Rickford, J. and Rickford, A. (1995) "Dialect readers revisited," *Linguistics and Education*, 7 (2): 107–28.

Rickford, J. and Rickford, R. (2000) *Spoken Soul*, New York: John Wiley and Sons.

Romaine, S. (1982) *Socio-Historical Linguistics: Its Status and Methodology*, Cambridge and New York: Cambridge University Press.

Smith, E. (1998) "What is Black English? What is Ebonics?" in T. Perry and L. Delpit (eds) *The Real Ebonics Debate*, Boston, MA: Beacon Press.

Smitherman, G. (1977) *Talkin and Testifyin: The Language of Black America*, Boston: Houghton Mifflin (reissued Wayne State University Press, 1986).

—— (ed.) (1981) *Black English and the Education of Black Children and Youth: Proceedings of the National Invitational Symposium on the King Decision*, Detroit, MI: Wayne State University Center for Black Studies.

—— (1997) "The chain remain the same: communicative practices in the Hip Hop Nation," in G. Smitherman, *Talkin That Talk: Language, Culture and Education* (2000), New York and London: Routledge.

—— (2000) *Talkin That Talk: Language, Culture and Education in African America*, New York and London: Routledge.

Smitherman, G. and Baugh, J. (2002) "The shot heard from Ann Arbor: language research and public policy in African America," *Harvard Journal of Communication*, 13 (1): 5–24.

Spady, J.G., Lee, C., and Alim, H.S. (1999) *Street Conscious Rap*, Philadelphia, PA: Black History Museum Umum/Loh Press.

Spears, A. (1982) "The Black English Semi-Auxiliary *COME*," *Language*, 58 (4): 850–72.

Taylor, O. (1985) "Standard English as a second dialect?" *English Today*, April 2.

Turner, L. (1949) *Africanisms in the Gullah Dialect*, Ann Arbor, MI: University of Michigan Press [1974 edition].

Williams, R. (ed.) (1975) *Ebonics: The True Language of Black Folks*, St. Louis: Institute for Black Studies (reissued 1997, St. Louis: Robert L. Williams and Associates, Inc.).

Winford, D. (2000) "Plus ça change: the state of studies in African American English," *American Speech*, 75 (4): 409–11.

Wolfram, W. (1969) *A Sociolinguistic Description of Detroit Negro Speech*, Washington, DC: Center for Applied Linguistics.

Yasin, J. (1999) "Rap in the African-American music tradition: cultural assertion and continuity," in A. Spears (ed.) *Race and Ideology: Language, Symbolism, and Popular Culture*, Detroit, MI: Wayne State University Press.

3

Sound and power: the language of the Rastafari

Velma Pollard

Introduction

"People evolve a language in order to describe and thus control their circumstances or in order not to be submerged by a reality they cannot articulate." Thus writes James Baldwin in a 1981 article about African American Language in the US. His comment, however, can easily be applied to the creation of the language of the Rastafari. This group decided that the language available to them, Jamaican Creole, an English-related creole, could not adequately describe their circumstance. They created a code sharpening the linguistic tools available to them in the direction toward which they wanted them to point.

The speech associated with Rastafari, labelled variously "I-ance," "I-yaric," "Rasta Talk," and "Dread Talk," is one of a small number of codes created to serve the specific ends of a particular group. Other such codes, however, have not spread beyond the narrow confines of their constituency. Today the language of Rastafari has spread not only beyond that group to the wider Jamaican society, but also beyond the boundaries of Jamaica to the international community.

The movement, its philosophy/religion

The language of Rastafari is the expression of the philosophy of a movement, a way of life which emerged in Jamaica in response to a social reality which placed the poor Black man at the bottom of society. The intention was to give that man pride in himself and his race. The Supreme Being was not to be the white Christian's Christ, but Haile Selassi, Emperor of Ethiopia, sprung from the house which began, it is believed, when the Queen of Sheba returned pregnant from King Solomon's court. The group took its name from Selassi's earlier title "Ras Tafari." The movement began around the year 1930, but the language emerged some two decades later.

The Rasta man saw himself as dispossessed, pressed down economically and socially by the establishment. He wanted to bend the words he had to use to represent that reality and to include his religious and philosophical point of view.

He was investing words with the power to represent him accurately. So, for example, pressed DOWN by society, he refused to label his condition "oppressed," whose direction is UP. Instead, he created the word "DOWNpressed" in a clear correspondence between sound and meaning, a correspondence alien to English, the principal lexifier of all language in Jamaica. The sound of the word became as important as the meaning.

This chapter will focus on the creation of words within the lexicon (wordology) of Dread Talk, particularly on the importance of wordSOUND in that language. This chapter will comment as well on the movement of the word/the philosophy/the way of life that is Rastafari and the role that the sound of Reggae music has played in its spread from Jamaica to countries in almost every continent.

"Artistry" describes the processes these wordsmiths used as they crafted words from the raw material of English. "WORDWORKS" is how Bongo Jerry, a Rastafarian poet of the 1970s, describes the battery of improved words. He sees these words as enlightening meaning, that is, throwing some light on it.

> Enlightening is BLACK
> hands writing the words of
> black message
> for black hearts to feel
>
> (Bongo Jerry, "Mabrak," 1970)

The pun is intended. One meaning of the verb "to lighten" in Jamaica is to make closer to white. And what is considered "enlightened" is usually a point of view which comes in from the white world. What is white is likely to be right in a society described elsewhere as a pigmentocracy (see Introduction, this volume). The plantation pecking-order of white planter at the top, African slave at the bottom, shifted only slightly during colonial times to divide the Black masses into a "brown" middle and a "black" base. Further modification in postcolonial Jamaica was proceeding at too slow a pace to satisfy an increasingly frustrated Black majority. The founders of Rastafari were part of that dissatisfied majority. Their method of resistance was a kind of *marronnage*. Like the maroons before them, they settled into exclusive communities. They developed a definitive lifestyle. Their habits of dress, eating, religious observance, and eventually language were different from those of the majority of Jamaicans. Further, when they did move and live outside of those communities the habits of that *marronnage* were maintained.

The resistance of Rastafari may well have foreshadowed the turbulent 1930s, which saw restive workers rioting in many islands and heralded the beginning of the Trade Union movement in Jamaica. To reach enlightenment through the writing of a Black message by Black hands was revolutionary at the time when Rasta came forth and was still so to a great extent at the time of Bongo Jerry. The Black message sought to reverse the accepted order of power, forcing DOWN to become UP. Another strong symbol of the inversion in Jerry's poem is the reversal of "Sir," the English term of respect, pronounced "Sar" in Jamaican Creole, to read "Ras," the early title of Haile Selassi (Ras Tafari). "Ras" became the title used by several of the brethren as well. Haile Selassi became the Supreme Being replacing the white Christian God.

Nettleford in the introduction to Father Joseph Owens's *Dread*, described Rastafari as "one of the most significant phenomena to emerge out of the modern history and sociology of Plantation America" (1976: vii). Later, quoting Theodore Adorno, he commented that "Social protest manifests itself in language change. For defiance of society includes defiance of its language" (1978: 18). The language of Rastafari evolved in defiance of the language spoken by the average poor Jamaican. Dread Talk reflects the impact of the Rastafari Movement on the Jamaican speech situation and shares the Movement's significance. The Rasta man became a maker of words reshaping Jamaican Creole (Patwa), the language of the man in the Jamaican street, to accommodate his religion and his philosophy. He identified "sound" as paramount. The vibrations associated with certain words were important. The language of the Rastafari illustrated a consistency between word-sound and word-meaning in many of its categories. In others, new meanings were assigned to old words from the lexicon of English and Jamaican Creole, the languages to which Dread Talk was counterpoised.

The sound /ai/ (I)

The sound /ai/ emerged as the most powerful sound in the language of Rastafari. Many meanings come together in that sound. English, the major lexifier of all language in Jamaica, would see little relationship between "I" (ego) and "eye," the organ of sight. In the code of the Rastafari, however, where sound is paramount, the relationship between the two is close and obvious. The "I," the ego, is that most important self, and "eye," that window of the soul, represents the most important of the senses: sight. In Dread Talk, when one truly understands something, one sees it. "Seen, ayah" is a response that indicates complete comprehension. "Ya no siit" (gloss: don't you see it?) is a reinforcing tag that comes at the end of most statements in normal Rasta discourse. A believer will speak of his conversion as the time when he "sight up Rastafari." Yawney (1972) comments on the fact that /sii/ (see) occurs at the beginning and end of the name "Selassi." Within the very word Rastafari there is power assigned the organ of sight where "fari" becomes "far eye," the "far seeing eye," which allows access to the deepest reaches of things. The Rasta man, comparing himself to the non-Rasta individual, confidently states, "Eyes they have and see not, only Fari could see" (Rastafari Movement Association 1976: 3). Given this logic it is easy to understand how blindness is seen to have negative overtones. "Cigarette," which is a negative item, not good for the body, is not allowed to retain the positive sound /sii/ (SEEgarete) but becomes /blain/ (BLINDgarete). And the university, the seat of Western orthodoxy (non-Rasta thinking) becomes not /yuu sii/ (UC: shortened form of UCWI, University College of the West Indies), but /yuu blain/ (UBLIND).

In the Jamaican setting the importance of seeing is not unique to Rastas. A person who has troubles and cannot find their origin might go to a "Doctor" (a man some might label "Obeah Man") and ask him to "look" to "see" (gloss: find out) what may be the trouble. It might be said, then, that Rasta coopted, rather than invented, this particular meaning. Nor is the notion of a personality trait associated with the sound of certain letters unique to Rastas. A child character in a recent novel, poring over the word "rape" in a newspaper report, wonders "what the letter *p*, usually so gentle, was doing in the middle of a word held in such horror that no one would utter it aloud" (Coetzee 1999: 160). What is different about the Rastas' identification of the sound /ai/ as a higher sound is the number of different significancies that come together within it.

So highly is the sound regarded among the brethren that in a reasoning in May Pen, Clarendon, Jamaica, not so long ago, one of the brethren explained to me and others present that "A" as the first letter of the alphabet is a ridiculous notion, rejected by Rastas. "I," he said, should replace it in that favored position. Homiak quotes one of the brethren as further strengthening the case for elevating "I": "Anyhow you turn 'I' is de said 'I'" (gloss: however you turn "I," it is the same "I"). By contrast, some other words can take on a different meaning by inversion; thus "if yuh take God an turn it around yuh get 'dog'" (1998: 172).

It is this powerful /ai/ that replaces the initial sound in any word from Jamaican English or from Jamaican Creole and transforms it into a word from Rasta "wordology." (Note "I-ance" mentioned earlier as one of the names for the Rasta language.). Thus, /vaital/ "vital," which describes food that is good for the body, becomes /aital/ "ital." The man who is happy and psychologically comfortable is /airii/ "I-ree," a transformation from "Free." A popular greeting between Rastas is /aits/ "Ites!," a version of "Heights." This particular category of Rasta words is the easiest to create. In fact, young men in the 1970s, wishing to associate themselves with the Movement, created and used these words at will.

Pollard (1980) identifies four categories of words in Dread Talk. Within Category III (I-words), there are two sections: (a) the pronominal function in which "I," "I-man," "the I" are equivalent to English "I" or "me," and "I-an-I" becomes equivalent to "I, me, you"; (b) the initial sound replacement described above, which yields words like "I-laloo" and "I-bage" ("callaloo" and "cabbage") among food items, and "I-mands" and "I-bernacle" ("demands" and "tabernacle") among non-food items. In this way ordinary words assume the force and power of "I." Outside the influence of English, "I" loses some of its power. Thus the lexicon of Rasta might be said to be somewhat weakened when it is transferred to foreign language environments. In French Creole territory, for example, the pronominal function may be reduced. "I an I" is sometimes rendered "nom et nom." The initial syllable function remains, however, since most of the words are imported unchanged into the local Rasta wordology.

Other categories within wordology

Let us look at the transformation within other categories:

Category I: known items bearing new meanings. ("Known" here refers to English usage.) Two examples in which the words originated within the framework of the formal Christian religious observance should suffice to trace the thinking behind this transformation. "Chant" means to discuss, talk about religious matters usually to the accompaniment of Niabinghi drums. In the Christian church, "chant" has to do with singing or reciting Psalms. The parallels are clear here. The Niabinghi drums replace the organ. "Chalice" is the chillum pipe (for smoking marijuana), known also as "kutchie." In the Christian church "chalice" is a gold or silver cup containing the wine at Mass. It could be that these words were chosen out of studied disrespect for the church of the white God although I have not heard this view put forward. Other significant words in this category are "Babylon" (of biblical notoriety), to represent the establishment and more narrowly the police, and "baldhead" to refer to a non-Rasta individual, literally one who keeps his hair cut, as opposed to one who allows it to grow (a "locksman" or "dreddy").

Category II: words that bear the weight of their phonological implications. (I have already mentioned "DOWNpressed" as the replacement for "oppressed.") "OVERstand" replaced "understand," taking into consideration the fact that to be in control of an idea you must stand over it. "LIFEline" replaced "deadline," taking the negative overtones out of a positive idea. "AppreciLOVE" replaced "appreciate" because in Jamaica, "h" may be added to or taken from words at random, and "appreciate" may be pronounced "apprecihate," rendering the negative idea of "hate" in a positive word. The creator of the Rasta Patois Dictionary on the Internet attempts a transformation of "appreciate," but the result is an internally inconsistent word: "Lovepreciate." "Love" and "(h)ate" cannot live within the same word.

Category III words were described above (see pp. 63).

Category IV: words that are entirely original (new) items. "DUNNY/ DUNNEY/DUNZA" is the word for "money," perhaps so named because it is easily and quickly used up ("soon done"). "FREENANA" is an unexpected transformation. One might expect "I-nana" following the more common process that marks Category III words. "Banana" got so named because it is so easily obtained without money (i.e. "free"). Banana is next to sugar in terms of major agricultural products of Jamaica. It is so commonly cultivated that a farmer may not object to your having a bunch or a "hand" from a bunch without charge. Another item in this category is "ATAPS," a word for "beer," which is "HOT HOPS," understandable because many Jamaicans drink their beer hot and "hops" is metonymically "beer." The use of "H" described in the discussion of Category II words above accounts for the sound of this word. Other significant words in this category are "DEADAHS," a word for meat which the Rasta man, a vegetarian, treats with disdain. In this connection, note that the Category I word for the place where meat is stored is "morgue," replacing "fridge." Artistry, resistance, power are all words which may be used to describe the processes by which Rastafari arrive at words to describe their experience and environment. It is a tribute to the innovative skill of this group that the words have, with little fanfare, become more and more integrated into the lexicon of the official language of Jamaica as well as into the informal speech of countries separated from Jamaica by many miles of water. Bongo Jerry's poem from which I quoted earlier ends significantly: "Mostofthestraightening is in the tongue-SO HOW?" The single word the poet makes of "most of the straightening" introduces what has become the most famous line of that poem.

Dread talk in the lexicon of Jamaican English

Within Jamaica signs of Dread Talk's movement into social arenas not considered its natural place have been obvious from the 1970s when young people consistently tried to "spice-up" their talk with words from the vocabulary of Rastafari. Almost imperceptibly the language moved from being an in-group code to being one associated with youth of all classes. What could hardly have been predicted is that the words of Rasta would become absorbed into the formal/official language of the island. But this has happened, if to a limited extent. Consider two examples of the use of a word ("trod": to walk, leave, move away from, Category I, in *The Daily Gleaner*, the premier daily newspaper of the island.

> A modern day Marco Polo *trods* Jamaican soil [my emphasis]
> > (headline, *Daily Gleaner*, October 24, 1985)

> Let us put firmly behind us the not so clean lyrics, bury the gun talk and the badman mentality, *trodding* [my emphasis] carefully with the foreign cover versions, for obvious reasons and let's rock the globe with our music.
> > (Claude Wilson, "Whither dance hall music," *Daily Gleaner*,
> > February 21, 1992)

"Trod," the past tense of the English verb "to tread" becomes the single form of the verb in Dread Talk and the base form in Jamaican English. The unwary researcher might consider this item an addition to Cassidy's list of verbs whose English past tense form becomes the unmarked form in Jamaican Creole (1971: 58). The verbs "lost," "broke," and "left" belong to that list. While such an analysis might identify a contributory reason and provide some reinforcement for the feature, I do not think it is the main determinant. "Trod" (frequently pronounced /trad/ following the Jamaican habit of replacing the sound /o/ with the sound /a/) only begins to replace "tread" in oral and written Jamaican after the Rasta man has made innumerable journeys on foot (spoken of as "traditions/tradishanz") from one point of Kingston to another and has described himself and been described as "trodding down creation." In other words, the Rasta man's constant use of this form of the verb forced its integration into Jamaican English and led to the almost total disappearance of the form "to tread." Indeed Bob Marley, the king of Reggae himself, immortalized the Dread Talk usage in his song "Buffalo Soldier" a song in which the soldier goes "trodding" through his land. Finally, in terms of the preference for "trod" over "tread," one might want to look at other choices made within Dread Talk and hypothesize about which word sounds have more power than others, bearing in mind the importance of sound which is the main focus of this chapter.

Not surprisingly, creative writers in the society were among the first to acknowledge the Rasta man's language and have long used it to include him in the Jamaican manscape. As early as 1967, Brathwaite, in "Wings of a Dove" in *Rights of Passage*, discussing the condition of "Brother Man the Rasta man," exploits the resonance of the sound and power of /ai/.

> And I
> Rastafar-I
> in Babylon's boom
> town . . .
> . . . rise and walk through the now silent
> streets of affliction . . .
>
> (41–2)

Given the discussion above, one might wish to speculate about whether Brathwaite might have replaced the verb "walk" with "trod," had he been writing at a later point in time, and what difference that sound might have made to the line.

Goodison, in "Ocho Rios II," in the collection *Tamarind Season*, begins a second observation of what happens in that tourist city with the voice of the Rasta man soliloquizing: "Today I again I forward to the sea" (1980: 53). Here the Rasta man is invoked not only by the sound /ai/ but also with the word "forward," which in Dread Talk is a verb which translates to English "advance," "step," or simply "go."

Scott begins the title poem of his collection *Dreadwalk* with a line isolating the sound /ai/. Like Goodison, he begins his poem with the entrance of a Rasta man:

> blackman came walking I
> heard him sing his
> voice was like sand
> when the wind dries it
>
> (1982: 39)

The reader understands that this "blackman" is a Rastafarian because the use of "I" at the end of the line is a Dread Talk commonplace. But the poet allows that

"I" to apply as well to the next line; so there are, in fact, two people, the Rasta man and his interlocutor, one line representing each: "blackman came walking I/I heard him sing." There is an economy here of a type frequently practiced by those poets who use language to identify the different people they want to write about in a situation where all language is English-related.

While the poetic lines discussed above are all from poets of Jamaica, the influence is not limited to Jamaica. Indeed Rohlehr (1985), a well-known Caribbean critic, discusses the influence of Rastafari on the thought and language of Kendell Hyppolyte, a brilliant young poet writing in St. Lucia using English, English creole, the occasional French creole, and Dread Talk words.

Sound and music: moving the message

Elsewhere (Pollard 1984) I described the transformations performed on the words of Rastafari as they interacted with the popular languages of St. Lucia and Barbados following the spread of the "word" to those islands. I discussed the debt owed to Reggae music for the spread of the philosophy and language of Rastafari and the popularity of this language in Reggae lyrics coming from the tongues of its more charismatic exponents, such as Bob Marley, Peter Tosh, Jimmy Cliff, Burning Spear and U Roy. I argued that "the transference of philosophy and language by remote control is new and could not have happened before technology advanced as far as it has today" (1984: 255). The literature discussed in the following section demonstrates the truth of that statement and indicates how much farther the message has spread in the intervening twenty years since I made that analysis.

Neil Savishinsky, making a general point about processes relating to the diffusion and globalization of culture, points to the significance of "low cost/highly sophisticated technologies" and cites the spread of the philosophy of Rastafari as an example of the effect of the one on the other (1994a: 259). Frank Jan van Dijk, reviewing Rastafarian communities outside of Jamaica, mentions migration and travel as vehicles of diffusion but points to radio and television as means by which "the message of Jah people . . . travels almost without restriction and sweeps 'Rastology' into even the remotest corners of the earth" (1998: 179). Among other cultures into which the philosophy of Rastafari has penetrated, Savishinsky identifies the Havasupai Indians of North Miami whose initiation into Reggae music is traced from the arrival of three Indians from California with a large collection of Bob Marley cassettes. In his discussion (1994a: 264), he cites Arnold Shaw, Director of the Popular Music Research Center at the University of Nevada, who speaks to a point I have made (Pollard 1984) about other populations: "Unquestionably, the initial appeal of Reggae to the Havasupai was its sound and beat. But the Indians also found parallels between their oppressive and deprived lives and those of Black Jamaicans among whom Rastafarianism developed as a socio-political religion."

Early in the 1980s a researcher from the Netherlands came to discuss Rastafari with me and wondered why in a country like his, where social services are so good that joblessness need not mean deprivation, a philosophy which evolved among the deprived would take root. I understood then that he was not extending the definition of "deprivation" beyond physical satisfaction and was entirely ignoring the psychological needs of the individual. I spoke to him, *inter alia*, about identity and oppression, and I think he began to understand. It is not remarkable that the philosophy of Rastafari has spread to all the corners of the world. The vehicle that facilitated its spread may be unlikely but that, as we shall see, is not the result of chance. The intent to use the music, and the auspicious timing in terms of the development of that music by the 1970s, must not be overlooked in accounting for the history of the spread of the philosophy of Rastafari.

Sociologists and literary critics alike have commented on the 1960s musical explosion in Jamaica and on the social and economic situation which influenced it (see, for example, Rohlehr [1969] and Brodber and Greene [1979]). At a time when the poor of Jamaica were ready to articulate their position, the language of Rastafari was ready and in place as a vehicle to carry the message. The musical geniuses were predominantly Rastafari brethren. Count Ossie (of blessed memory), the leader of the group of drummers and singers known as the "Mystic Revelations of Rastafari," speaking in the early 1970s, described the role of the music in these words: "We were fighting colonialism and oppression but not with the gun and bayonet, but wordically, culturally" (*Swing*, September/October 1972). Brodber and Greene, discussing the song as a communicative device, explain that one of the characteristics of the theocratic world government, which all Rastafarian sects see as the next phase of social and political evolution, is that the "singers, as well as the players of instruments, shall be there" (Psalm 87.7, quoted in Brodber and Greene 1979: 13). They suggest that there is, therefore, divine sanction for the work of singers and other musicians.

At a time of political, musical, and religious ferment, Reggae music moved onto the world stage, taking with it the message of Rastafari which would speak to the situation of all the oppressed/downpressed peoples of the world and give them not only hope but advice in terms of how they might change their situation. Bob Marley, speaking to a people with a history of subjugation, tells them to take their lives into their own hands and to stand up for their rights. He indicates that this is something the individual has to do for him/herself. His (1980) words have become a mantra for dispossessed people all over the world: "Emancipate yourself from mental slavery/none but ourselves can free our minds." More recently, in support of self-conscious determination for the use of Reggae music, Ras Mortimer Planno, perhaps the most highly respected Rastafari brethren alive, mentor of the young Bob Marley of the 1960s, in an interview on Bush Radio, South Africa, said: "So that was the purpose of having Bob Marley in Trenchtown, that we use Bob Marley as our messenJah who carry the messages around the whole world" (quoted in Yawney 1999: 157). DeCosmo, referring to that same period of mentorship with Mortimer Planno, writes:

"From that point on, Marley knew that what he had to offer would come from his words" (1995: 75). She quotes Marley himself, who explained in an interview that "Music is the biggest gun, because it save. It nuh kill" (gloss: Music is the biggest gun because it saves, it does not kill).

Chevannes refers to Peter Lee's 1991 tribute to Bob Marley in which the love of Marley's music is seen as "the common bond linking a blues guitarist in Mississippi, a Black South African soldier serving in Namibia, a young accordion player in a South African township, and a group of Australians, New Zealanders and Scotsmen in London" (1995: 269). The spread of the word, predictably, was first to the communities where large numbers of Jamaicans had migrated (predominantly England and the US) and to other Caribbean islands which, like Jamaica, had recently gained independence from England. These islands had attempted, in the early 1960s, to become one political unit and had failed. Later, less comprehensive units, predominantly to foster external trade, were attempted. Black Stalin, Trinidadian calypsonian, himself a Rasta man (quoted in Craig 1980), compares these attempts unfavourably with the Rastafari Movement. He suggests that there is something Rastas know that politicians do not know.

The question of what Rastas know and why the philosophy found such fertile ground so quickly in these islands, then later everywhere, is answered by Black Stalin when he describes a community of people who were all brought from the same place on the same ships. It is this common history that accounted for the easy spread in the Caribbean, and in North and Central America, of the UNIA (United Negro Improvement Association), the brainchild of Marcus Garvey, who became famous in the Black World in the decade before Rastafari came forth and who is consided the main philosophical ancestor of Rastafari. Researchers into Rastafari, particularly Chevannes (1971, 1995), offer detailed discussions of these matters.

I am suggesting that that sameness of journey and ship, if treated as a metaphor for any journey into degradation and lack of self-respect, joins all people whose sociopolitical image is similar to that of the poor Black man in the Jamaica of the early twentieth century when Rastafari came forth. And this, more than anything else, accounts for the fertile ground on which the seed of the Rastafari philosophy falls wherever Reggae music has moved it. Tracing the spread of Rastafari over the whole world (outernational), van Dijk mentions the islands of the Pacific and the effect of Reggae on Black youth (chiefly, but not exclusively, Maori and Samoans) in New Zealand, "subjugated and stripped of their cultural traditions by European powers . . . struggling to regain their heritage and identity." He reports that Bob Marley and the Wailers performed in Australia and New Zealand in 1978 and gave a "major boost" to what had before been only small inroads (1998: 193–4). By 1983, Bill Hawkeswood, a New Zealand anthropologist, had written an MA thesis ("'I'n'I' Rastafari: identity and the Rasta movement in Auckland") which remains the definitive work on Rasta in that part of the world and is cited by most later anthropologists researching Rasta. A quotation from one of Hawkeswood's informants under-scores the link between music and message:

> Most of the street kids got into Rasta through the music. And Reggae music has a message. This message is what the knowledge is. So once they get into the music, the message is reaching them. I'spose that's how we all got into it. We heard about Ras Tafari, Macus Garvey, and all these things in the songs.
>
> (Reported in Savishinsky 1994a: 273)

The preeminence of the notion of a particular sociopolitical image as a factor in the predisposition of any group to accept the message of Rasta accounts for the fact that the Rasta man at this time is not necessarily Black and need not have been taken out of Africa, though that was a *sine qua non* when the Movement began in Jamaica. He may be white in Europe, and in Africa he may be a Black person who has never left or been taken from Africa. This view also gives credi-bility to the notion that the possibility of Rasta exists in everyone and comes alive when a light is turned on in the self and the individual "sights up" Rasta-fari, becomes, as it were, illumined with the truth of the message. This notion, long accepted in Jamaica, recurs in interviews elsewhere, as for example, in those reported by Jan DeCosmo of Rastas in Brazil who said they had been "born Rastafari but had 'assumed the posture' in the late seventies or early eighties after being exposed to Reggae music" (1999: 6). The particular music which bore the message carried within it, because of its origins, something that would call out to people who already had a relationship with certain kinds of music in their religious observances.

Music, message, and religion

The drum sound, however it is re-created, is the favored sound in Reggae music. The Niabinghi drums have their origins in the Kumina and Pukkumina (Poco-mania) drums of Afro-Caribbean religions in Jamaica. In fact, if you close your eyes and eliminate location as a consideration, it is sometimes hard to tell whether church music or dance music is what you hear. A foreign researcher in the early 1980s, traveling from Western Jamaica where he had attended a number of religious meetings, to Kingston where he attended dances, mentioned the close relationship he felt between the music and the body movements of what he described as the "national religion" on a Sunday night and the music and movements of the secular congregations in Saturday night halls in Kingston. This is by no means surprising. It is the drum that defines the sound and move-ment in both sacred and secular contexts. The existence of these religions in the other Caribbean islands, as well as the primacy of the drum in much of popular music, has allowed the drumming associated with Rasta to merge imperceptibly with other sounds in the receiving societies. Elsewhere (Pollard 1984) I discuss

Kele in St. Lucia and the Shakers in Barbados. I also believe that the fact of the existence of an Other to the Euro-Christian concept of religion already predisposes people within a society to being open to a new religion/philosophy. So for example in Brazil, where there is Candomble, and in Cuba, where Santeria and Palo Monte are alive and well, there is less strangeness attached to Rastafari than one might expect.

While there is no one explanation to account for the phenomenal spread of Rasta philosophy, it is safe to say that certainly outside of Jamaica the initial interest has been the call of the music as attested to above in the commentary about New Zealand. Music, even when it is without words or when the words are not understood, has the capacity to move the human soul. Diallo, writing about his people, the Minianka, sees music as a bridge between the visible and invisible realms and a "potent force for maintaining or restoring human harmony with the cosmos" (quoted in DeCosmo 1995: 69). Brodber and Greene, commenting on the response to music among people of African origin, quote from Haitian writer Jacques Romaine's *Masters of the Dew* where the fictional Diaspora man says, "I enjoyed myself like a real negro. When the drum beats I feel it in the pit of my stomach" (1979: 2). DeCosmo reports the impassioned response of an informant from Brazil:

> It comes without saying that I didn't know a word in English. When I heard Reggae the first time, I discovered it was the beat of my heart. Something happened to me. I felt like light. And it was not important what the words were saying because I was made conscious to my spirit; it made me feel good to my soul, to my being . . .
>
> (2000: 43)

Hansing, researching Rastafari in Cuba, records similar dramatic responses to Reggae music by people in that country who would eventually "sight-up" Rasta (2001).

Savishinsky reports that of the 100 or so Rastas he interviewed in Ghana, where both Ethiopian World Federation and Twelve Tribes of Israel, two of the houses/denominations of the Rastafari philosophy/religion, have communities, "80 percent admitted that their initial interest in Rastafari was stimulated by a prior exposure to Reggae . . . In the vast majority of cases, it was the music of Bob Marley in particular that made the greatest and most lasting impression on these young people" (1994b: 26–7). What is less easily explained is the effect of the music on non-Black populations with no history of the drum.

The first level of response has been to the music, to the rhythms of Reggae. Attention to the words and their meaning comes next. Interaction with people who are willing to "reason" with you, to expound on the knowledge associated with those words and the philosophy behind them is the third level of response. There are places where Reggae music has taken the Rastafari philosophy to the first level only; others have followed up on it and gone to the second level. A smaller number has reached the third level. Indeed in most communities all three levels coexist. Outside of Jamaica the response at the third level is associated with the presence, whether by design or chance, of Rastafari brethren who have been able to visit and give of their knowledge. Yawney (1999) gives details of this kind of involvement internationally from the Nyabinghi house, and Homiak (1999) comments on the use of video technology in this effort. Van Dijk mentions the visit to New Zealand in 1986 of the prophet Gad of the Twelve Tribes of Israel "to establish formally the first branch of the Jamaican organization in Pacific" (1998: 194). Bonacci (2002) writes of Italian Rastas going to England to meet brethren, to feel themselves part of a larger unit and to discuss doctrinal matters. The Bible and the speeches of Haile Selassi I are the more crucial documents involved in the reasonings. Initiates seek a deeper consciousness of what it means to be Rasta beyond the "Peace and Love" which is heard in so many of the songs and see examples of the day-to-day living (livity) of members of the different communities: how they prepare food, how they dress, how often they study the Bible and the other texts.

One of the variables influencing the level at which the response is made is language. Where words have meaning they are more likely to reach the listener's consciousness immediately. But the one can and frequently does lead to the other. DeCosmo's informant, quoted above, continues with regard to the history of his becoming Rasta: "I was very interested to know what the people were singing in the Reggae music. In truth what they said had a lot of things to do with me. And it was my own history that was being translated in the words of the songs" (2000: 43). Writing on Rastafari in Cuba, Furé Davis speaks of "the culture of Reggae in Cuba and the Rastafarian life associated with the music" (2000: 213). He too looks to the 1970s when "Cuba did not escape the internationalization of Reggae music that started mainly with the international tours of Bob Marley and the Wailers, the many Reggae bands that sprang up at that time and the growing interest of record companies in selling Reggae outside of Jamaican borders" (2000: 213). He quotes Angel Quintero Rivera, Puerto Rican musicologist, who sees music as representing one way in which man interacts with his world.

According to Furé Davis, the second level of appreciation came with the presence of Jamaicans who could facilitate the deepening of understanding for those individuals whom Reggae music had drawn to the philosophy of Rasta. Furé Davis quotes from the testimony of one of the earliest converts who links Rastafari in Cuba to the arrival of Jamaicans who came to Cuba to take courses. The testimony becomes lyrical remembering that "The walls of those camps where these Jamaicans were for five years working and learning are still painted in green yellow and red . . . I had the opportunity to share some time with them" (2000: 214). One of DeCosmo's Brazilian informants equally indicates a movement from first- to second-level involvement though his results from communal reasoning without the physical input of Jamaicans. Describing how he "sighted up" Rasta, this man remembers:

I started when I was eighteen years old, when I went into the army. I found some brothers who liked Bob Marley and who identified themselves with me because I had already heard Marley and I had heard Reggae music. And because of my own lifestyle and my environment I was touched by the Holy Ghost. Jah transformed my life, and I became his disciple, his lamb.

(2000: 49)

The response to Rasta has not been uniform. Brazil and Cuba represent foreign language environments which the philosophy of Rasta has penetrated. On the other hand, Giovannetti, writing from Puerto Rico (1995; forthcoming) into which Reggae music came through Puerto Ricans traveling between New York and their island, looks with dismay at a situation where the music and the external paraphernalia of Rasta have been appropriated by white upper-class youth (Blanquitos) for whom the words of the music have sometimes no meaning or sometimes inaccurate meanings. He points to the irony inherent in such a situation where such an unlikely population has "transformed the music and ethnic symbols of one of the best known social movements of the Caribbean (Rastafari) into fashion" (forthcoming: 10). Savishinsky mentions similar groups in West Africa within an environment which includes serious converts to the Rastafari way of life and comments:

One of the most conspicuous elements associated with the spread of the Rastafarian movement in West Africa is the fashion trends it has inspired, trends engendered in large part by the wide-scale popularity and proliferation of Reggae music. In a great many instances the appropriation of Reggae/Rastafarian fashions represents the total extent to which young people in West Africa personally relate to Rastafari, *especially those who are not connected to any of the local Rasta communities*.

(1994b: 29; my emphasis)

Commenting on Rasta in the Pacific, van Dijk makes reference to Gordon Campbell's comment in the *New Zealand Listener*, stating that "the majority of the youth began as Reggae fans rather than as potential Rastafarians . . . To them Rasta was music, style, coiffeur." There were others in that environment, however, for whom "Rasta was a vibrant and new political message; a successor to Black Power, emphasizing peace, love, and brotherhood; and a call for the unity of subjugated people around the world to fight oppression" (1998: 193–4).

Most researchers have placed the responses into categories ranging from flippant to devout; style to religion. One might establish two very broad categories, making allowance for the variations in between, and see how the models described in the literature fit them. "Rasta as style" could be one category for all those who use the symbols but do not recognize the contemplative philosophical aspects. This category would include the West African and Pacific youth

Savishinsky and van Dijk describe, the Puerto Rican group about whom Giovan-netti writes, as well as those Cuban affiliates who, in Furé Davis's words, took "the negative path towards the marginal activities, crime, and jiniterismo." The word "jinitero" is also applied to both male and female "hustlers" who attach themselves to tourists and support illicit practices. This group has nefarious intentions which the Puerto Rican, West African, and Pacific groups have not been said to have, but the superficial response to Rasta undeniably links them. This group would also include the "Dreadlocks" from Brazil who, according to DeCosmo "use the style of Rastafari but . . . really don't know Rastafarianism."

The other category, "Rasta Contemplative," might include all who are seri-ously involved with the social, philosophical, and religious concerns of Rastafari. This category would include the "Real Rastas" of Furé Davis's description. DeCosmo's informants in Brazil make a distinction between cultural/political and religious Rastafari (also called Orthodox and Protestant). Both, however, might be subsections of the "Contemplative" category. In Brazil further subdivisions would need to be made to account for the other religious alliances of these believers (a reasonable proposition in the Brazilian environment as DeCosmo describes it). Equally, in the Cuban situation, if Hansing's (2001) categories are used, several subdivisions would have to be set up within both basic categories.

Something torn and new

Transculturación, the term Furé Davis uses in his description was coined by the Cuban critic Fernando Ortiz. It is an excellent term to describe what is happen-ing as the culture of Rastafari spreads to new lands and interacts with other cultures. Nancy Morejón, famous twentieth-century Cuban poet, commenting on that term in a different context, writes that "Transculturation signifies con-stant interaction, transmutation between two or more cultural components" (quoted in Andrews 2001: 6). The variation inherent in such a spread (the het-erogeneity about which van Dijk writes) is part of what Furé Davis describes as "something new and different." This is a phrase reminiscent of "something torn and new" which Edward Brathwaite, writing three decades earlier, used to describe the rhythms of the steel pan, a metaphor for the new Caribbean man.

> now waking
> . . . making
> with their
> rhythms some-
> thing torn
> and new
> > (1969: 113)

Perhaps a new Rasta man or several versions of such a man is emerging. This is not likely to offend true Rastas who frequently quote the Bible—"In my father's house there are many mansions"—and who have the patience and the faith to wait and to accept change if/when it comes. (See also Yawney and Homiak 2001.)

I am particularly interested in the way the language of Rastafari interacts with languages outside of Jamaica. I have written about this as it happened in St. Lucia (Anglophone and Francophone Creoles) and in Barbados, and (with Furé Davis) am beginning to look at it in Cuba. I want to note which words from Dread Talk, Jamaica get integrated into the language of Rastas in other countries. Of these I want to see which are translated and which are retained as they are, which are given an extended meaning, and which words, non-existent in Jamaica, get created abroad. Indeed Furé Davis refers to the adaptation of language in a situation where Cuban Rastas "have to express themselves in Spanish about an imported topic with a foreign vocabulary" (2000: 210).

The place of Reggae music in the internationalization of the philosophy of Rastafari is clear and undeniable. It is interesting to note what has happened to that music as it has interacted with musical communities outside of Jamaica, especially those with their own strong traditions. Hawaii is a case in point. There, Jawaian Music, a mixture of Reggae and Hawaiian music, emerged soon after Reggae music "first made its way into Hawaii in the early seventies," taken there "first by internationally known acts such as Bob Marley" (Ku'ualoha Ho Omanawanui 2001: 141). Perhaps the same hybridity will strike the language of Rastafari. The auguries are that it will if the change in the attitudes and behaviors that have marked the development of the Movement itself are anything to go by. I have already indicated the variety of subsections possible within the two broad categories of Rasta I have set up. My categories have to do with seriousness and non-seriousness. But even within the "serious" subcategory, it is possible to note the extent to which attitudes toward some of the earlier tenets of Rasta have shifted within the last two decades, both at home in Jamaica and in the "new lands" to which the Movement has been exported. Commentary on two aspects of Rasta tradition, the attitude toward women and the attitude toward race, should suffice.

Although the woman, the Rasta man's partner (queen, dawta), has always been a highly valued person in the community, her deference to her "King man" in all things has been a given. Even child rearing, which in many traditional societies is thought of as woman's business, has very strong input from the male in Rastafari communities. The Rasta man's contribution to the upbringing of his "yout" (youth = child) is well recognized in Jamaica. There have always been people of a more modern/emancipated frame of mind who have seen this aspect of Rastafari as problematic. One Rasta woman's response to me on this issue was that what you have to do is choose a "King man" who is worthy of your respect and follow him. That answer, of course, is not sufficient for all women. The matter has come up for discussion over and over again. Barry Chevannes, in his definitive work, *Rastafari: Roots and Ideology*, treats the changing role of women and comments on discussions within the local communities. He cites the explanation given in the April/May 1981 volume of *Yards Roots* by

Sister Illaloo, who notes, in Chevannes's words, that "traditionally there was no such person as a 'Rastawoman,' but a girl taken from outside the movement and fashioned into the Rastaman's ways" (1995: 260). This, she says, changed in the 1970s, when women started coming into the Movement "independently of any man." Chevannes also quotes the impassioned plea of "Daughter Loi," who, in a 1985 issue of *Rasta Voice*, sent the following message:

> My black brothers, your black sisters are not your enemy. Your black sisters are not a threat to your masculinity. In this system she is in double jeopardy. Just as the white man system provide for the use, abuse and refuse of the black race, so too is the system of the black man on black woman. At this point-in-time black sisters are forced to recognize their role in the black brethren scheme of things to be one of inferiority.
>
> (1995: 257)

The evolutionary process has been at work within Jamaica for some time. In the "new lands" there has been even less tolerance for the traditional role of the female, especially in situations where it would have been counterproductive. In many cases the torch of Rastafari is being carried by women.

Attitudes toward race have been undergoing a similar change. Black consciousness and Black pride have been hallmarks of Rastafari from its earliest beginnings. The philosophy gave the poor Black man in Jamaican society pride in himself and his past and confidence in the possibilities for his future. It gave him a Black God in whose image he could have been made. The enemy was the white oppressor. A white Rastafari brethren would have been a contradiction in those early times.

The spread of the philosophy outside of the home communities where it began and the movement of the philosophy outside of Jamaica have meant that most Rastafari communities have accepted members of other races, including white people. Earlier I noted the existence of Rastafarian communities with no cultural connections to Africa. Giulia Bonacci describes the Rastafari community in Italy as one in which she observed "an endogenous population (non-immigrant, Italian, White) graft itself on an exogenous tradition (Jamaican, Black) with which *a priori* they have no common historical or cultural heritage" (2002: 1). Within some communities, however, it seems that there are rules governing racial behavior. Tafari, in a book that looks at Rastafari in Jamaica up to 1988, suggests that within the Nyabinghi, one of the foremost houses/denominations/communities of Rastafari, interracial unions are censured. Tafari writes: "Europeans, like other nations entering the fold, should embrace a partner of their own race" (2001: 317). Tafari seems to be critical of the Twelve Tribes, another Rasta community, for having no such restriction.

As the philosophy of Rastafari travels abroad, it is likely to develop in directions that serve the needs of the new communities. Racial and cultural relationship to Africa was perhaps the most important aspect of a movement started in the Jamaica of the 1930s. However, the fact that the philosophy speaks for the alienated, the depressed, the disenchanted allows it to appeal to widely different communities. It is too early to tell how the language of Rastafari will evolve in the different communities as it engages with languages not related to English. What seems certain, however, is that significant terms from Dread Talk, the language of Rastafari in Jamaica, will be part of all new lists. It is important to remember that the initiation into Rasta involves oral transmission of important doctrinal and life matters by interaction with older brethren who use Dread Talk. I believe that words like "Ital" to describe natural food approved of by Rasta, "Irie" to describe a positive feeling, and "Livity," which in Bonacci's words "encompasses the nutritious, spiritual, individual, and social rules specific to Rastafari" (2002: 5), will form the core of the language wherever and however it evolves.

References

Andrews, J. (2001) "Introduction: the poetry of Nancy Morejón," in N. Morejón, *Black Woman and Other Poems*, London: Mango Publishing.

Baldwin, J. (1981) interview with James Baldwin, *English Magazine*, 7, Inner London Education Authority.

Bonacci, G. (2002) "Rastafari talk in Italian: expansion of Rastafari movement in Italy," paper presented to the Second Conference on Caribbean culture, University of the West Indies Creole Mona, January 9–12.

Brathwaite, E.K. (1967) *Rights of Passage*, London: Oxford University Press.

—— (1969) *Islands*, London: Oxford University Press.

Brodber, E. and Greene, J.E. (1979) "Roots and Reggae: ideological tendencies in the recent history of Afro Jamaica," paper presented at the conference on Human Development Models in Action, Fanon Research Center, Somalia, June 1979.

Cassidy, F.G. (1966, 1971) *Jamaica Talk*, London: Macmillan Education.

Chevannes, B. (1971) *Rastafari: Roots and Ideology*, Kingston and Syracuse, NY: The Press, University of the West Indies and Syracuse.

—— (ed.) (1998) *Rastafari and Other African-Caribbean Worldviews*, New Brunswick, NJ: Rutgers University Press.

Coetzee, J.M. (1999) *Disgrace*, New York: Penguin Books.

Count Ossie (1972) Interview with Elean Thomas, "Groundations: Count Ossie and the MRR," *Swing*, September/October.

Craig, D.R. (1980) "Language, Society and Education in the West Indies," *Caribbean Journal of Education* 7 (1 and 2: 1–17).

DeCosmo, J.L. (1995) "To set the captives free . . . religion and revolution in Bob Marley's Music," *International Journal of Comparative Race and Ethnic Studies* 2 (2): 63–79.

—— (1999) "A new Christianity for the modern world: rastafari fundamentalism in Salvador, Bahia, Brazil," presentation at the 24th Annual Conference, Caribbean Studies Association, Panama City.

—— (2000) "Reggae and Rastafari in Salvador, Bahia: the Caribbean connection in Brazil," in H. Gossi and S. Murrell (eds) *Religion, Culture and Tradition in the Caribbean*, New York: St. Martin's Press.

Furé Davis, S. (2000) "Rastafari and popular culture in contemporary Cuba: A case study of Caribbean connections," *Caribbean Quarterly*, Rastafari Monograph.

Giovannetti Torres, J.L. (1995) "Rasta y Reggae: Del Campo de Batalla al Salon de Baile," *Revista Universidad* 7: 1.

—— (forthcoming) "Popular Music and Culture in Puerto Rico: Jamaican and Rap Music as Cross-cultural Symbols," in F.R. Aparicio and C. Jaquez (eds) *Musical Migrations*, Basingstoke: Palgrave Macmillan Ltd.

Goodison, L. (1980) *Tamarind Season*, Kingston: Institute of Jamaica.

Hansing, K. (2001) " Rasta, race and revolution: the emergence and development of the Rastafari movement in Socialist Cuba," unpublished PhD thesis, University of Oxford.

Homiak, J. (1998) "Dub history: soundings on Rastafari livity and language," in B. Chevannes (ed.) *Rastafari and Other African-Caribbean Worldviews*, New Brunswick, NJ: Rutgers University Press, 127–81.

Homiak, J.P. (1999) "Movements of Jah people: from soundscapes to mediascapes," in J. Pulis (ed.) *Religion, Diaspora and Cultural Identity: A Reader in the Anglophone Caribbean*, 87–123.

Jerry, Bongo (1970) "Mabrak," in *Savacou: Journal of the Caribbean Artists' Movement*, 3/4.

Ku'ualoha Ho 'Omanawanui (2001) "Yo brah, its Hip Hop Jawaiian style; the influence of Reggae and Rap on contemporary Hawaiian music," *Hawai'i Review* 56, 141–75.

Morejón, N. (2001) *Black Woman and Other Poems*, London: Mango Publishing.

Nettleford, R. (1976) "Introduction," in J. Owens, *Dread: The Rastafarians of Jamaica*, Kingston: Sangster.

—— (1978) *Caribbean Cultural Identity: The Case of Jamaica*, Kingston: Institute of Jamaica.

Owens, J. (1976) *Dread: The Rastafarians of Jamaica*, Kingston: Sangster.

Pollard, V.E. (1980) "Dread talk: the speech of the Rastafarian in Jamaica," *Caribbean Quarterly*, 26 (4): 32–41.

—— (1984) "Rastafarian language in St. Lucia and Barbados," *York Papers in Linguistics* *11*: 253–63.

—— (1994) *Dread Talk: The Language of Rastafari*, Kingston: Canoe Press.

Marley, B. (1980) "Redemption Song," Bob Marley Music Ltd B.V. (used by permission of the Bob Marley Foundation).

Rastafari Movement Association (1976) *Rastafari: A Modern Antique*, Kingston: RMA.

Rohlehr, G. (1969) "Sounds and pressure: Jamaica Blues," *Moko*, 16 and 17.

—— (1985) "The problem of the problem of form," *Caribbean Quarterly*, 31 (1): 1–52.

Savishinsky, N.J. (1994a) "Traditional popular culture and the global spread of the Jamaican Rastafari movement," *New West Indian Guide*, 68 (3 and 4): 259–81.

—— (1994b) "Rastafari in the Promised Land: the spread of a Jamaican socioreligious movement among the youth of Africa," *African Studies Review*, 37 (3) 19–50.

—— (1998) "African dimensions of the Jamaican Rastafari movement," in N.S. Murrell, W.D. Spencer and A.A. McFarlane, *Chanting Down Babylon*, Kingston: Ian Randle Publishers.

Scott, D. (1982) *Dreadwalk*, London: New Beacon Books.

Tafari, I. (2001) *Rastafari in Transition: The Politics of Cultural Confrontation in Africa and the Caribbean (1966–1988)*, Chicago, IL, Jamaica, and London: Research Associates School Times Publications, Frontline Distribution International and Miguel Lorne Publishers.

van Dijk, F.J. (1998) "Chanting down Babylon Outernational: the rise of Rastafari in

Europe, the Caribbean, and the Pacific," in N.S. Murrell, W.D. Spencer and A.A. McFarlane, *Chanting Down Babylon*, Kingston: Ian Randle Publishers.

Yawney, C.D. (1972) "Herb and chalice: the symbolic life of the children of slaves," paper presented at the annual meeting of the Caribbean Sociology and Anthropology Association, Montreal.

—— (1999) "Only visitors here: representing Rastafari into the 21st century," in J.W. Pulis (ed.) *Religion, Diaspora and Cultural Identity*, Amsterdam: Gordon and Breach Publishers.

Yawney, C.D. and Homiak, J.P. (2001) "Rastafari," in Stephen D. Glazier (ed.) *Encyclopaedia of African and African-American Religions*, New York: Routledge.

Part 2

CONCEPTUALIZATION AND STATUS OF BLACK LANGUAGES

4

Promoting African languages as conveyors of knowledge in educational institutions

Zaline M. Roy-Campbell

In most African countries, the language of education is a contentious issue. English, French, or Portuguese, each a remnant of the colonial legacy, remains steadfast as the dominant language of instruction for many countries in Africa. Despite the overwhelming evidence that the use of these foreign languages negatively impacts the acquisition of school knowledge by the vast majority of African students, throughout most African countries the foreign languages continue to be afforded dominance in the educational sphere. The colonial imposition of these languages as the languages of knowledge that should be valued and as the languages of cultural capital has contributed to the naturalization of English, French, or Portuguese as an indispensable part of what it means to be educated in many African countries. Those who are considered the *knowers* speak the language of power—English, French, or Portuguese—while the knowledge of those who do not speak the language of power is devalued.

This chapter discusses the juxtaposition of foreign languages and indigenous African languages in the educational arena. It reflects on the reasons countries have maintained English, French, or Portuguese as the primary language of instruction and on the continued impact of the dominance of these languages on indigenous languages. It also considers the possibilities for shifting the paradigm toward valuing African languages as conveyors of high-status knowledge. East and Southern Africa are the focus of this reflection, although parallels can be drawn with countries in other parts of Africa. The voices of African scholars who have addressed the language issue in Africa are central to this discussion. As linguists and educators who are indigenous to the communities they are analyzing, these African scholars are positioned to provide insights that may escape scholars unfamiliar with the intricacies of the local context.

Because language is such an important aspect of human interaction, there exist several general assumptions about language. One assumption, promoted by the power elite, is that there is a correct way of speaking, and anyone who does not conform to the expected norm is deficient. The specific representation of this norm differs from one society to the next and is linked to the disagreement about what constitutes a language or dialect. For example, in the United States, children who come to school speaking African American Language (also referred to as Ebonics) are often perceived as deficient because they do not speak the standard American English.[1] In African countries the aforementioned norm is manifested in the perception that those people who do not speak English (or French, or Portuguese) are not educated, or are inferior to those who are fluent in the respective European language. This view has arisen from the devaluing of the indigenous linguistic forms people have used in their daily lives for centuries, and the valuing of more recent European languages which brought with them Western education.

Another critical assumption is that children cannot be proficient in more than one language, despite overwhelming global evidence to the contrary. The clearest manifestation of this perspective is the dichotomization of African and European languages as the languages of instruction. Posing the language issue as necessitating a choice between an African and a European language establishes the framework for the belief that the European language is a "neutral" choice in the face of the difficulty posed by selecting one from the many African languages. It is crucial to dispel these myths. Understanding the terminology used in reference to African languages is an important beginning in this effort.

Terminology

Within African countries, indigenous linguistic forms are typically referred to as *vernaculars* or *dialects*, whereas European linguistic forms are called *languages*. This terminology was part of the colonial discourse that stigmatized African languages in relation to European languages. To date, linguists have not succeeded in drawing a clear distinction between a dialect and a language. Technically, the term *dialect* refers to a language variety associated with a regionally or socially defined group of people. However, the term is also commonly used to refer to a social or geographical language variety that is not the "standard" one. *Standard* refers to the socially preferred language variety, considered by the gatekeepers of the language as the correct use of the language. A question that arises in this respect is: *who decides what the standard is?* One widely quoted example that illustrates the complexity of this distinction is the contrast between Chinese and Nordic languages. Different spoken varieties of Chinese are regarded as dialects though their speakers cannot understand each other, while Swedish and Norwegian are regarded as separate languages although their speakers generally understand each other. Kamwangamalu (1998) points out that language forms with higher social value are called *languages*, while varieties with lower social value are called *dialects*.

Although the technical definition of a *vernacular* is a language of a particular locality, within African countries the term is often stigmatized to refer to linguistic forms that are considered less than a language. Herbert Chimhundu (1993) outlines the manner in which African languages have been "vernacularized," or reduced to a vernacular. He uses the UNESCO definition of a vernacular as the language of a group that is politically or socially dominated by a group that speaks another language. Among many educated Africans, the terms *the vernacular* and *the dialect* are coterminous with African languages. In Tanzania, I have even heard Kiswahili (spoken by more than 90 percent of the population) referred to as *the vernacular*, juxtaposed to English. These terms are an indication of an internalized perception that devalues African languages in relation to European languages.

Other terms used to refer to African languages are: indigenous languages, local languages, the mother tongue, and tribal languages. The latter term is often used in contrast to *national* or *official* languages. *Indigenous languages*, in the context of Africa, refers to *local languages*, those linguistic forms that originate in Africa and for whom the predominant speakers are native to African countries. This term is often used in contrast to *foreign languages*, or *colonial languages*, which typically refer to those languages introduced by the colonialists—English, French, and Portuguese—but includes other languages for whom the predominant native speakers originate outside of the African continent. *Mother tongue* is a term often used broadly to refer to indigenous or local languages. It specifically refers to the first language that a person learned and spoke at home as a child. In this discussion, it is used in the broader sense.

A *national language* is the language of a political or social entity, usually a country or nation state. Ayo Bamgbose (1991) points out that the idea of a national language originated from the notion that language is a unifying factor in national integration. It is one of the symbols of a nation, alongside a national flag and a national anthem. When many African countries emerged from colonial rule in the 1950s and 1960s, the new African leadership assumed that a common language was necessary to integrate the diverse linguistic groups of the new nation state.[2] Bamgbose notes, however, that one-language-one-nation is an outmoded nineteenth-century concept. Many contemporary African leaders have designated several African languages within their countries as national languages, used for intra- and inter-ethnic communication and as languages of wider communication.

The *official language*, on the other hand, is that used for most areas of government administration, including education. In most African countries, foreign languages—English, French, or Portuguese—serve as the official language. In a few countries there are joint official languages, e.g. Tanzania (Kiswahili and English), Lesotho (Sesotho and English), Botswana (Setswana and English), Rwanda (Kinyarwanda and French), and Madagascar (Malagasy and French). One widely proffered rationale for retaining the European language as the official language was the concern that the choice of one language over another would create inter-ethnic conflict. Post-apartheid South African leadership has circumvented this issue by selecting eleven languages as official languages—nine indigenous languages, plus English and Afrikaans.

Pejorative terminology is often used by Africans, in reference to their own languages, and by Europeans (and others who originate outside of the African continent). One of the first stages of valuing African languages is to recognize that all languages have the capacity to serve whatever functions are required of them. Some linguistic forms are less developed than others, but that is more a reflection of the uses to which those languages have been put rather than of an innate characteristic of those languages or the people who speak them. Kahombo Mateene, former Director of the Inter-African Bureau of Languages,[3] has affirmed that African languages are underdeveloped in scientific and technical expression because they have not been used in these fields. He explains that the poverty or underdevelopment of African languages is quite voluntary. "These languages are poor because we do not want to enrich them, by not wanting to use them in certain fields such as education and translation, which are all factors of language enrichment and development" (Mateene 1980: 26). All languages are important for the knowledge that they embody as expressions of life experiences and for the people who speak them. They are vehicles for storing and reproducing the society's knowledge as well as purveyors of culture.

Language and the production of knowledge in African countries

Language is often closely associated with thought and culture. Peter Mwaura (1980) relates language to the way we perceive reality and maintains that speakers of different languages see the universe differently. This perspective has been used to lend support to arguments in favor of instruction in the mother tongue. Ngũgĩ wa Thiong' o (1986), in describing colonial education, maintains that children were made to see the world and their place in it as defined by the culture of the language of imposition. He has linked the domination of African peoples' languages to the domination of their mental universe. To reaffirm the dignity of African languages and attempt to counteract the influences of European language on African minds, Ngũgĩ broke from the tradition of writing literary works in the English language and began writing in his native Gikuyu language. This symbolic affirmation has been wildly acclaimed as his books now must be translated from Gikuyu into English, to make them available to a wider audience.

On the other hand, several scholars—e.g. Alamin Mazrui—caution against viewing language as determining the manner in which we perceive reality (Mazrui and Mazrui 1998). Mazrui contends that this perspective can generate a cause–effect relationship between European languages and mental colonization and conversely between African languages and mental decolonization. Drawing on the work of Frantz Fanon, Mazrui describes the colonizing effect of European languages, arising from alienation. Fanon (1967) points out that this alienation results from the colonized person internalizing the cultural stereotypes of the colonizer and describes ways in which language and its uses serve to reinforce the subjugated position of the Black colonial subject. Within this vein, those Africans who continually invoke the inadequacy of their languages for use in certain domains are impugning Africans' importance as human beings with a culture worthy of respect. In the African colonial experience, European language and culture were presented as superior to everything African. It is within this context that formal education has come to be associated with the European languages. Reflecting on this meshing of language and education, Afolayan (1978) maintains that because the use of a foreign language as the medium of education is the norm in most postcolonial African countries, scholars, and policy makers tend to equate education for the African with knowledge of the European language.

Yet, language is not education; it is the vehicle for storing, passing on, and reproducing knowledge. The absence of a script for recording many of the languages spoken throughout the African continent, prior to the advent of the Europeans, did not mean that knowledge was not produced in African societies. Before the development of written language, knowledge was passed on from one generation to the next through the oral tradition. This was primarily facilitated through storytelling by elders and griots[4] in the society. Where knowledge was recorded in African languages, it was in a script that was not accessible to the European explorers. Ge'ez, one of the oldest forms of written language, was found in Africa, in the area currently known as Ethiopia, and the earliest Mande inscriptions date to 3000 BC.[5]

In the nineteenth and twentieth centuries, European missionaries transliterated many of the African languages into Latin script, in order to ensure that the Bible was accessible to Africans. They developed grammars and dictionaries for African languages to assist them in their dual mission of proselytization and colonization. As they opened schools, they provided basic education in the African languages,[6] while what was perceived as high-status knowledge, schooling beyond a few years, was made available in the colonial language. In other words, as Africans moved up the colonial educational ladder, they transitioned from instruction in their own language to instruction in English.[7] This was part of the process of naturalizing the foreign language as the language of education. Bamgbose (1991) points out that the few Africans who had access to this education succeeded in English, often to the detriment of their own languages, and became alienated from the masses of Africans. This privileged section of the African population became the educated elite that stepped into the shoes of the Europeans at the end of the anti-colonial struggle. This new leadership of African men continued the colonial policy of using English as the national/official language and the language of education. At the onset of their countries' political independence, many of these new leaders, enveloped in the nationalist fervor that led to the demise of colonial rule, considered the options of using an African language or retaining the colonial language as the national language (Mwankate 1968). However, citing the plurality of indigenous languages, the political leadership opted for the colonial language as a "neutral" language. The prevailing sentiment at the time was that one language should be chosen as the "unifying language." Further, so this line of thought went, the selection of one African language over another would have created dissension. This decision perpetuated and helped to naturalize the linkage between high-status knowledge, education, and the European language.

In many African countries, indigenous languages were used as the media of instruction for the first few years of schooling. This was a result of the 1953 UNESCO policy on Mother Tongue Education. However, nearly half a century later, Mother Tongue Education in most African countries continues to mean only a few years of using indigenous languages as media of instruction, rather than indigenous-language use throughout the entire educational system. The legacy of colonialism yet prevails.

Tanzania as a beacon of light

Tanzania was the only African country that, at the time of independence, had a unifying language, Kiswahili (despite the 120 other languages spoken in the country). This was due to Kiswahili's unique history. Before the arrival of European colonialists, Kiswahili was used as a language of trade from the coast to the inland sections of Tanzania. The German colonialists took advantage of this trading language and further developed it as the language of colonial administration. German missionaries transliterated Kiswahili into Roman script and constructed grammars and dictionaries for the language. However, they developed written Kiswahili only for use as the medium of basic education.[8] During the anti-colonial struggle, African nationalist leadership was able to capitalize upon the widespread use of Kiswahili as the language of unification. This was politically possible because Kiswahili was not the language of a numerically dominant ethnic group. Rather, it cut across ethnic lines, gaining and sustaining acceptance throughout the country.

While the colonialists encouraged the use of Kiswahili as a lingua franca in Tanzania, they opposed its use as a lingua franca in the neighboring countries of Kenya and Uganda. In these countries, they favored the use of other indigenous languages, which they referred to as the vernaculars.[9] In reflecting on the impact of Kiswahili as a unifying language in Tanzania, creating a common Tanzanian identity rather than a Mchagga or Msikuma identity, one might speculate on the effects of the construction of an East African identity around the Kiswahili language.

The British colonial administration facilitated the exercise of power through a policy of divide-and-rule. In Kenya (with about forty languages) and Uganda (with about twenty-five languages), there are strong ethnolinguistic identities, making it difficult for the selection of any one indigenous language as the unifying language. Consequently, English has remained the dominant language of government and education. However, Kiswahili has greater acceptance in Kenya than in Uganda.[10] Since 1984, Kiswahili has been a required subject for all primary school pupils in Kenya. It is now necessary to pass English and Kiswahili as subjects at the secondary school level, and, with the vast Kiswahili literature produced by Kenyans and Tanzanians, students in both Kenya and Tanzania can major in Kiswahili at the university level. Kiswahili is also spoken in the Democratic Republic of the Congo, Rwanda, and Burundi, as well as in the northern part of Mozambique. The valuing of Kiswahili as a language on the same level as English or French has vast potential for the development of a regional linguistic identity, with Kiswahili as a language of education in the aforementioned countries.

In Tanzania the colonial legacy remains strong. Although the policy of using Kiswahili as the medium of instruction throughout primary school was mandated in 1968, the political leadership remains reluctant to accept Kiswahili as the language of education at the post-primary school level more than thirty years after plans for this move were announced (Roy-Campbell 2001). One reason for the refusal to move ahead with Kiswahili may have been its perceived isolation. Mulokozi (1991) points to this as one of the reasons proffered by some of the opponents to Kiswahili as the medium of instruction for post-primary school. If Kiswahili had been more widely accepted in the neighboring countries where it is spoken, Tanzania would have had allies as well as access to a greater resource base to develop Kiswahili as the language of advanced education.

Another argument against using Kiswahili-medium instruction beyond the primary school level has been that it lacks adequate linguistic sophistication to reproduce high-status knowledge, particularly in the sciences. This notion has been refuted by the work of the Institute of Kiswahili Research, the National Kiswahili Council, and the Institute of Education in Tanzania. All three bodies have been engaged, for more than thirty years, in expanding the lexical base, constructing monolingual dictionaries and writing textbooks in Kiswahili. The first monolingual Kiswahili dictionary developed by Tanzanian linguists at the Institute of Kiswahili Research, *Kamusi ya Kiswahili Sanifu*, was published in 1981. Since Kiswahili is the medium for primary school education, Kiswahili-medium textbooks have been produced for all primary school subjects, including math and science. During the 1970s, the Institute of Education had begun writing secondary school textbooks in Kiswahili in preparation for the change in medium at the secondary school level. By 1987 a *Primary Technical Dictionary of English–Kiswahili* had been completed. This was followed three years later by a dictionary of scientific terms, *Kamusi Sanifu ya Biolojia, Fizika na Kemia*. The Department of Kiswahili at the University of Dar es Salaam developed a technical lexicon for talking about linguistics in the Kiswahili language (Roy-Campbell 2001). All of these initiatives are concrete evidence of the capacity of African languages to expand their lexical base to meet new requirements.

Despite the efforts of linguists and educators to demonstrate that Kiswahili can sufficiently function as the medium of instruction at the post-primary school level, the political leadership has refused to budge on this issue. At several points during the 1970s and 1980s, amidst preparations for the transition to Kiswahili as the medium of instruction at the secondary school level, government rhetoric suggested that the change would occur (Roy-Campbell 2001). However, anticipation of this change was laid to rest in 1984 when the Minister of Education announced that English would remain for some time to come. This was a setback for Tanzania as well as neighboring countries who were watching the developments of Kiswahili-medium instruction.

One result of Kiswahili-medium instruction at the primary school level has been a perceived fall in the standard of English at the secondary school level and above. Numerous studies have documented the difficulties secondary school students encounter with English-medium instruction in Tanzania. In the 1970s, two Tanzanian cultural leaders, Penina Mlama and May Matteru (1976), conducted a study that illustrated the vast difference in performance of students in Kiswahili and English. This study pointed to the importance of Kiswahili as the medium through which students can access knowledge.

In the 1980s, additional studies reinforced the importance of Kiswahili-medium instruction at the secondary school level. The 1980 Presidential Commission on Education conducted a study of the entire educational system, with a view toward recommending improvements. Although it was not mandated to look specifically at the language issue, nonetheless the language of instruction issue arose as a concern. In its Report, the Commission recommended that Kiswahili be used as the medium of instruction at the secondary school level and set a timetable to begin in 1985.[11] One member of this Commission told this author in an interview that members of the Commission were concerned that English did not seem to be facilitating education, but was blocking it (Roy-Campbell 2001).

Another study, conducted by two British researchers, examined the reading levels of students at all levels of schooling (Criper and Dodd 1984). Their report stated that the level of English in secondary schools was totally inadequate for the teaching and learning of other subjects and that it was hard to see how any genuine education could take place at the lower secondary school level using English as the medium. However, their recommendation was to reinvigorate English as a viable medium of instruction at the secondary school level. Implicit in this recommendation was the message that Kiswahili could not adequately serve this function, despite preparations for this very purpose by the National Kiswahili Council, the Institute of Education, and the Institute of Kiswahili Research. Findings of both studies were buttressed by a survey of reading competence of secondary school students in English, conducted by Roy-Campbell and Qorro (1998).

Although all of these studies highlighted the difficulties with English-medium instruction in Tanzania, the political leadership opted to retain English as the medium of instruction. This is one of the clearest manifestations of the strength of the colonial legacy. Commenting on the political leadership's decision, the former Head of the Tanzanian Institute of Education stated

> When the Presidential Commission on Education (1982) came up with the recommendation for medium-switch to Kiswahili for secondary education, this was a result of some research carried out among educationists and students. However, when in 1983 the government decreed against the use of Kiswahili medium in the secondary school, this was not a result of any research; certain beliefs, values and prejudices came into play.
>
> (Katigula 1987: 16–17)

In addition to Tanzania, Ethiopia and Somalia mandated African languages as media of instruction beyond the initial years of primary school education. In Somalia, where 99 percent of the population speak Somali, it took a Presidential decree for this to occur. However, following the decree a Linguistic Commission was appointed to produce grammars, dictionaries, and textbooks. The Ministry of Education appointed Somali teachers to research-writing committees to prepare textbooks, and within eight years more than 100 textbooks in the Somali language had been produced. Reliance on written Somali in public administration resulted in the development of a suitable vocabulary and style to cover all aspects of life—politics, law, education, economics, sociology, culture, science, and technology (Andrzejewski 1979).[12] One consequence of the strengthening of the Somali language was that it encouraged Somali intellectuals to publish scholarly and artistic works in their own language, thereby releasing energies and talents that were denied an outlet for expression in the past (Warsame 2001).

The Ethiopian experience was more complex. Amharic, the indigenous language mandated as the language of schooling, was the language of the ruling class in Ethiopia, not the language of the largest linguistic group. Other ethnolinguistic groups viewed Amharic as an imposition that devalued their languages.[13] In 1992, the new Ethiopian leadership stated that all children are entitled to study in their mother tongue. In practice, however, territorial languages are used as languages of instruction as it would be impractical to use all of the more than eighty languages. Michael Ambatchew (1996) points out that instruction in the mother tongue proved difficult for some regions and that they returned to Amharic-medium instruction and taught the mother tongue as a subject.

Valuing African languages in Southern Africa

Angola, Mozambique, Namibia, South Africa, and Zimbabwe regained majority rule more than fifteen years after other African countries had been politically independent. (Most African countries secured their independence in the 1960s.) Therefore, the political elite of these Southern African countries had opportunities to learn from the experiences of other African countries. Learning from the past, the political leadership in each of these countries recognized two or more indigenous languages as national languages although English or Portuguese was retained as the official language and the language of education, particularly at and above secondary school level.

In Zimbabwe, the two major languages, Shona and Ndebele, were recognized as national languages. However, English has remained the primary official language and the language of instruction for most of primary and all of post-primary school education. Shona and Ndebele are required subjects up to the secondary school level in the respective regions where they are spoken. In 1996, a group of Zimbabwean linguists formed the Zimbabwe Languages Association to engage issues of language policy and the development of indigenous languages as viable tools for Zimbabwe's development. This would seem to be a laudable goal. However, although these linguists seek to develop indigenous languages, the underlying principles of what constitutes "development" in terms of language need to be investigated more thoroughly.[14]

At the University of Zimbabwe, the Department of African Languages has embarked on a project to develop monolingual dictionaries for the indigenous languages, researched and prepared by indigenous speakers of the languages. The first, a Shona language dictionary, *Duramazwi RechiShona*, was published in 1996. Work on the Ndebele monolingual dictionary is currently underway. There are plans to produce glossaries of scientific and technical terms and glossaries for other disciplines. There are also plans to develop bilingual dictionaries in Shona and other African languages. The intent is to begin with Ndebele and other Zimbabwean languages, then extend to other languages spoken in the region. The fact that the dictionaries are being developed by mother tongue speakers of African languages, with linguistic expertise, is a major advance over the past sociolinguistic situation. Nonetheless, the major limitation in the development of the dictionaries is that the dictionary models which are used assume a level of literacy that is unrealistic for most ordinary users.

In Namibia, English is the official language although it is spoken by less than 1 percent of the population. However, ten indigenous languages have been given the status of media of instruction for functional literacy and for the lower primary school. Eight of these languages are taught as subjects up to tenth grade, and three are taught as undergraduate courses at the University of Namibia. To prepare teachers to teach African languages, the University of Namibia has introduced a training program for language multipliers (Legere 1996). These courses offer promise for the future through the provision of a core of teachers who can both teach the indigenous languages and use them as media of instruction. There is, however, a strong sentiment for English-medium instruction at the lower primary school owing partially to the absence of textbooks in the Namibian languages and to the parents' concern that their children will be at a disadvantage if they do not begin their studies in English medium (Brock-Utne 2000).

Both Angola and Mozambique, which were colonized by Portugal, adopted Portuguese as the official language upon political independence in 1975. Katupha (1994) points out that because the Portuguese colonialists devalued African languages and punished Africans for speaking them in school, these languages were associated with humiliation. Since 1990, when the revised National Constitution acknowledged the value of indigenous languages, efforts have been underway to produce textbooks and to develop orthographies for Mozambican languages. There are also plans to introduce two Mozambican languages as media of instruction in the first four years of primary school.[15] Six indigenous languages have been given the status of national languages in Angola. In 1977, the National Language Institute was created as a scientific institution to assist with the implementation of language policy. Linguists at this Institute have established alphabets for six languages to enable the translation of textbooks and literacy work.[16] Mozambique is increasingly showing interest in the development of its indigenous languages. At the same time, though, since it joined the British Commonwealth, the country is also increasingly moving toward a policy of official status for English.

Post-apartheid South Africa has gone further than any other African country by enshrining linguistic rights in its Constitution. The political leadership has recognized eleven official languages (nine indigenous languages, plus English and Afrikaans). South Africa has a peculiar history with regard to African languages since use of indigenous languages as media of instruction was the norm under the policy of Bantu Education. This policy of racial separation sought to condemn Africans to a mediocre education as the development of these languages was circumscribed, therein providing only that level of knowledge that the Afrikaner government wanted Africans to have access to. This has contributed to a resistance by some South Africans to the use of African languages as media of instruction, as they associate this practice with keeping them confined within a linguistic prison.

The official recognition of African languages affords South African educators and linguists the impetus to ensure that the indigenous languages are sufficiently developed to be used as languages of advanced education. It also provides the space for the development of a trifocal language policy within each region, with two of the most widely spoken languages within each region plus English. Benjamin (1994) maintains that South African nationals should be able to speak the official languages of the region in which they live, while Maake (1994) recommends that no person should be allowed to teach in a South African school without evidence of the mastery of at least one South African Bantu language. The goal of multilingualism in South Africa notwithstanding, the Constitutional language policy is such that, in practice, there is at present no pressure for a South African citizen to learn a language beyond her/his own, other than English which is a language of instruction in all regions of South Africa.

Too many languages to choose from

One of the greatest challenges facing African countries in addressing the issue of using indigenous languages as media of instruction is the large number of languages within the different geographical borders. This social reality has contributed to the depiction of African countries as being afflicted with the "curse of Babel," and has been used as a rationale for retaining the European languages. However, Bamgbose (1991) argues that this multilingualism should be viewed as an asset to the community, not a liability. The majority of Africans do not regard the availability of several languages as a problem. If anything, they regard it as an asset, for it means that there are more linguistic resources to exploit for their social goals.

Currently, many African countries have begun to debunk the myth of "Babel" by selecting two or more indigenous languages as national languages. I have already cited the examples of Namibia, Angola, and South Africa. Other countries in East and Southern Africa are also actively engaged in promoting indigenous languages. A Center for Language Studies was set up in Malawi to develop and promote indigenous languages. Textbooks have been produced for all subjects, up to fourth grade, in four languages: Creole Chichewa (Chinyanja), Chiyao, Chitumbuka, Chilomwe (Kamwendo 1994). The Kenyan Institute of Education has produced reading materials in twenty-four of the forty Kenyan languages. Although Kitula King'ei (1996) critiques this policy as not including the other languages, it is an advance over many other countries. However, teachers are not trained to teach these languages; rather they must rely on their rudimentary knowledge of the language. The Luganda Language Academy in Uganda has embarked on a project to articulate scientific terminology for Luganda. They are involving former and current math and science teachers, university lecturers, and linguists in this process through workshops where they test the new terms (Mukasa and Kiingi 1996). This procedure offers promise as a model for other Ugandan languages.

In Botswana, where about 80 percent of the population speak Setswana, there are five organizations involved in the development of other indigenous languages. These organizations, registered as NGOs, are involved with developing orthographies, translation of religious texts, development of reading materials, making grammatical descriptions, and conducting adult literacy classes. Lydia Nyati-Ramahobo (1996) points out that the underlying aim of these efforts is to provide literacy in the mother tongue to as many citizens as possible and to promote linguistic and cultural pluralism, cultivating unity in diversity. Setswana is used as the medium of instruction for the early years of primary school, but English remains the primary language of education.

Breaking the paradigm

It is argued that the plurality of languages, as individual linguistic entities, will remain a major barrier to the more widespread use of indigenous African languages in education. The number of speakers of different languages ranges from less than 1,000 for some languages, to millions for others. Critics argue that many of these languages do not have developed orthographies, and thus the cost of developing these languages and educational materials in so many languages would be phenomenal. Once the argument is posed in this way, it tends to be conclusive. Rather than generate discussion and ideas about surmounting this challenge, the discussion is usually terminated. However, enlightened African linguists and scholars have begun to engage in conversations around the standardization and harmonization of African languages as one way to cope with the challenge of multilingualism. In 1996, Kwesi Prah brought together African linguists and educators from different African countries to address the issue of harmonizing and standardizing languages in different parts of the African continent. Their contributions have been published in an edited volume entitled, *Between Distinction and Extinction: The Harmonisation and Standardisation of African Languages* (1998).

In the 1980s Neville Alexander revisited a proposal, made by Nlapo in the 1940s, to harmonize two groups of languages in South Africa, reducing eight languages to two: Nguni (Xhosa, Zulu, Swazi, South Ndebele and North Ndebele) and Sotho (North Sotho, South Sotho, Tswana).[17] Similar proposals could be made for many groups of languages throughout the African continent. Prah points out that African languages can be pooled into wider clusters that enjoy significant degrees of mutual intelligibility. These clusters straddle and cross territorial borders. He gives the example of the "Fula, Fulani, Peul, Tuculor, Fulful, Fulbe cluster which would account for about 50 million speakers and Hausa and its varieties for another 40–50 million" (Prah 1998: 7). There is also Xitsonga spoken in Zimbabwe, Mozambique, Zambia, and South Africa, and related languages, like the Southern Luo cluster which includes seven languages spoken in Kenya, Uganda, and Tanzania.[18]

Peter Mwikisa (1996) points out that Sesotho, Setswana, and Silozi are spoken in Zambia, Mozambique, Botswana, Lesotho, and Namibia, and that there are traditional bonds of cultural and linguistic similarity among groups within these countries. He notes, however, that mutual intelligibility drops significantly as one moves from spoken to written forms of the languages, as there are different orthographic conventions. This would be the area of greatest challenge for African linguists. They could be charged with developing standardized forms for the written languages for each language cluster, similar to the situation of Chinese, with its mutually unintelligible dialects but standardized written form. Monolingual dictionaries, similar to the Shona dictionary described earlier, can incorporate varied spoken forms of similar words that are acceptable in the different languages. A strategy in which the same dictionary has words from different languages could help in showing how multilingual material could be developed. Rather than being defeated by the tower of Babel, African linguists and educators can begin galvanizing the power of Babel.

Maurice Tadadjeu (1980) offers another alternative for addressing the plurality of African languages in a proactive manner. He argues for a trilingual model, whereby children learn first in the mother tongue, then another African language (national or regional), then a European language. Both alternatives will undoubtedly require a great deal of re-education. The strength of the notion that education means using a European language must be broken.

African countries are undoubtedly multilingual. However, Tsonope (1995) characterizes the linguistic situation in African countries as neglected multi-lingualism and unbalanced bilingualism. In the daily lives of the vast majority of Africans, most indigenous languages tend to be assigned to family, social, and cultural domains. These languages continue to be downgraded because of the lack of attention by the official sector of the society. He notes that there is a mis-conception that encouragement of several languages militates against national unity and highlights the risk of accentuating cleavages between communities. However, the examples of Rwanda, Burundi, and Somalia testify to the fact that a common language does not guarantee national unity. Within each of these three countries, the people speak a common language, yet they have been frag-mented into antagonistic cleavages.

The African continent abounds with positive experiences of bi- and multi-lingualism. The six-year primary school project in Nigeria is illustrative. In select schools, Yoruba was used as the language of instruction from Primary 1 to 6, with English taught as a subject. At the end of the six-year period, students who had learned through Yoruba medium generally performed better in the exami-nations than students who had studied through English medium. Further, the English proficiency of the students who studied through Yoruba medium was higher than that of those who had English-medium instruction (Fafunwa *et al.* 1989). This study clearly demonstrated that the use of African languages does not have to come at the expense of proficiency in European languages. The Rivers Reader Project in Nigeria is another illustrative example. This Project began in 1970. It was designed to produce initial literacy in about twenty languages and to use these languages as media of instruction for other subjects (Elugbe 1994).

The examples of Somali in Somalia, Afrikaans in South Africa, and even Kiswahili in Tanzania, all languages that have been elaborated, with grammars and dictionaries being produced as well as teaching materials, are indications of what is possible for African languages. Fufunwa (1990: 105) points out that "Once a particular mother-tongue has been fully developed as a medium of education in a given country, it is relatively easy to apply the same principle to other languages."

The work of Cheik Anta Diop (1981), and others who have built upon it, doc-uments the vast achievements of Africans, during the age of Antiquity, in mathematics, architecture, chemistry, astronomy, and medicine, all areas that required technical vocabulary and conceptual frameworks.[19] This refutes the assumption that scientific and technical knowledge is naturally constructed in European languages, or that African languages, by their very nature, cannot incorporate knowledge and modern science. If African languages were capable of expressing concepts in these areas at one point in history, why are they less capable of serving as languages of science and technology in the present era? Uti-lizing African languages in education opens the space for indigenous knowledge, through indigenous languages, to become an essential part of the knowledge base of African societies.

The OAU Language Plan of Action for Africa (1986) affirmed the premier place of African languages as instruments of national communication and all national economic and social development. However, this did not translate to indigenous languages becoming the media of instruction beyond early primary school in African countries. Ten years later, African leaders at the Intergovernmental Conference of Ministers on Language Policies in Africa, held in Harare, Zimbabwe, March 1997, declared as part of their vision for Africa that scientific and technological discourse should be conducted in the national languages as part of Africa's cognitive preparation for facing the challenges of the next millennium. As part of the strategies for implementation, it recommended that economic and practical forms of value should be given to the African languages by specifying language requirements for specific domains such as education, training, employment, and citizenship. The conference declaration endorsed the Pan African Project for Training and Educational Materials Production in African Languages (PATPAL), which was established at the Pan African Seminar on "The Problems and Prospects of the Use of African National Languages in Education," held in Accra, Ghana, 1996. This project seeks to attain a critical threshold in the training of personnel, in every African country, and the production of educational materials that would help make the use of African languages as media or co-media of instruction a normal practice in African educational systems (Tadadeju 1996).

Kamwangamalu (1998) suggests the need to rethink the ethnolinguistic map of Africa to promote the use of African languages in education. This could be one of the tasks of regional linguistic bodies in Africa. Chumbow and Tamanji (1998) have proposed a sharing of ethnic, cultural, and linguistic identity across borders to build bridges of cooperation between countries. They have drawn on Phiri's (1984) proposal that the international boundary should be seen not as a barrier but as a meeting point. A similar perspective could also be applied to ethnolinguistic groups who speak mutually intelligible languages within countries. The Bantu Education policy in South Africa encouraged the use of indigenous languages to isolate Africans into separate ethnolinguistic groupings. However, the harmonization and standardization project offers great potential for building bridges rather than divisions through indigenous languages in Africa. Mazrui and Mazrui contend that "far from being a divisive force that weakens the bonds of nationhood and wider relations of political identity, linguistic pluralism can be one powerful force of a new humanity within a world of tremendous diversity" (Mazrui and Mazrui 1998: 198).

Consolidating a new vision

In the twenty-first century, there is need for a conception of language different from that of the twentieth century. Bilingualism, multilingualism, and bidialec-

talism should be important components of the new vision. These concepts need
to be analyzed, taking into account the perceptions of and orientations toward
language which are characteristic of speakers of various languages. The language question in African countries should be addressed such that it ensures that
as many children as possible are given a meaningful education, that illiteracy is
eradicated among both children and adults, and that conceptions of language
and literacy are not in conflict. Contradictory notions about language and literacy might disempower and undo serious efforts to develop literacy in indigenous
languages. History has shown that such objectives cannot be accomplished by
the use of foreign languages.

Although efforts are currently being undertaken by linguists and educators in
various countries toward valuing African languages by elaborating these languages and providing reading materials in them, most often these scholars do
not have the power to ensure that these languages are used as media of education in schools. There is an urgent need for greater lobbying within and among
countries, language boards, linguistic associations, and other bodies that are
engaged in the further development and valuing of African languages. Although
the political leadership ultimately makes the policy decisions within a country,
nonetheless it is imperative that scholars examine the responses of ordinary
speakers to language and educational policies formulated by governments
because the everyday people are the constituencies of political leadership. And
in that constituency, there is the power to bring about sociolinguistic change.

With computer technology, through the Internet and websites, the possibilities
are infinite. Several websites, many based at US universities, currently promote
African languages. These contain ethnologues of African languages spoken in
each country, as well as on-line courses, grammars, dictionaries, and translations. The use of desktop publishing and web pages has made the cost of
producing materials in several different African languages manageable.

The challenge that faces African scholars of African languages is to consoli-
date the experiences of developing and utilizing indigenous languages across the
African continent. It is crucial to be informed about language issues and language developments in various African countries. Each country need not
reinvent the wheel. Similar attitudes about the inadequacy of African languages
exist in all African countries, even among those who utilize indigenous languages as a medium of instruction, such as Tanzania. Apprehension about less
commonly spoken languages being devalued is continent wide. Working through
projects like PATPAL, African scholars can collectively begin to address these
issues, sharing experiences of how they cope with particular problems in their
respective countries. This form of cooperation could also facilitate the harmonization and standardization of languages across borders.

African scholars, linguists, and educators, as indigenous speakers of these languages, are uniquely positioned to take leadership in the valuing and promotion
of African languages. At the turn of the nineteenth century, Europeans were
engaged in elaborating African languages for their own purposes. By the end of

the twentieth century, Africans in some countries had begun to reappropriate their languages. The challenge for African scholars in the new millennium is to extend this vision to empower African languages.

Notes

1 There is a wealth of literature addressing this issue. See e.g. Alim, Winford, this volume; also Baugh (1999), Rickford and Rickford (2000), and Smitherman (2000a and 2000b).
2 In many of these countries, English or French was selected as the national language since it was difficult to choose one from the many African languages to serve this function.
3 OAU refers to the Organization of African Unity. This bureau was created in 1966 by the Assembly of the Heads of State and Government of the OAU. It was to serve as an organ of the OAU in the linguistic decolonization and unity of the African continent.
4 Griots originated in West Africa and were the oral historians, the keepers of the history of the village and the genealogy of its members.
5 See Van Sertima, 1994: 211. Ge'ez is still used as a liturgical language in Ethiopia.
6 Territories colonized by the British tended to make use of the indigenous languages for basic education. French and Portuguese colonies, however, tended to proscribe the use of indigenous languages for basic education.
7 I detail this process with respect to Tanzania in Roy-Campbell (2001).
8 The history of the development of this language is beyond the scope of this chapter; see Roy-Campbell (2001) for a fuller discussion.
9 See Roy-Campbell (2001) for a discussion of this issue.
10 One reason for the resistance to Kiswahili in Uganda is its association with Idi Amin and his army. Because it was the language of the army, which was perceived as being largely comprised of uneducated Northerners, Kiswahili was despised by the Baganda and other groups in Uganda. It was later viewed as a language of repression under the regime of Idi Amin's army, which used Kiswahili to exercise their control.
11 I discuss the work of this Commission with regard to the language of instruction issue in detail elsewhere. See Roy-Campbell (2001).
12 All of this work occurred prior to the disintegration of the government of Somalia in the 1990s.
13 Mekuria Bulcha discusses the repression of the linguistic rights of the Oromo and other linguistic groups in "The politics of linguistic homogenization in Ethiopia and trends in the development of the Oromo language," in Prah (1998).
14 Sinfree Makoni provides a critique of the way in which Shona has been developed. See Makoni (1998), "In the beginning was the missionaries' word—European invention of an African language: the case of Shona in Zimbabwe," in Prah (1998: 157–64).
15 Da Barca (1996) discusses the project to introduce two languages, Cnyanja and Xitsonga, in primary schools, and four languages, Cisena, Cidau, Xitsonga, and Emakua for adult literacy programs.
16 Ana Maria Mao-de-Ferro Martinho (1994) discusses these efforts and points to the problems of the ongoing civil war that has hindered the progress of this project. See "Educational and linguistic problems in Portuguese speaking Africa," LOGOS, 14.
17 See Alexander (1989) for a discussion of this proposal.
18 Nyombe (1998) has classified this grouping of languages based on mutual intelligibility.
19 See, in particular, Diop (1981) and Van Sertima (1994).

References

Afolayan, A. (1978) "Towards an adequate theory of bilingual education for Africa," in J.J.E. Alatis (ed.) *International Dimensions of Bilingual Education*, Georgetown University Round Table on Languages and Linguistics, Washington, DC: Georgetown University Press, 330–90.

Alexander, N. (1996) "Models for multilingual schooling in a democratic South Africa," in K. Heugh, A. Siegrühn, and P. Plüddemann, (eds) *Multilingual Education in South Africa*, Johannesburg: Heinemann, 79–82.

Ambatchew, M.D. (1996) "Mother tongue, national language or international language? The case of Ethiopia," paper presented at the International Seminar on Language and Education in Africa, Cape Town, South Africa, July 15–19.

Andrzejewski, B.W. (1979) "The development of Somali as a national language and medium of education and literature in Somalia," *African Languages*, 5 (2): 1–9.

Bamgbose, A. (1991), "Language and the nation," *The Language Question in Sub-Saharan Africa*, Edinburgh: Edinburgh University Press.

Baugh, J. (1999) *Out of the Mouths of Slaves: African American Language and Educational Malpractice*, Austin, TX: University of Texas Press.

Benjamin, J. (1994) "Language and the struggle for racial equality in the development of a non-racial Southern African nation," in R. Fardon and G. Furniss (eds) *African Languages: Development and the State*, London: Routledge, 97–111.

Brock-Utne, B. (2000) *Whose Education for All? Recolonization of the African Mind*, New York: Falmer Press.

Bulcha, M. (1998) "The politics of linguistic homogenisation in Ethiopia and trends in the development of the Oromo language," in K.K. Prah (ed.) *Between Distinction and Extension: The Harmonisation and Standardisation of African Languages*, Johannesburg: Witswatersrand University Press, 91–124.

Chimhundu, H. (1993) "The vernacularization of African languages after independence," *Diogenes*, 161, Spring: 35–42.

Chumbow, B.S. and Tamanji, P. (1998) "Linguistic identity across the borders of the Cameroon triangle," in Kwesi Prah (ed.) *Between Distinction and Extinction: The Harmonisation and Standardisation of African Languages*, Johannesburg: Witwatersrand University Press, 75–90.

Criper, C. and Dodd, W. (1984) *Report on the Teaching of English and its Uses as a Medium of Instruction*, London: ODA/British Council.

da Barca, N.D. (1996) "Production of textbooks in Xitsonga (Xichangana): problems of choosing the variety to be used in the textbooks," paper presented at the International Seminar on Language and Education in Africa, Cape Town, South Africa, July 15–19.

Diop, C.A. (1981) *Civilization or Barbarism: An Authentic Anthropology* (translated from the French by Yaa-Lengi Meema Ngemi, 1991), New York: Lawrence Hill Books.

Elugbe, B.O. (1994) "Minority language development in Nigeria: a situation report on Bendel and River States," in R. Fardon and G. Furniss (eds) *African Languages, Development and the State*, London: Routledge, 62–75.

Fafunwa, B.A. (1990) "Using national languages in education: a challenge to African educators," in *African Thoughts on the Prospects of Education for All*, Selected Papers Commissioned for the Regional Consultation on Education for All, Dakar: UNESCO–UNICEF.

Fafunwa, B.A., Iyabode Macauley, J.I., and Sokoya, J.A.F. (eds) (1989) *Education in the Mother Tongue: The Primary Education Research Project (1970–1978)*, Ibadan: University Press Ltd.

Fanon, F. (1967) *Wretched of the Earth*, New York: Grove Press.

Kamwangamalu, N. (1998) "Linguistic frontiers in Africa: reality and implications for education and development: the Zaire–Zambia border area with respect to the Bemba Cluster," in Kwesi Prah (ed.) *Between Distinction and Extinction: The Harmonisation and Standardisation of African Languages*, Johannesburg: Witwatersrand University Press, 187–202.

Kamwendo, G. (1994) "Promotion of foreign languages at the expense of Malawian indigenous languages: language policy in the Malawian education system during Dr. Banda's rule (1964–1994)," paper presented at the Pan African Colloquium: Educational Innovation in Postcolonial Africa, Cape Town, December 12–15.

Katigula, B.A.J. (1987) *Factors Affecting the Achievement and Non-Achievement of the Objectives of National Language and Mother Tongue Policies and Teaching Programmes in Africa: The Case of Tanzania*, Dakar: UNESCO.

Katupha, J.M.M. (1994) "The language situation and language use in Mozambique," in R. Fardon and G. Furniss (eds) *African Languages, Development and the State*, London: Routledge, 86–96.

King'ei, K. (1996) "Critical issues in Kenya's multilingual education curriculum," paper presented at the International Seminar on Language and Education in Africa, Cape Town, South Africa, July 15–19.

Legere, K. (1996) "Languages in Namibian education, achievements and problems," paper presented at the International Seminar on Language and Education in Africa, Cape Town, South Africa, July 15–19.

Maake, N.P. (1994) *Dismantling the Tower of Babel*, in R. Fardon and G. Furniss (eds) *African Languages, Development and the State*, London: Routledge, 111–22.

Mateene, K. (1980) "Failure in the obligatory use of European languages in Africa and the advantages of a policy of linguistic independence," in *Reconsideration of African Linguistic Policies*, Kampala: OAU/BIL, 11–41.

Mazrui, A.A. and Mazrui, A.M. (1998) *The Power of Babel: Language and Governance in the African Experience*, New York: Oxford University Press.

Mlama, P. and Matteru, M. (1977) *Haja ya Kutumia Kiswahili Kufundishia Katika Elimu ya Juu*, Dar es Salaam: Baraza la Kiswahili la Taifa.

Mukasa, L. and Kiingi, K. (1996) "Report on testing workshops for articulation of scientific concepts in Luganda," paper presented at Colloquium on Harmonising and Standardising African Languages for Education and Development, Cape Town, South Africa, July 11–14.

Mulokozi, M.M. (1991) "English versus Kiswahili in Tanzania's secondary education," in J. Blommaert (ed.) *Swahili Studies*, Ghent: Academic Press, 23–38.

Mwankate, J.M. (1968) *The Growth of Education in Zambia since Independence*, Nairobi: Oxford University Press.

Mwaura, P. (1980) *Communication Policies in Kenya*, Paris: UNESCO.

Mwikisa, P.W. (1996) "African languages in education and development: challenges for the 21st century: the case of Sesotho, Setswana and Silozi," paper presented at Colloquium on Harmonising and Standardising African Languages for Education and Development, Cape Town, South Africa, July 11–14.

Ngũgĩ wa Thiong' o (1986) *Decolonising the Mind*, Harare: Zimbabwe Publishing House.

Nhlapo, J. (1944) *Bantu Babel: Will the Bantu Languages Live?* Cape Town: The African Bookman.

Nyati-Ramahobo, L. (1996) "Language in education policy and practice: the case of Botswana," paper presented at the International Seminar on Language and Education in Africa, Cape Town, South Africa, July 15–19.

Nyombe, B.G.V. (1998) "Harmonizing, standardizing and classifying Nilotic languages for education," in Kwesi Prah (ed.) *Between Distinction and Extinction: The Harmonisation and Standardisation of African Languages*, Johannesburg: Witwatersrand University Press, 125–42.

OAU (1986) *Language Plan of Action for Africa*, Document CM/1352 (XLIV), Addis Ababa: OAU Secretariat.

Phiri, S.H. (1984) "National integration, rural development and frontier communities: the case of Ngoni astride the Zambian boundary with Malawi and Mozambique," in A.I. Asiwaju (ed.) *Partitioned Africans*, Lagos: Lagos University Press.

Prah, K.K. (1995) *African Languages for the Mass Education of Africans*, Bonn: German Foundation for International Development.

—— (ed.) (1998) *Between Distinction and Extinction: The Harmonisation and Standardisation of African Languages*, Johannesburg: Witwatersrand University Press.

Rickford, J. and Rickford, R. (2000) *Spoken Soul: The Story of Black English*, New York: John Wiley and Sons, Inc.

Roy-Campbell, Z.M. (2001) *Empowerment through Language: The African Experience, Tanzania and Beyond*, Trenton, NJ: Africa World Press.

Roy-Campbell, Z.M. and Qorro, M. (1998) *Language Crisis in Tanzania: The Myth of Kiswahili versus English*, Dar es Salaam: Mkuki na Nyota.

Smitherman, G. (2000a) *Talkin That Talk: Language, Culture and Education in African America*, London and New York: Routledge.

—— (2000b) "Language and democracy in the United States of America and South Africa," in S.B. Makoni and N. Kamwangamalu (eds) *Language and Institutions in Africa*, Cape Town: Center for Advanced Studies of African Society, 65–92.

Tadadjeu, M. (1980) *A Model for Functional Trilingual Education Planning in Africa*, Paris: UNESCO.

—— (1996) *Pan-African Project for Training and Educational Materials Production in African Languages (PATPAL)*, prepared for Intergovernmental Conference on Language Policies in Africa, Harare, Zimbabwe.

Tsonope, J. (1995) "Prospects for the indigenous languages of Botswana: implications of the Government White Paper No. 2 of 1994," *Journal of Botswana Educational Research*, 3 (1, 2): 5–14.

Van Sertima, I. (1994) *Blacks in Science: Ancient and Modern*, New Brunswick, NJ: Transaction Books.

Warsame, A.A. (2001) "How a strong government backed an African language: the lessons of Somalia," *International Review of Education*, 47 (3–4): 341–60.

5

Language policies and language education in Francophone Africa: a critique and a call to action

Hassana Alidou

Introduction

The purpose of this chapter is to critically assess language education policies and practices in Francophone Africa, using Burkina Faso, Mali, and Niger as case studies. The sociolinguistic character of Francophone Africa has undergone fundamental change since the demise of colonialism. Thus, there is a crucial need to revisit current language policies and pedagogical practices in the so-called "French-speaking" countries and to develop new language education systems and instructional strategies to address the plague of illiteracy and non-education that continues to haunt these nations. The critique presented here calls into question the established philosophical paradigm of "mother tongue" medium of instruction. At the same time, this critique challenges the postcolonial advocacy of "French-only" medium of instruction. Given the diversity of sociocultural, economic—and linguistic—conditions throughout Francophone Africa, there is a need to develop forms of education to accommodate this diversity. It is no longer the case (if it ever was) that one size fits all. A serious reevaluation of the status and roles of African languages and the French language as well is long overdue. My position is grounded in fifteen years of involvement in international development and in my experience as a first-language speaker of Hausa and Zarma-Songhay, two main languages spoken as national languages in Niger. My work and research in international development involved professional development training for language teachers, extensive observations of primary school classrooms, and policy formulation for governmental institutions and international donors.

It is crucial that linguists, educators, policymakers, and other stakeholders recognize that, since colonization, the role of French has evolved in Africa. Scholars cannot continue to view this sociolinguistic condition as merely reflecting the inherited colonial language or as a case of an oppressive language promoted to official status. On the one hand, it must be acknowledged that African schools designed by French colonial power not only served as a significant space for cultural and linguistic imperialism, but also, in the postcolonial era, have become a large textbook market for French publishing companies which produce most of the educational materials currently used in Francophone Africa (Alidou-Ngame 2000). In order to preserve this market, French support for African education is strictly tied to the maintenance of a French-based educational policy from primary school to higher education. Such a policy is an essential factor in the French government's financial and technical support of African education. On the other hand, because of this colonial history, French is becoming the first or second dominant language of a significant number of African children concentrated in urban centers. This sociolinguistic development has implications for the use of French in the classroom. Such an educational consideration was not possible in the 1960s when the acquisition of French was not as widespread. Thus, African scholars such as Bokamba and Tlou (1980) rightfully criticized the use of French as the first language of instruction for African children. However, this critique is not totally applicable today. The teaching and use of the French language in classrooms must be revisited in light of this new sociolinguistic development.

For several decades now, linguists and educators have argued for the use of African languages as media of instruction in schools (e.g. Bokamba 1984; Fafuna et al. 1989; Alidou 1997; Bamgbose 1997; Moumouni 1998; Mazrui 2000). African political leaders have also recommended that these languages be used in education. However, their support for this cause has been more visible in political discourse than in actual policies backed by financial investment. In Francophone Africa, only Guinea Conakry's former President, Seku Toure, fully implemented the use of national languages as the dominant means of instruction in primary and secondary education. Unfortunately, this language education policy ended with his death in 1984. The lack of sufficient financial support from government and private donors has seriously affected corpus planning efforts undertaken by linguists since the 1960s. Consequently, there are very few African languages that have been fully described, updated, and modernized to serve as media of instruction in education. In all Francophone countries the promotion of national languages in education currently remains mainly an educational experiment, rather than a generalized language policy implemented in government schools.

It is my contention that European languages which serve as official languages must be adopted as "African" languages imbued with an African identity. These languages can then be used as effective languages of instruction. By the same token, African languages can and should be used as media of instruction and also taught as a subject in African schools. Governments and the private sector must develop forms of language education that fit the needs of children living in various sociocultural, economic, and linguistic conditions.

Based on the language(s) of instruction, there are three types of formal primary schools in Burkina Faso, Mali, and Niger:

1   French medium only from first to sixth grade; this characterizes mainstream governmental or private schools;
2   French and Arabic as co-equal media of instruction from first to sixth grade; this type of school is the madrasa;
3   experimental bilingual schools that use national languages as media of instruction in the first three years of schooling, with French being introduced as the dominant language of instruction from the fourth grade onward.

The focus of this critique is the government mainstream and experimental bilingual primary schools. The first two sections of this chapter deal with language and curriculum issues in these two types of schools. The third section issues a call to action and provides recommendations to address language education and literacy issues in Francophone Africa.

Educational language policy in Francophone schools: post Jomtien conference

In 1990, UNESCO, the World Bank, national ministries of education, and several international organizations gathered in Jomtien, Thailand, to evaluate the state of education in the world. Not surprisingly, the evaluation of the African educational system, as with other socioeconomic sectors and domains in African countries, was depressing. The whole world recognized that Africa is experiencing a serious educational crisis related to the irrelevance of the curriculum, the languages of instruction, and the centralized organizational structures of the educational systems. A call for investments and reforms that take into consideration African people's socioeconomic and cultural backgrounds was made. While most developed countries pledged increased financial and technical support, African governments produced policy papers renewing their interest in designing reforms to influence the adaptation of African curricula to the reality and needs of people and in the use of national languages as media of instruction to promote education for girls.

The use of African languages was particularly viewed as a strategy to promote gender equity and cultural and linguistic diversity in schools. In Burkina Faso, for example, the use of community languages as instructional media facilitates girls' active participation in classroom activities while the use of French tends to intimidate them. As a secondary school teacher and university lecturer in Niger, I observed that, in the classroom, girls and women were reluctant to speak out because they were afraid to make mistakes in speaking French. (However, they adequately expressed their opinions in writing in French, and in some cases they did better than their male classmates.) Creating a classroom environment in which they were permitted to speak their community languages reduced their level of fear and increased dialogue, interaction, and involvement in the classroom.

After Jomtien, several high-level political gatherings took place to revive the use of African languages for formal basic education. The ministers of education of African states met with linguists and education specialists in Segu, Mali (1992), Mamou, Guinea (1992), Accra, Ghana (1995), and Cape Town, South Africa (1996) in order to produce policy papers related to the use of African languages in education. Each conference ended with a specific declaration favoring the use of African languages as media of instruction in schools. These conferences were supported not only by government agencies but also by the international donor community.

In April 2000, UNESCO and the World Bank organized a ten-year evaluation of the "Education for All by Year 2000" programs. The follow-up meeting that took place in Dakar, Senegal, revealed that in Africa very limited progress had been made. For instance, the implementation, at the grass-roots level, of the curriculum and language education reforms designed in the early 1990s by Francophone African countries has been extremely slow. Further, at the end of primary schooling, African students' performance on achievement tests administered in official languages, e.g. French and English, continues to remain far below international standards (UNESCO 2000).

The question of language of instruction was barely addressed owing to the reluctance of the World Bank and France to support the promotion of national languages in formal education. In fact, since Jomtien, the World Bank and the French government have expressed more resistance to than support for language education reforms proposed by African governments, particularly those of Burkina Faso, Mali, and Niger. However, these governments have endeavored to maintain the momentum and have obtained some technical and financial support from a few international organizations. Currently, only these three Francophone countries have systematically intensified efforts for the creation or revitalization of their experimental bilingual schools. In Burkina Faso, the Ministry of Basic Education (MEBA) and UNICEF created the "Ecoles Satellites" (Satellite Schools). In Mali, the ministry of Basic Education obtained the support of several international organizations and created "Les Écoles de la Pédagogie Convergente" ("schools of convergent pedagogy") developed by Professor Waumbach from Belgium. This pedagogical approach is based on the oral development of the national language and the inclusion of local performing art (dance and singing). Niger's Ministry of Basic Education received technical and financial support from two German development agencies to revitalize the forty-six bilingual education schools that had been created since 1973. It is in these educational contexts that one can observe pedagogical innovations related to the adaptation of the school curriculum and languages of instruction to students' cultural, linguistic, and economic backgrounds. However, the mainstream schools have remained generally the same, as if the Jomtien conference had never occurred. Consequently, the current sociolinguistic profile of urban students, particularly as it relates to their proficiency in French, is not taken into consideration by mainstream teachers and curriculum developers specializing in the teaching of French as medium of instruction or subject in the primary school curriculum.

Language issues in mainstream schools

Mainstream primary schools in Francophone Africa are mere copies of colonial schools. The organizational structure of the schools, the curriculum content, and language of instruction policies were modified only slightly after independence, for example simple changes in the names of characters in reading textbooks. "René" is replaced by "Musa" or "Hamidou" and "Mary" by "Mariama." However, there has been no fundamental change in language teaching methods since the colonial era. French is still taught as the exclusive language of instruction, even though for 95 percent of rural and poor urban children French can be considered a foreign language. In rural settings particularly, French remains strictly the language of school and homework. Children never use it as the means of communication in their families or communities. In these settings, local languages are the main means of communication.

In urban centers, particularly in the capital cities of Burkina Faso, Mali, and Niger, French is rapidly becoming the first or second language of children from upper- and middle-class families. These children come to school with some oral and written proficiency in French that allows them to understand instruction delivered in this language. They participate actively in class, and the teachers often give them more attention. The educational experience of these children is generally positive, as they achieve academic success. However, these privileged students constitute a minority. The majority of students in both urban and rural schools come from poor, non-literate families where French is not the means of daily communication. Unfortunately, the educational experience of this group of students is characterized by class repetition and a high drop-out rate between fourth and sixth grades. The average rate of drop-out in primary schools of French-speaking countries is nearly 25 percent according to most World Bank and UNESCO annual reports. In Francophone Africa, the majority of primary school students experience exclusion in the classroom. Owing to a lack of proficiency in French, they are silenced and spend most of their time listening to the teacher and the very few students who can speak French. Most of the non-French-speaking students experience academic failure owing, in part, to the lack of proficiency in the language of instruction and, in part, to the use of inappropriate language teaching methods by their classroom teachers.

Most of the teachers currently serving in primary schools in Francophone Africa (whether certified or not) do not speak the French language very well. In the sixty schools (half mainstream and half bilingual) I have visited in Burkina Faso, Mali, and Niger since 1990, the majority of teachers have great difficulty teaching in general and using the French language as the means of instruction in particular. Therefore, they frequently code-mix and code-switch. So do their students. This situation is prevalent mainly in rural schools and in schools located in poor urban neighborhoods.

During the colonial era, schoolteachers used the teaching of grammatical rules, drill repetition, and memorization as language teaching pedagogy. To force pupils to speak the French language, they used drastic physical and psychological measures involving the beating and shaming of students (Moumouni 1967; Mateene 1985). Such pedagogical, physical, and psychological methods are still used in Francophone African classrooms, particularly in rural areas. These practices prevail in spite of governments advocating non-violent pedagogy and student-centered and constructivist language teaching approaches.

Teachers construct materials, lessons, and tests that lend themselves to regurgitation. Since most students fear physical punishment, they do their best to memorize the lessons they copied or the reading materials they used in the classrooms. Like parrots, they develop very good repetition skills, but they can barely write their names. Students spend most of their time memorizing lessons for the tests instead of trying to understand the relevance or meaning of what they read. This lack of proficiency in French negatively affects their understanding of knowledge transmitted in that language. Consequently, they perform poorly on achievement tests that require mastery of French and the ability to perform highly cognitive tasks in French.

A review of Burkina Faso, Mali, and Niger Ministry of Education statistics since 1965 shows that 65 percent of sixth graders annually fail the achievement tests administered in French even though most of them have had six to eight years of instruction in the language. Another problem inherent in mainstream primary schools in poor rural and urban areas in Burkina Faso, Mali, and Niger is the high rate of grade repetition (35 percent) and the drop-out rate (25 percent) between fourth and sixth grades (UNESCO 1990, 1999, 2000; Human Sciences Research Council 1999).

As noted above, the majority of students who experience academic success in Francophone primary schools come from urban middle- and upper-class families, with highly educated parents. In these students' homes, French is the dominant language. A literate culture is also developed in this setting. Children are exposed at a very early age to reading and writing in French. Their parents take them to the local French library, and they are also exposed to television broadcasting in French. TV5, Canal plus, and Antenne 2 are all French channels which are watched daily in these family living rooms. Most of these children also have the chance to attend early childhood education that systematically introduces them to reading and writing in French. In short, these children come to school prepared for instruction delivered in the French language. They represent the majority of students who successfully pass the end of primary school exam. These urban children from the middle and upper classes who are regularly exposed to French represent 70 percent of the students who graduate from primary school, compared to 30 percent primary school graduates from poor urban and rural schools. However, the academic success of this particular group of students has nothing to do with governmental education or language policies, but reflects their parents' educational background, social status, and deliberate decision to promote French language and literacy at home.

It is imperative that social class and parental education be carefully analyzed in designing effective educational reforms in Africa. Failure to consider social class as a unit of analysis in educational policy in Africa will contribute to the retention of inadequate educational systems and further promote social inequalities in school and society. In urban settings where more and more kids from prominent families come to school with some proficiency in French, it is important to recognize the reality of the sociolinguistic situation by familiarizing teachers with issues of linguistic diversity and equity and the use of pedagogical approaches that will facilitate learning in classrooms where students have various levels of proficiency in the language of instruction. If social class and differential language proficiency are not taken into consideration in the classroom, the learning of the majority of children who come to school without a knowledge of French will be negatively impacted. African classrooms, far from becoming a space for the eradication of societal inequality, will continue instead to serve as a space for maintaining or perpetuating inequality through the promotion of students who have French-language competence prior to enrolling in school. Language policies must be sensitive to sociolinguistic transformation in African societies and include language education programs that are socially just.

One would think that in the 1980s and 1990s African educational reformers and policymakers would have taken into consideration applied linguistic research findings in order to promote the development of adequate language proficiency in primary schools. Krashen's (1976) findings about the significance of meaningful linguistic input in promoting adequate proficiency in a second or foreign language is particularly crucial for addressing language issues in African schools. Identifying appropriate second-language teaching methods that include culturally relevant pedagogy is crucial in promoting language competence in French. Instead of forcing on students the variety of French spoken in France and reading materials produced with French children in mind, it is important to recognize the cultural and social reality of African students in Francophone countries. The teaching—and learning—of French must be organized around what students know already and what they ought to know in order to become effective second-language learners who can understand knowledge acquired in French and use it effectively to further their learning.

The adoption of effective language teaching methods must be accompanied by the development of a literate environment in the community. The language of instruction must be used outside the classroom in order for learners to enhance their proficiency and competence in that language. The creation of community libraries and the promotion of literacy in French and the national languages among adults can provide needed linguistic support for students and teachers. However, such initiatives do not currently exist. In the sixty schools I visited, in almost all cases there was only one source of French language reading material, the official textbook used by the teacher (often produced by French textbook publishers and the ministries of education with World Bank funding). The language teaching methods involved in national reading textbooks used in Burkina Faso, Mali, and Niger are still based on phonics, drills, and memorization.

Textbook prefaces commonly suggest the use of active methods with very limited pedagogical information about the meaning of such methods or how to effectively conduct language lessons using this approach.

A careful analysis of the pedagogical units included in a given text reveals that drills, repetition, and memorization are still the guiding pedagogical principles. These books are not comprised of authentic texts or stories that students can read and enjoy. In this context, reading and writing are never taught as activities that have social and cultural functions. Therefore, very few students develop a desire for reading and writing, and most of them finish primary school with very limited literacy skills in French. In this regard Mendo argues that grammatical rules learned during French lessons are never used in natural conversations because, in Cameroon, French is mainly used for specific formal purposes: school and writing letters. Thus, children are unable to acquire adequate language proficiency in French. Yet, at the end of primary school they are expected to take high-stakes and cognitively demanding tests that assess their mastery of the French language and their ability to solve problems in French. These achievement tests are not only unjust, they are also unreliable indicators of students' abilities.

Specific issues related to experimental bilingual schools

In the early 1970s, a few Francophone countries developed experimental bilingual schools. A review of available data from Burkina Faso, Mali, and Niger ministry of education documents indicates that preservation and promotion of African languages and cultures through literacy were the main purposes of the bilingual schools. In that respect, bilingual schools have been part of both nationalization and Africanization of primary schools in the postcolonial period. The second main goal of bilingual education, as stated in Bamgbose's well-known book, *Mother Tongue Education: the West African Experience* (1976), is the acquisition of adequate literacy in both national languages and the dominant languages of instruction, namely French, English, Portuguese, or Spanish depending upon a country's colonial history.

After twenty to thirty years of experimenting, the use of national languages in primary schools has not been expanded to all primary schools. There are still fewer than 200 bilingual schools (as opposed to more than 3,000 mainstream schools) in each Francophone country. Most of the experimental bilingual schools are marginalized. They are located mainly in poor urban and rural areas. In Burkina Faso, Mali, and Niger, the bilingual schools survive largely because of international development aid. Therefore, depending upon availability of funding, these schools experience short periods of success often followed by long periods of stagnation and academic failure. Demonstration schools (such as the bilingual school located in Segu, Mali) which serve as scientific and pedagogical laboratories for linguists, educators, and policymakers benefit not only from funding and educational materials but also from political attention. They are therefore high-performing schools which produce highly successful students. Indeed, students attending such schools perform far better than mainstream students located in the same geographical area. Of course not all experimental bilingual schools benefit from such attention. However, one can objectively say that whenever governments and educators invest adequately in bilingual schools, the schools tend to produce better educational outcomes.

In Burkina Faso the Ecoles Satellites were created with the financial support of UNICEF, in Mali, Les Ecoles de la Pédagogie Convergente have the technical support of GTZ, and a few international organizations (non-French based) and the Ecoles Expérimentales from Niger are technically and financially supported by the German Technical Agency (GTZ). In these three countries, the German Foundation for International Development has been contributing to the revitalization program through its professional development training projects for curriculum developers and authors of national language textbooks. I have been involved in these projects as the Academy Director of the workshops organized by the German Foundation for International Development in Burkina Faso, Mali, and Niger. The account I provide below reflects, therefore, an active participant's perspective.

In the experimental bilingual schools, national languages that serve as regional languages were selected as media of instruction along with French. These languages are used for the first three years of instruction, and French is taught as a subject in the curriculum. In fourth grade, French becomes the main language of instruction even though the use of national languages is acceptable whenever students have difficulty comprehending instruction delivered in French.

For most students attending bilingual schools, national languages used as media of instruction are their dominant languages, and French can be considered a foreign language. The use of these languages as means of instruction in the first three years of education facilitates students' involvement in all classroom interactions.

While most mainstream teachers have at least one year of training in teacher training colleges, teachers serving in bilingual schools have very limited training in teaching French and national languages. In Mali and Niger, bilingual teachers are recruited from among regular schoolteachers. These teachers are identified as enthusiastic volunteers, and they are provided with intensive three-month workshops on national language orthography and transcription in addition to general classroom management workshops. Bilingual teachers from Mali and Niger are civil servants and as such are paid directly by the ministries of education. Their salary is similar to that of teachers serving in mainstream schools. This is not the case in Burkina Faso where Ecoles Satellites teachers hold a very special position. They are considered not civil servants but community teachers. As such, wherever they serve, the population is responsible for their lodging and salary. Here there are serious teacher turnover problems owing to the fact that poor rural populations cannot always pay the teachers. Again, poor rural children and parents pay the price for an unsustainable educational reform. By contrast, in mainstream schools, even in rural areas, the government does not expect the population to pay teacher salaries.

Teacher enthusiasm cannot substitute for qualifications required for teaching in national languages and French. Many bilingual teachers face serious professional challenges. They may be able to speak the language of instruction, but they have not mastered reading and writing in that language. Participation in a three-month workshop is not sufficient to master literacy skills. The profile of bilingual teachers described here shows that, from the outset, bilingual school students tend to face serious problems. They are taught by unqualified teachers with very limited knowledge of language pedagogy. "Amateurism" is the best word to describe the situation.

It is important to mention the exceptions to this bleak educational picture: demonstration schools that produce highly successful students. These are the laboratory schools—found in all three countries—that benefit from extensive research, funding, and the involvement of linguists from national universities and international consultants sent by organizations such as GTZ, DSE, USAID, or the Swiss Development Agency (OSEO). In these model bilingual schools, teachers benefit from professional development training related to researchers' interests in mother tongue education. As a result of this pedagogical and linguistic training, teachers in these schools develop transcription skills as well as a stronger knowledge base about teaching in the mother tongue. Their students successfully pass the end of primary school achievement examinations. The performance of bilingual school students attending the demonstration schools is often better than that of students in mainstream schools.

The number of students attending demonstration schools is unfortunately very small in comparison to the overall population of students. Since most African countries rely heavily on international aid, ministries of education and governments in general have very limited power to implement education and language policies not favored by the major donors to a given country's educational programs. It is clear that technical and scholarly arguments in favor of bilingual education and the proven success of demonstration schools are not the only factors influencing the use of research-based results to shape language education policies. While I was conducting research for my dissertation (Alidou 1997), I interviewed a former Secretary of Education in a Francophone African country. I posed the question of why the ministry of education was not reformulating its language education policy in primary schools, given the positive outcomes of experimental schools with both national languages and French as media of instruction. Although this former Secretary was an ardent advocate of national languages, he straightforwardly stated that as long as his country relies on French resources and support, it would never implement such schools on a grand scale. Further, he contended that a direct appeal to the World Bank for resources to expand the use of national languages in primary schools was not a possibility since France remains the main advocate for Francophone African countries at the World Bank. Moreover, he pointed out that the World Bank's lack of support for these demonstration/experimental schools flies in the face of UNESCO's positive evaluation of these schools in the mid-1980s. (The reaction of this former Francophone government official is frequently echoed by other officials if the interviewer promises not to disclose their identity.)

In North America, several studies conducted in bilingual schools indicate that there is a high positive correlation between literacy in one's first language and literacy in one's second language (Cummins 1979). That is, learning and literacy developed in a student's first language facilitate learning and literacy development in a second language. This correlation is due to the existence of a common underlying linguistic proficiency which allows bilingual learners to transfer linguistic and general knowledge acquired in their first language to their second language. Cummins's argument has become axiomatic, and it is used in several policy papers to argue for the promotion of African languages in formal education (Mazrui 2000). Indeed, in Africa one could make a similar argument for the promotion of African languages as media of instruction if these languages had the same type of status and development as English, French, or Spanish in the North American context. However, the languages used in bilingual schools in Burkina Faso, Mali, and Niger (as well as in other Francophone countries) have very limited writing and literary traditions. The lack of a literate culture and tradition in these languages impedes the development of adequate literacy skills. It is difficult, therefore, to apply Cummins's theory of linguistic interdependence between first and second languages in Francophone countries.

In Burkina Faso, Mali, and Niger, bilingual schools also present fundamental equity issues. Students attending these schools who fail to pass the end of primary school achievement tests face serious social problems. They easily relapse into illiteracy, and their access to jobs becomes very limited. Typically, they have not acquired basic literacy and proficiency in French. Owing to underdevelopment in most African villages, there are no paying jobs in rural areas that require literacy skills in national languages, or in French for that matter. Even when there are development projects, if there is a literacy component, one or two people from the village can carry out the task. This situation renders bilingual education even less equitable than mainstream education, with its focus on French as the language of instruction. A primary school drop-out from a mainstream/government school will have at least limited proficiency in French which will give him access to working-class positions in urban areas—e.g. gardener, mailman in government or private organizations.

Conclusion and recommendations

This critique of the language education issue in mainstream and bilingual education schools indicates the inadequacy of language education in Francophone Africa, as manifested in the case studies of Burkina Faso, Mali, and Niger.

Improvement of the Francophone African educational system, particularly in primary schools, requires an accurate assessment of the situation. As a children's advocate, I strongly believe that parents should have the right to determine the type of school their children attend. Therefore, governments should create diverse types of schools to accommodate the diverse linguistic and cultural needs of the population. Equal financial and technical support should be given to all public schools regardless of the language policy of these schools. I call, therefore, for improvement of language teaching in both mainstream and bilingual schools in Francophone Africa. Governments should encourage competition among schools. This would force schools to improve their performance. Further, governments should develop language teaching/learning programs that take into account both linguistic and socioeconomic diversity.

Intensive workshops organized irregularly, with the support of international donors, cannot be a sustainable strategy for school improvement. Instead of these costly emergency teacher training projects, I call for serious reform of the curriculum in teacher education programs. The teacher training curriculum has not been significantly reevaluated since the colonial period. An analysis of the curriculum content of Ecoles Normales located in Burkina Faso, Mali, and Niger indicates that the courses have not been changed in spite of the various educational reforms undertaken by ministries of education. After each reform, sporadic workshops are organized to familiarize teachers with the policy being implemented and the few pedagogical methods that sustain the reform. Often, these workshops last ten days, and there is no follow-up to determine whether/how teachers are using the new knowledge acquired during the workshops. The serious gap between language education policy and classroom practice must be addressed. Teacher education programs must be redesigned in order to effectively train all new teachers for both mainstream and bilingual classrooms. The ministries of education should make dual teacher certification mandatory for new teachers. Dual certification will allow ministries of education to address teacher shortage problems in both mainstream and bilingual schools.

In the same way that African countries experience food hunger, there is a long-lasting book hunger in Africa. Research has established a high correlation between the availability of books and educational materials and high academic performance. Literacy cannot develop without a literate environment. Such an environment is defined not only by the availability of print material in a community, but also by the use of language in both its oral and written forms for all types of cultural and socioeconomic purposes. It is critical, therefore, that the effort to use national languages and French in schools must be backed up by the promotion of a literate culture in both urban and rural contexts. Availability of libraries that contain reading materials in all languages used in schools and the promotion of literacy among adults and children will provide children with access to meaningful linguistic input both in national languages and in French. Such input is needed in order to develop adequate language proficiency in the languages of instruction (Krashen 1981).

One of the main problems facing teachers and students in bilingual schools is the lack of uniform orthography for a given African language. National languages used in the bilingual schools have at least two or three orthographies. Teachers are thus confronted with the issue of teaching children literacy skills using several different orthographic representations of their language. (See Makoni, this volume, for discussion of this issue in South African primary schools.) This orthographic diversity has a potentially negative impact on students learning to read because consistency in the representation of the writing system is important to children struggling to develop literacy skills. When the various dialects of a language are mutually intelligible (generally the case), ministries of education should select a single orthographic system to be used by all educational institutions involved in formal basic education. Importantly also, uniform orthography and textbooks will be cost-effective and answer those critics who charge that the production of educational materials in African languages is costly.

For languages used transnationally, such as Hausa, Fulfulde, and Songhay, which are spoken in several countries in West Africa, regional efforts are needed, involving curriculum developers, linguists, and authors, to identify the dialect in those languages that can be used for educational purposes. Such joint efforts can result in the production of textbooks in national languages that can be used by a significant number of students. This strategy will promote the creation of a large market for reading materials in national languages and lead to investment in local publishing companies specializing in the production of these materials (Alidou-Ngame 2000).

In conclusion, I call for an accountability system that adequately addresses national and international language education policies in Francophone Africa. Many reforms have been undertaken in Africa. Unfortunately, when these reforms fail, African students end up paying a heavy price: exclusion from the educational system at a very young age, thus limiting their chance for upward mobility in their own society.

References

Alidou, H. (1997) "Education language policy and bilingual education: the impact of French language policy in primary education in Niger," unpublished doctoral dissertation, University of Illinois-Champaign-Urbana.

Alidou-Ngame, H. (2000) *Stratégies pour le développement un secteur editorial en langues nationals dans les pays du sahel Burkina Faso, Mali Niger et Sénégal*, London: Groupe de Travail sur les Livres et le Matériel Educatif.

Bamgbose, A. (1976) *Mother Tongue Education: The West African Experience*, London: Hodder and Stoughton.

—— (1997) *Language and the Nation: The Language Question in Sub-Saharan Africa*, Edinburgh: Edinburgh University Press.

Bokamba, E.G. and Tlou, J. (1985) "The consequences of the language policies of African states vis-à-vis education," in K. Mateene, J. Kalema, and B. Chomba (eds)

Linguistic Liberation and Unity of Africa, Kampala, Uganda: OAU Inter-Africa Bureau of Languages, 45–66.

Cummins, J. (1979) "The role of primary language development in promoting educational success for language minority students," in J. Cummins (ed.) *Schooling and Language-Minority Students: A Theoretical Framework*, Sacramento, CA: California State Department of Education.

—— (1991) "Interdependence of first- and second-language proficiency in bilingual children," in E. Bialystok (ed.) *Language Processing in Bilingual Children*, Cambridge: Cambridge University Press, 70–89.

Fafunwa, A.B., Macauley, J.I., and Funnso Sokoya, J.A. (1989) *Education in Mother Tongue: The Ife Primary Education Research Project (1970–1978)*, Ibadan: University Press Limited.

Federici, S., Caffentzis, G., and Alidou, O. (2000) *A Thousand Flowers: Social Struggles against Structural Adjustment in African Universities*, Trenton, NJ: Africa World Press.

Human Sciences Research Council (1999) "With Africa for Africa: towards quality education for all," in V. Chinapah (ed.) *Education for All: 2000 Assessment Survey, 1999 MLA Project*, draft regional report, Pretoria: HSRC.

Krashen, S.D. (1976) "Formal and informal linguistic environments in language acquisition and language learning," *TESOL Quarterly*, 10: 157–68.

—— (1981) "Effective second language acquisition: insights from research," in Atlatis *et al.* (eds) *The Second Language Classroom: Directions for the 1980s*, Oxford: Oxford University Press.

—— (1982) *Principles and Practice in Second Language Acquisition*, Oxford: Pergamon.

Mateene, K. (1985) "Colonial languages, as means of domination, and indigenous languages as necessary factors of liberation and development," in K. Mateene, J. Kalema, and B. Chomba (eds) *Linguistic Liberation and Unity of Africa*, Kampala, Uganda: OAU Inter-Africa Bureau of Languages, 45–66.

—— (1996) "OAU strategy for linguistic unity and multilingual education," paper presented at the International Seminar on Language Education in Africa, Cape Town, South Africa.

Mazrui, A.A. and Mazrui, A.M. (1998) *The Power of Babel*, Chicago, IL: University of Chicago Press.

Mazrui, A.M. (2000) "The World Bank, the language question and the future of African education," in S. Federici, G. Caffentzis, and O. Alidou (eds) *Thousand Flowers: Social Struggles against Structural Adjustment in African Universities*, Trenton, NJ: Africa World Press.

Moumouni, A. (1998) *L'Education en Afrique*, Paris: Présence Africaine.

UNESCO (1990a) *World Declaration on Education for All and Framework for Action to Meet Basic Learning Needs: The Amman Affirmation*, World Conference on Education for All, Jomtien, Thailand, March, 5–9 1990.

—— (1990b) *Compendium of Statistics on Illiteracy*, 1990 edition, no. 31, Paris.

—— (2000a) *Global Synthesis: Education for All, 2000 Assessment*, Paris: International Consultative Forum on Education for All Publications.

—— (2000b) *Status and Trends 2000: Assessing Learning Achievement*, Paris.

6

Contradiction or affirmation? The South African language policy and the South African national government

Nkhelebeni Phaswana

Introduction

After nearly half a century of apartheid rule in which only English and Afrikaans were official languages, the Republic of South Africa adopted a new democratic Constitution that provides for eleven official languages. Clause Six of the Constitution stipulates: The official languages of the Republic are Sepedi, Sesotho, Setswana, siSwati, Tshivenda, Xitsonga, Afrikaans, English, isiNdebele, isiXhosa, and isiZulu. (See Makoni, this volume, for the full excerpt of the Founding Language Provision in the Constitution.) Now, more than six years after the drafting of the Constitution, the question arises as to the success of the eleven-languages policy. The fact that the South African national government has been charged by the new Constitution with the tasks, *inter alia*, of the promotion of multilingualism and multiculturalism on the one hand, and the promotion, as well as the elevation, of the status of African languages on the other, makes the issue of the language/s used and preferred by the national government crucial. The sociolinguistic study presented in this chapter seeks to investigate the extent to which South Africa's eleven official languages are used by the national government in carrying out its duties. That is, to what extent is the South African national government affirming the demands of the Constitution as provided for in the founding provisions of the Constitution? As a backdrop for understanding the crisis around and preoccupation with the language question, South African language policy must be located within its sociohistorical context, from the seventeenth to the twenty-first century.

A sociohistorical overview of South African language policy

During the apartheid era, Afrikaans and English were used as gate-keepers for political power and dominance, as instruments for preserving certain privileges for whites, and ultimately as tools for unfair and unequal distribution of the country's economic resources. McLean, in a discussion of how language was used as a tool for divide-and-rule in South Africa, pointed out: "The basis on which Black people have been stripped of their South African citizenship and forcibly removed to bantustans has been their ethnic identity, of which language has often been the only index" (1992: 152). When Jan Van Riebeeck and his crew arrived at the Cape, they encountered the indigenous population which consisted of two groups, the Khoikhoi and the San people.

Maartens (1998) records that in the early years the Dutch language had no direct influence on the two indigenous languages. Instead of the settlers learning and studying these indigenous languages for communication and business, interpreters were used where trade, and later missionaries, required direct contact with the indigenous people. The interpreters happened to be indigenous people who over the years acquired some Dutch or English. In 1658, Portuguese and Malay-Portuguese became the linguae francae among the slaves who were brought to the Cape from countries such as Angola, Madagascar, Bengal, Guinea, and later South East Asia. To counteract the dominance of these two languages, the Dutch East India Company, before the end of 1658, decreed that only Dutch should be used. Maartens (1998: 26) noted that this decree constituted the first language policy of South Africa.

Once Dutch became an official language, the Khoikhoi, the San people, and the enslaved had no choice but to speak the language of their masters. Even among themselves, the indigenous people and the enslaved used Dutch as the medium of communication. Thus, slave–master and slave–slave communication contributed to the emergence of what is today called Afrikaans in South Africa. Alexander (1989) and Brown (1992), discussing how Afrikaans came into being as a language in South Africa, confirm that Afrikaans was born in the Western Cape as the language of trade, education, and social intercourse between white and non-white. Its early form, as they indicate, was, by the end of the seventeenth century, spoken as a lingua franca by most of the inhabitants of the Cape. Although Afrikaans, or what was known in that period as "Cape patois" or "kitchen Dutch," was regarded as inappropriate for educational discourse, as Moodie (1980: 40) points out, Afrikaans and Dutch (Holland) coexisted such that by the end of 1795, most of the Khoikhoi and the enslaved people were part of an Afrikaans–Holland language community.

The English first occupied the Cape in 1795, but it was not until the second British occupation of the Cape in 1806 that the British policy of Anglicization was implemented. Because of the Anglicization policy, English became the commonly accepted language in the Cape Colony while the indigenous languages, together with Afrikaans, were relegated to inferior status. In 1853 English was made the exclusive language of Parliament, and Dutch and Afrikaans were used in the church and the family respectively. In 1882 Dutch, rather than Afrikaans, was again recognized as the official language of the Cape Parliament along with English. When the first Anglo-Boer War broke out in 1899, a war eventually won by the British in 1902, the official status of Dutch was withdrawn. However, in 1910 when the Act of Union was signed, Article 137 of the Constitution accorded Dutch equal status with English as the official languages of the Union. This Constitution did not even acknowledge the existence of the indigenous African languages, let alone allocate them any status. As Dutch regained its status (it had judicial equality and rights and privileges with English), it was used in schools together with English. A great challenge to Dutch was mounted by Afrikaans speakers who claimed that Dutch, as enshrined in the Constitution, referred to Afrikaans as well. Because of the endless resistance waged by Afrikaners against the policy of official recognition of Dutch, but not Afrikaans, in 1925 an amendment to Act 137 of the Constitution made Afrikaans one of the official languages. However, Cluver (1992) and Moodie (1980) argue that essentially that 1925 amendment replaced Dutch with Afrikaans as the official language, and thus its legal equality with English was written into the Constitution.

Cluver (1992) notes that the victory of Afrikaans over Dutch became an effective strategy for maintaining the ethnic identity and solidarity of the Afrikaner and ultimately formed the political power base of the National Party (NP). After the NP took over the government in 1948, Afrikaans was developed and elevated to a position to compete with English. This language policy had a serious impact on the educational language policy as well. Unlike the language policy in Black schools, the language of teaching and learning in the education of a white child was determined by the child's mother tongue. However, in the fifth year of schooling, either English or Afrikaans took precedence as the language of learning and teaching for the African child. Article 15 in the 1948 education policy document stipulated:

> We believe that . . . the teaching and education of the native must be grounded in the life and world view of the whites, most especially those of the Boer nation as the senior white trustees of the native . . . [who] must be led to an . . . independent acceptance of the Christian and National principles in our teaching . . . The mother tongue must be the basis of native education and teaching but . . . the two official languages must be taught as subjects because they are official languages, and . . . the keys to the cultural loans that are necessary to his own cultural progress.
>
> (1948, quoted in Hlatshwayo 2000: 54, 56)

The stipulations of Article 15 were implemented through the system known as Bantu Education introduced through the Bantu Education Act of 1953. This Act was designed to accomplish three goals: to promote Afrikaans and reduce the influence of English in Black schools; to impose in Black schools the use of Afrikaans and English as equal media of instruction; and to extend mother tongue education for Blacks from fourth grade to eighth grade (Kamwangamalu 1997: 6).

Black South Africans vigorously opposed the use of Afrikaans as a language of instruction as well as the promotion of African languages as media of teaching and learning beyond the fourth year of schooling. The expansion of African languages as media of instruction was perceived by Blacks as part of the Afrikaners' divide-and-rule policy.

When South Africa became a Republic on May 31, 1961, under the leadership of H.F. Verwoerd, the Republic of South Africa Act reinforced the equality of English and Afrikaans. However, there was no mention of the status or position of African languages. Although Afrikaans and English were the two official languages of learning and teaching beyond the fourth year of schooling, the Black majority clearly favored English over Afrikaans, which was regarded as the language of the oppressor. As an international language, English was considered the language to be used for liberation. When the Department of Bantu Education discovered that Africans were rejecting Afrikaans as a medium of teaching and learning, it issued a policy document indicating that Afrikaans and English were to be co-equal media of instruction in Black schools. This language-in-education policy was intended to curb the dominance of English in Black schools. A number of efforts were made to have the policy withdrawn. For example, the African Teachers Association of South Africa (ATASA) and the Urban Bantu Council met with the Regional Director for Bantu Education, pleading for a reversal of the policy. However, a deadlock was reached, and both languages (English and Afrikaans) were to be used and treated equally in Black schools. The implementation of this policy was planned to start in the high schools in the Southern Transvaal, including Soweto (Southwestern Township).

In June 1976, this language-in-education policy was met with insurmountable opposition in the Soweto uprisings. Students in the townships west of Johannesburg marched from school to school defying this language policy and protesting the imposition of what was perceived as the oppressor's language in their education. Indeed, some of the protest signs stated that if Black students have to learn Afrikaans, then B.J. Vorster, the Premier at the time, should learn isiZulu. The South African Police and the South African Defense Force viciously confronted these young students and ruthlessly gunned them down. A month later, in July of 1976, the apartheid government was forced to withdraw its language policy. It was a bittersweet victory. Many young students had lost their lives in the uprising, but Black schools were given the right to choose the language they preferred as the medium of teaching and learning.

The Soweto rebellion marked the first time in the history of South Africa that the people had resisted the apartheid government's language policy. Ninety-six percent of the Black schools chose English, not one of their African languages, as the language of teaching and learning after the first four years of primary schooling. Education in African languages was perceived as a governmental ploy to promote ethnicity and prevent Black unity (Cluver 1992: 114) and as a means to offer Black students education of inferior and undesirable quality. An additional factor in the choice of English was that African nationalists and South African leaders—e.g. Z.K. Matthews of the African National Congress (ANC)—viewed English as a linguistic vehicle of wider African unity and nationalism (Brown 1992: 84).

The birth of South Africa's democratic language policy

Given the history of language issues and policies in South Africa, it is not surprising that in the early 1990s, when the apartheid government opened negotiations with political parties in South Africa, the language issue was high on the agenda. These deliberations, with both the ANC and the NP serving as major players, gave birth to the new democratic language policy in South Africa. The primary goal of the NP (the party in power at the time) was to protect the position of Afrikaans as an official language. However, it lacked, as Heugh (1994: 4) reports, a clearly defined strategy for maintaining the status quo. As a political tactic, the NP found it imperative that its apartheid tendencies be obscured and thus supported the retention of Afrikaans and English, and all other languages, especially African languages (which, however, would be accorded a lower status than Afrikaans and English). The ANC's position on the language question was that of multilingualism, favoring the elevation of South Africa's nine major African languages to the position of English and Afrikaans. As a result of these negotiations the new Constitution of the Republic of South Africa, adopted on May 8, 1996, and amended on October 11, 1996 by the Constitutional Assembly, recognizes all the eleven major languages spoken in South Africa as national official languages.

Prior to the negotiations, African languages were only used as official languages in the various homelands where they were dominant, and even there they shared linguistic space with English or Afrikaans or both. Thus, during the apartheid era, African languages in South Africa, as in many postcolonial African states today, were relegated to a lower status and pushed to the periphery while English and Afrikaans enjoyed official, higher status. However, unlike most postcolonial governments in Africa, which ignored and sacrificed the multilingual and multicultural nature of their societies for a Eurocentric monolithic approach to language and culture, the ANC-led South African government recognized and embraced both multilingualism and multiculturalism, granting all major languages spoken in the country equal status at national level. This language policy was perceived by sociolinguists as an ideal democratic step toward the development and empowerment of South Africa's Black majority. Mateene Kahombo, head of the Division of Language Policy for the Organization of African Unity (OAU), congratulated South Africa for being the first member state to put in its Constitution a language policy similar to the one proposed by the OAU Language Plan of Action for Africa (1996).

The new Constitution of South Africa poses some essential linguistic demands that the South African national government must address. First, the ANC-led government is charged, both explicitly and implicitly, with the responsibility of addressing the problem of linguicism and linguistic hegemony in South Africa. Second, the Constitution calls upon the national government to take practical and positive measures to elevate the status, as well as advance the use, of African languages in South Africa. The Constitution requires that all official languages enjoy parity of esteem and equitable treatment. Given the continuing controversy around language policy in South Africa, it remains open to question whether South Africa will live up to these expectations of linguistic democratization. As Maartens observes, it is

> becoming increasingly apparent that a considerable mismatch appears to exist between emerging language policy on the one hand, and actual language practice in the spheres of government and education on the other. Whereas language policy expressly professes to promote multilingualism in South Africa, language practitioners in languages other than English are complaining more and more that their languages are being marginalised to an even greater extent than in the past.
>
> (1998: 16)

Maartens's critique suggests that there is a contradiction between the Constitutional commitment to empower the indigenous languages, whose status was diminished by the apartheid regime, and the actual realization of such a commitment. The government's perceived lack of commitment toward the implementation of the multilingual policy was signaled early on by Heugh (1994, 1995), who claims that the ANC has taken a *laissez-faire* position on the question of language. She argues that there is a policy decision but no formulation of strategies for implementing that decision.

Since language is both power and resource, the use of language has serious repercussions. Only the people whose languages are used (especially by those in power) are likely to become empowered, and it will be at the expense of those people whose languages are not used and who thus become marginalized. It is for this reason that Tollefson (1991) argues that there is a dynamic relationship between social relations and language policy. He contends that hierarchical social systems can be associated with language policies which ultimately give advantage to groups speaking particular varieties (1991: 17).

To ascertain the extent to which the South African national government is affirming the entrenchment and implementation of the policy of multilingualism and multiculturalism in South Africa, a study was conducted, which focused on Members of Parliament (MPs) and Parliamentary deliberations and proceedings.

Methodology

Qualitative methodology was used in this study. Data were primarily collected through in-depth unstructured interviews with MPs. Parliamentary documents which could be classified as internal documents and external communication were also collected as primary sources, for example official minutes and related sources such as notices, internal memoranda, minutes of meetings, programs, and agendas of meetings. Reports from various portfolio committees, reports from the NCOP (National Committee of Provinces), bills and acts of Parliament, newsletters circulating in Parliament, the Constitution, and other documents became part of the data for this study. Systematic observations of Parliamentary meetings and sessions were another source of data for the study. These observations focused on both the entire Parliament and the various portfolio committees—for example, Portfolio Committee on Finance, Portfolio Committee on Arts, Culture and Language, Science and Technology, Portfolio Committee on Land Affairs. More attention was given to the Portfolio Committee on Arts, Culture and Language, Science and Technology since this was the committee that had been holding hearings on the Pan South African Language Board Amendment Bill which directly affected the implementation of the Constitutional language policy.

Interviews, observations, and collection of documents took place in Cape Town during February and March of 1999. For the interviews, snowballing sampling technique was used, whereby interviewees were asked to recommend their colleagues to be interviewed.

In-depth interviews

All interviewees were asked about the mismatch between what the Constitution demands and what they as Parliamentarians practice in Parliament. In other words, the Parliamentarians were asked to account for their language practices *vis-à-vis* what the South African Constitutional language policy requires.

In response to this open-ended question, one NNP (New National Party) representative acknowledged that 80 to 90 percent of the speeches delivered by MPs in Parliament are in English, 10 percent are in Afrikaans, and the balance in other languages (African languages). In addressing and acknowledging that there is a mismatch between Constitutional demands and language practices in Parliament, he pointed out that there always exists a difference between theory and practice. He said: "Our official policy is to support that because we voted for the Constitution; on that issue we did not disagree. We disagree with some other issues in the Constitution but not this one. But in practice it [the use of all eleven languages] *just does not work*" (my emphasis).

In response to this question, another NNP representative argued that time has already proven that there is something fundamentally and inherently complicated about the approach to the South African language situation set out in the Constitution. Like one African National Congress (ANC) representative, who argued that the eleven-languages policy is an ideal policy which practically cannot work, this second NNP representative said that there is no way that the eleven official languages could be used equitably as the Constitution demands.

Thus, she challenged the Constitutional approach and proposed her own: "The ideals embodied within the Constitution do not work. To my way of thinking, the approach that there should be eleven official languages universally across South Africa is impractical. The more practical approach would have been an incremental approach." Although this NNP representative recognized the mismatch between Constitutional demands and Parliamentary practice, she still supported the maintenance of the status quo, i.e. that Afrikaans and English continue to be the official languages. She argued that the dominance of English and Afrikaans could be justified in that these two languages, unlike African languages, are already completely developed. This NNP representative considered African languages underdeveloped, cultural languages whereas she considered English and Afrikaans developed, practical languages which should be the ones used in Parliament.

A second ANC representative, responding to the question about the mismatch between what Parliamentarians practice and what the language policy requires, indicated that since English and Afrikaans are the two languages which are still privileged in South Africa, they are likely to dominate all other languages in Parliament. Acknowledging that some Parliamentarians refrain from using their mother tongues (although they are official South African languages), this ANC representative gave the following explanation:

> We must remember that there has been a very systematic and conscious oppression of African languages in this country. Also, there has been a very systematic and conscious discrediting of anything African in this country. Of course in this short space of time, it will be reflected.

This MP further argued that since the ANC government had only been in power for five years, many of the policies that have been put in place are just beginning to work. He expressed optimism that South Africa would set an example of how the language issue in a multilingual country could be handled.

A third ANC representative stated that the implementation of the eleven-languages policy simply is not possible in Parliament. He regards English as a functional language that should be utilized in Parliament and argued that it had been correctly chosen as the language of record in Parliament. He reasoned:

> We are not speaking English just because we want to speak English, but because it is convenient . . . We are speaking English because we want to communicate, not because we want to sound educated . . . It is easy and it is cheap; it is a *lingua franca*.

Two MPs representing the Inkatha Freedom Party (IFP) supported the use of English as the sole language of Parliament. One made the following argument in legitimizing the position of English only in Parliament:

> We are already noticing what is happening in other countries of the world, that the English language is the one that is the most robust and generally pushes all other languages to one side whether it is in India, whether it is in Australia, or whether it is in America.

This IFP representative pointed out that since English has now become the global language, there are so many varieties of English that people have made their own, it should dominate all other languages in Parliament. He further argued that the dominance of English is realized partly because science and technology, internet, and computers and all the modern technologies utilize it more than any other language. He commented that wherever people from different language backgrounds come together, one language, which is Eurocentric, is always going to dominate all other languages. A Eurocentric language, as this MP stated, could be used cross-culturally and for the purposes of educational research as well as for communication with the outside world. He further explained that the new language policy, which he argued is not practical, emanated from President Mandela who had been very anxious, during the Constitutional deliberations, not to cause anyone to rock the boat. Rather, Mandela wanted the language matter to be settled over time and not the way the apartheid government had done—through force and compulsion. Finally, this MP pointed out that allowing language use in Parliament to unfold as it is doing is a diplomatic way of allowing language practice to dictate the language/s that should be used in the long run in Parliament.

A Freedom Front (FF) representative, who was on the language committee during the drafting of South Africa's new Constitution, also addressed the question of the mismatch between Constitutional requirement and MP linguistic practice. He argued that it was a matter of political correctness to say that eleven languages are official. He further pointed out that in the committee rooms, where, according to another FF representative, "big debates are taking place," and where there are no interpreting facilities, only English is used, and other languages are seriously sidelined. Both FF representatives contended that what the Constitution demands is quite a symbolic thing, for multilingualism is not practiced at the highest level of the government.

One DP representative I interviewed asserted that he had no problems with English being dominant in Parliament. However, he acknowledged that in spite of what the Constitution demands, only a few languages are heard in Parliament, and thus, he concluded, this makes a mockery of the Constitution.

Obstacles in the promotion of African languages

According to the MPs I interviewed, there are three main obstacles to the promotion and elevation of the status of African Languages: cost, attitudes toward African languages, and need for corpus planning.

The interviewees in this study pointed out that it would be costly to utilize all the official languages in Parliament equally. One of the IFP representatives whom I interviewed argued that languages are not used equally in Parliament or elsewhere in South Africa because of the lack of an efficient interpreting system that would require a lot of money which the government does not have. In elaborating on why it would be financially impossible to use all eleven official languages in Parliament, one of the ANC representatives asserted that the implications would be enormous, for there would need to be massive libraries and archives in Parliament to store all the documents, records, bills, and other official Parliamentary material that would be in different languages. She further indicated that however the situation turns out in South Africa, there should be a language used as a common denominator because it could be extremely expensive to utilize all the eleven official languages simultaneously in Parliament.

An FF representative had also mentioned cost as a stumbling block in the use and elevation of the status of official languages other than English in Parliament. However, an ANC and a FF representative took a different position. They pointed out that cost should not stop parliamentarians or the government from implementing the demands of the Constitution.

On the issue of attitudes toward African languages, one ANC representative said that one who speaks in Tshivenda or any other African language in Parliament is perceived as uneducated and uncivilized, while invariably those who speak in English are said to be well informed and better educated. This representative went on to say that people do not feel honored when using their African languages. Two ANC representatives also argued that because of colonization, Black South Africans see themselves as inferior to their white counterparts. They explained that now that people are building a new South Africa, they no longer feel at ease using their African languages. Rather, they feel as though they are perpetuating apartheid policy (i.e. creation of separate bantustans on the basis of language). As a consequence, they regard a European language (English) as superior.

Yet another ANC representative stated that although one cannot be comfortable expressing oneself in a language other than one's mother tongue, it is surprising that in Parliament, even though there are interpreting facilities, parliamentarians still ignore their mother tongue for English. She expressed her disappointment in the top leadership of all parties whose supporters are Blacks, going to villages speaking English and sidelining the village languages in order to look and sound different from their communities.

An issue often debated in multilingual African contexts is the question of corpus planning for African languages. "Corpus" planning refers to consciously engineered changes, such as the creation of new words, to a language. In the case of African languages, corpus planning often has to do with modernizing the language. Do African languages need to be revamped and updated for life in the twenty-first century? Or perhaps, *can* they be updated? These questions were also raised by another ANC representative who maintained that since African languages, which she called "cultural languages," are still undeveloped, they could not be utilized in Parliament. She said that African languages lack the vocabulary necessary to discuss topics in various fields or areas—hence it becomes difficult to use them in Parliament. This observation was also shared by another ANC representative who said that one of the constraints in using African languages is lack of the terminology required in deliberations and speeches in Parliament. Yet a different ANC representative also pointed out that it is not only demanding and taxing to a parliamentarian to prepare his/her speech in an African language, it can also be difficult for interpreters and translators because of the lack of relevant, sufficient terminology and jargon in African languages.

Parliamentary reports, speeches, bills, newsletters, Hansard, and other documents

As part of this study, I examined various written documents in Parliament, such as reports, legislative acts, bills, meeting minutes and agendas, and other official written documents. All demonstrate the widespread preference for English in Parliament. The LANGTAG (1996) Subcommittee on Language in the Public Service reports that the RDP (Reconstruction and Development Programme) report was never written or translated into any language other than English. Paradoxically, while this LANGTAG subcommittee makes this charge about the RDP, all the LANGTAG reports, including the final comprehensive report, appear in English only.

Governmental/departmental annual reports

The following are some of the reports sent to Parliament on an annual basis:

> Report of the Auditor-General on the Dairy Board Liquidation, Account (Verslag van die Ouditeur-Generaal oor die Suiwelraadlikwidasierekening) (1996, 1997 and 1999), in both English and Afrikaans
> Report of the Auditor-General on the Accounts of Vote 31—South African Revenue Service (Verslag van die Ouditeur-Generaal oor die Rekenings van Begrotingspos 31—Suid-Afrikaanse Inkomstediens) (1996–7), in both English and Afrikaans
> Report of the Auditor-General on the Local Authorities Loans Fund for 1997–8 (Verslag van die Ouditeur-Generaal oor die Leningsfonds vir plaaslike Besture vir 1997–8), in both English and Afrikaans.

Speeches

Although a few parliamentarians deliver their speeches in the language of their choice, some high officials, for example, ministers and deputy ministers, consistently deliver their speeches in English. For example, the address to Parliament by the Deputy Minister of Arts, Culture, Science and Technology, on the Pan South African Language Board Amendment Bill, in February 1999, was entirely in English. The Minister of Arts, Culture, Science and Technology also delivered his talk in English. President Nelson Mandela's last and final address to Parliament on February 5, 1999 included not a single expression from an indigenous African language; his address was entirely in English.

Acts and bills

Several acts and bills in Parliament still reflect the apartheid past, i.e. English and Afrikaans are still the only two languages in which acts and bills appear. The following acts and bills are in English or in English and Afrikaans only: Public Investment Commissioners Amendment Bill (B 8–99) (Wysigingswetsontwerp op die Openbare Beleggingskommissarisse) is in both English and Afrikaans. Domestic Violence Bill (B 75D–98) (Wetsontwerp op Gesinsgeweld) is in both English and Afrikaans. Witness Protection Bill (W 130B–98) (Wetsontwerp op Getuiebeskerming) is in both English and Afrikaans. Criminal Procedure Amendment Bill (B 132B–98) (Strafproseswysigings-Wetsontwerp) is in both English and Afrikaans. The Pan South African Language Board Act No. 59 of 1995 is in English.

Hansard documents

Hansard documents contain the debates of the National Council of Provinces and the National Assembly. Some of the Hansard documents contain interpellations, questions, and replies which are only in English. The two Hansard documents: *Debates of the Senate Second Session—First Parliament (No. 9) of the 6th to the 13th of June 1995* and *Debates of the National Assembly Second Session—First Parliament (No. 14) of the 5th to the 6th of September 1995* contain interpellations, questions, and replies which are in English. It is clear from these documents that very few MPs express themselves in any language other than English. For example, of the 117 MPs who made contributions to the discussion about the bills as documented in the *Debates of the Senate Second Session—First Parliament (No. 9) of the 6th to the 13th of June 1995*, only three were in an African language: two in Sepedi, one in isiXhosa.

Newsletters

Both the Newsletter of the National Council of Provinces (*NCOP News*) and the *Newsletter for Members and Staff of Parliament* are in English-only.

Meeting agendas and minutes

The agenda and minutes of the meetings are always obtainable in both English and Afrikaans. For example, the National Assembly Order Paper (Nasionale

Vergadering Ordelys) of February 9, 1999 and the National Assembly and National Council of Provinces Meetings of Committees (Nasionale Vergardering en Nasionale Raad van Provinsies Vergaderings van Komitees) of February 9, 1999 appear in English and Afrikaans. Although English and Afrikaans are used alongside each other in the agenda and minutes of the meetings, African languages are not.

Systematic observation

Observations made in both the committee rooms and the National Assembly demonstrate the hegemony of English in the Republic of South African Parliament. All fourteen meetings of the various portfolio committees were conducted in English. In the National Assembly, where there are interpreting facilities, only a few speeches and responses were made in various official languages. Although the majority of the MPs are Black Africans who have African languages as their first language, virtually all speeches and deliberations observed during this period in 1999 were in English. This appears to be the norm throughout Parliamentary sessions.

Conclusion

English remains the dominant language used by MPs in South Africa's National Assembly and portfolio committee rooms. The perceived "dangerous power" of English in the South African Parliament will definitely have a negative impact on the enhancement of multilingualism and multiculturalism that the Constitution enshrines. Similar to Dua's proposal (1994) with reference to the Indian language situation, unless the newly emerging Black politicians associated with the indigenous African languages organize themselves to counter the hegemony of English, and fight for a different political, social, and cultural arrangement of power and knowledge, they will not only fail to curb the dominance of English, but also contribute to the marginalization of their languages and cultures.

Afrikaans also continues to hold an elevated position in the South African Parliament. In this way, Boer privilege continues to exist. In order to alter this situation, some drastic changes and creative thinking are needed on the part of supporters of Black language use. What would happen if African MPs insisted that at least one African language be used regularly in Parliament? Or if all politicians were required to demonstrate mastery of at least one African language in order to run for office? What would happen if the urban vehicular Zulu that is currently emerging in the big cities and on local television stations was recognized as a lingua franca or vehicle of wider communication that would be promoted by the government and used in local politics? Such moves would constitute creative action on the part of those who support not only the recognition, but also the use of African languages in all sectors of society.

The lack of political will to publicly promote African languages could "result in the betrayal of the cause of both the language and cultural renaissance and the destiny of mankind" (Dua 1994: 133). Although English and Afrikaans are currently dominating all other languages in Parliament, the privileging of these languages must be resisted. It is unfortunate that Members of Parliament are the ones who have created this situation. As pointed out above, the effects of this language policy at macro-level are detrimental. Although English is currently perceived as the language of politics and economics in South Africa, we, as Black linguists, must help politicians rethink language issues so they reflect a movement toward Black empowerment in South African and globally. So long as the national government uses English and Afrikaans as the only languages of record in Parliament, those who continue to fight for the use and recognition of African languages will continue to be regarded as uneducated and uncivilized, and their voices ignored and ultimately silenced. That will be the betrayal of our freedom and democracy, for freedom can only be fulfilled when the languages of the people are utilized in all segments of the society.

References

Alexander, N. (1989) *Language Policy and National Unity in South Africa/Azania*, Cape Town: Buchu Books.

—— (1995) "The economic and political importance of language policy in the new South Africa," paper presented to the Inter-Governmental Technical Committee, Pretoria.

Brown, D. (1992) "Language and social history in South Africa: a task still to be undertaken," in R.K. Herbert (ed.) *Language and Society in Africa: The Theory and Practice of Sociolinguistics*, Braamfontein: Witwatersrand University Press, 71–92.

Cluver, A.D. de V. (1992) "Language planning models for post-apartheid South Africa," *Language Problems and Language Planning*, 15 (2): 1–37.

Criminal Procedure Amendment Bill (W 132B–98), Republic of South Africa: Creda Communications.

Debates of the National Assembly (Hansard), Second Session, First Parliament, No. 5, September 5–6, 1995, Cape Town: Creda Press.

Debates of the National Assembly (Hansard), Second Session, First Parliament, No. 14, April 15–18, 1997, Cape Town: Creda Press.

Debates of the National Council of Provinces (Hansard). First Session, Second Parliament, No. 8, November 18–21, 1997, Cape Town: Government Printer.

Debates of the Senate (Hansard), Second Session, First Parliament, No. 9, June 6–13, 1995, Cape Town: Creda Press.

Domestic Violence Bill (B75–98), Republic of South Africa: Creda Communications.

Dua, H.R. (1994) *Hegemony of English*, Mysore: Yashoda Publications.

Heugh, K. (1994) "The implementability of South Africa's eleven language policy," paper presented at the First World Congress of African Linguistics, Kwaluseni: Swaziland, July.

—— (1995) "Disabling and enabling: implications of language policy trends in South Africa," in R. Mesthrie (ed.) *Language and Social History: Studies in South African Sociolinguistics*, Claremont, South Africa: David Philips, 329–50.

Hlatshwayo, S.A. (2000) *Education and Independence: Education in South Africa, 1658–1988*, Westport, CN: Greenwood Press.

Kamwangamalu, N.M. (1997) "Multilingualism and education policy in post-apartheid South Africa," in *Language Problems and Language Planning*, Amsterdam and Philadelphia, PA: John Benjamins.

LANGTAG (1996) *Towards a National Language Plan for South Africa: Final Report of the Language Plan Task Group* (1996), Department of Arts, Culture, Science and Technology.

Maartens, J. (1998) "Multilingualism and language policy in South Africa," in G. Extra and J. Maartens (eds) *Multilingualism in a Multicultural Context: Case Studies on South Africa and Western Europe*, The Netherlands: Tilburg University Press, 15–36.

Mandela, N.R. (1999) "Presidential address to Parliament," Cape Town, South Africa, February.

Mateene Kahombo (1996) "OAU's strategy for linguistic unity and multilingual education," paper presented at the International Seminar on Language in Education in Africa, University of Cape Town, July.

McLean, D. (1992) "Guarding against the bourgeois revolution: some aspects of language planning in the context of national democratic struggle," in R.K. Herbert (ed.) *Language and Society in Africa: The Theory and Practice of Sociolinguistics*, Braamfontein: Witwatersrand University Press, 151–61.

Moodie, T.P. (1980) *The Rise of Afrikanerdom: Power, Apartheid, and the Afrikaner Civil Religion*, Berkeley, CA: University of California Press.

National Assembly and National Council of Provinces Meetings of Committees: Third Annual Session, Second Parliament, February 1999, Parliament of the Republic of South Africa.

National Assembly Order Paper: Third Annual, Second Parliament, February 9, 1999, Parliament of the Republic of South Africa.

Newsletter for Members and Staff of Parliament (January 1999), produced by a Project of the European Union Parliamentary Support Programme.

Report of the Auditor-General on the Accounts of Vote 30: South African Police Service for 1996–97, Pretoria: Government Printer.

Report of the Auditor-General on the Accounts of Vote 31: South African Revenue Service for 1996–97, Pretoria: Government Printer.

Report of the Auditor-General on the Dairy Board Liquidation Account for the Period Ended on 22 April 1998, Pretoria: Government Printer.

Report of the Auditor-General on the Local Authorities Loans Fund for 1997–98, Pretoria: Government Printer.

Report of the Auditor-General on the Secret Services Account, the Related Departmental Accounts and the Security Services Special Account for 1996–97, Pretoria: Government Printer.

The Constitution of the Republic of South Africa (1996) South Africa.

Tollefson, J.W. (1991) *Planning Language, Planning Inequality: Language Policy in the Community*, London: Longman.

Witness Protection Bill (W130B—98), Republic of South Africa: Creda Communications.

7

From misinvention to disinvention of language: multilingualism and the South African Constitution

Sinfree Makoni

The aim of this chapter is to explore the political significance of the analytical categories used in discussions about language in the South African Constitution. That Constitution has been heralded as intellectually progressive and politically enlightened because of the significance it attaches to human rights and its acknowledgment of multilingualism in the African context. In giving official status to nine African languages, South Africa has charted a course in opposition to that of other African countries, for example Malawi and Namibia, whose constitutions stipulate English as the official language. In fact, the Malawian Constitution goes even further by stipulating proficiency in English as a pre-requisite for public office. I will argue, however, that the South African Constitution, by recognizing nine African languages as neatly divided, "bounded units" (Cook 2002), or "hermetically sealed units" (Makoni 1998a; Nuttall and Cotzee 1998), is socially alienating and cognitively disadvantaging to the very people it is intended to serve. Furthermore, I will argue that the South African Constitutional language policy creates a self-serving amnesia by encouraging Africans to "unremember" the historical and material contexts in which the so-called African "languages" were invented, or "cobbled together" as Brutt-Griffler (2002) prefers to put it.

The final version of the South African Constitution, which forms the basis of the analysis in this chapter, was approved in 1996. The Founding Provisions are: the Sovereignty of South Africa, the Supremacy of the Constitution, Citizenship, National Anthem, and Languages.

The language provisions are as follows:

1   The official languages of the Republic are Sepedi, Sesotho, Setswana, siSwati, Tshivenda, Xitsonga, Afrikaans, English, isiNdebele, isiXhosa, and isiZulu.

2   Recognizing the historically diminished use and status of the indigenous languages of our people, the state must take practical and positive measures to elevate the status and advance the use of these languages.

3(a) The national government and provincial governments may use any particular official languages for the purposes of government taking into account usage, practicality, expense, regional circumstances and the balance of the needs and preferences of the population as a whole or in the province concerned; but the national government and each provincial government must use at least two official languages.

3(b) Municipalities must take into account the language usage and preferences of their residents.

4   The national government and provincial governments, by legislative and other measures, must regulate and monitor their use of official languages. Without detracting from provisions of subsection (2), all official languages must enjoy parity of esteem and must be treated equitably.

> (Chapter One, Founding Provisions, The Constitution of
> the Republic of South Africa 1996: 4)

The language provisions continue:

5   A Pan South African Language Board established by national legislation must—
(a) promote and create conditions for the development and use of—
   (i)   all official languages;
   (ii)   the Khoi, Nama, and San languages;
   (iii) sign language;
(b) promote and ensure respect for—
   (i)   all languages commonly used by communities in South Africa, including German, Greek, Gujarati, Hindi, Portuguese, Tamil, Telegu, and Urdu;
   (ii)   Arabic, Hebrew, Sanskrit, and other languages used for religious purposes in South Africa.

> (Chapter One, Founding Provisions, The Constitution of
> the Republic of South Africa 1996: 4–5)

The Bill of Rights in the final version of the Constitution protects the rights of individuals to "use the language of their choice." Sections (30) and (31) state that individuals have the right "to receive education in the official languages or language of their choice where that is practicable." Section (35) provides for the right of an accused person to be tried in a language that he/she understands or, if that is not practicable, to have the proceedings interpreted. The Founding Provisions make it imperative for the State to "take practical and positive measures to elevate the status and advance the use" of the "indigenous" languages. The Provisions also make it mandatory for the State to "ensure respect for all languages commonly used by communities in South Africa"—e.g. Hindi, Gujarati, Portuguese, Tamil, Telegu, Urdu, other languages used for "religious purposes"—the list of languages is indeterminate!

The South African Constitution, then, on which the country's national language policy is founded, recognizes eleven separate languages as official, nine of them constructed as "indigenous." What makes these languages separate and indigenous is far from clear. When did they become separate and indigenous, and for whom, and under what circumstances? These are crucial questions which are not addressed even in radical sociolinguistics (e.g. Phillipson 1992; Makoni and Kamwangamalu 2000) where the existence of separate indigenous languages is taken as self-evident, unproblematic, and an uncontested sociolinguistic fact. Increasingly one finds this matter addressed only in endnotes to academic work on the sociolinguistics of South Africa (Hornberger 2002).

The development of the indigenous languages to prepare them for their new Constitutional role is placed in the hands of various sectors of government, the key one being the Pan South African Language Board (PANSALB). The architects of the Constitution were fully aware that "the new Constitutional provisions relating to language are messy, inelegant and contradictory," as Albie Sachs, a South African judge who played a key role in the construction of the South African Constitution, so aptly put it. The extent of the inelegance, contradiction and messiness, however, has not been explored, nor even recognized by most sociolinguists.

To begin with, we should note that the discourse that constructs African languages as separate categories has its genesis in colonial thinking, namely in an ideology of "linguistic fixity" that disregards the sociohistorical contexts in which they were invented (Ranger 1985; Chimhundu 1992; Harries 1995; Makoni 1998b). The construct of "invention" or the related notions of "narration" and "imagination" (Anderson 1983; Bhabha 1990) have been productively deployed in research dealing with cultural formations of ethnicity, national identity, and traditional legal systems. The upshot of arguments about "invention," "narration," and "imagination" has been to convincingly demonstrate that ethnicity and cultural institutions, such as traditional legal systems, are a product of colonial ideology and did not exist unproblematically out there in African space. Linguists dealing with African sociolinguistic issues have been slow to exploit the advantage of the insights generated from "invention" and related concepts. If traditional systems and ethnicity were part of colonial ideology, it is logical to ask to what extent other cultural formations, such as so-called "African languages," are part of the same colonial ideology. In this chapter, I seek to examine the analytical usefulness of the construct of invention as it applies to African languages. The question is of interest because it shows how languages are constituted historically and thus allows for the possibility of languages being deconstituted. The issue is also of current interest because it reflects the extent to which some of the contemporary problems with implementability of language policies in Africa are situated in the conceptualizations and ways of thinking about African languages.

Different languages were invented out of what was one language through a process marred by "faulty transcriptions and mishearings," mediated through partial competence in African languages, and motivated by an overly sharp separation between language structure and language use (Campbell-Makini 2000) reinforced by the use of different orthographic systems. Initiatives for rendering African speech ("languages") in written form resulted in "an exaggerated multi-ethnic, multi-lingual, and multi-tribal picture of African colonies [that] has been painted through misinterpretation and inadequate study on the part of the early missionaries and manipulation for administrative convenience on the part of colonial governments" (Chimhundu 1992: 88). For example, the speech of the Sotho and Tswana, whose languages are productively conceptualized as a continuum, were defined as separate languages. The Xhosa and Zulu peoples, whose languages are closely related, were defined as speaking different languages because of the rivalry between the different missionaries working with these two groups. Setswana, Sesotho, and Sepedi, three of the languages officially recognized within the South African Constitution, are very similar grammatically, morphologically, and lexically. The differences between these three languages are mainly in the area of phonology. These related speech forms were codified as separate languages because of missionary politics.

In some cases even the names given to some of the African speech forms were invented by Europeans. The most telling example is the name "Shona," a language spoken in Southern Africa, mainly in Zimbabwe. (However, because of massive migration from the north, it is also spoken in parts of South Africa as well, for example by the Tswana people.) Prior to European colonialism, the Shona peoples did not have a collective term to refer to themselves. In 1931, the name "Shona" was used for the purpose of facilitating administrative classification. The recommendation did not come from Shona language users themselves, but from a committee of missionaries who subsequently commissioned a language expert, Clement Doke, Professor of Linguistics at the University of Witwatersrand in Johannesburg, South Africa, to design an orthographic system for Shona—in spite of his lack of knowledge about the language.

> It has been widely felt that the name Shona is inaccurate and unworthy, that it is not the true name of any of the peoples whom we propose to group under the term "Shona-speaking people," and further, it lies under strong suspicion of being a name given in contempt by enemies of the tribes. It is pretty certainly a foreign name, and as such is very likely to be uncomplimentary like the name "kaffir."
>
> (Southern Rhodesia 1929: 25)

After Shona was decreed into existence, a standard grammar was subsequently constructed under Clement Doke's direction and a vocabulary was created "of as many and as representative words as possible which shall include words from the major dialects." The vocabulary was largely drawn from missionary converts who were working as "laboratory assistants." The famous laboratory assistants were David Mandisodza, Joseph Chamunorwa, and Paul Malanga, converts to the American Methodist Church (Southern Rhodesia 1929). In this context, there was no pretense of linguistics operating under the banner of objective science. Rather, this was linguistics clearly being utilized to serve the interests and politics of missionaries and colonial administrators (Campbell-Makini 2000; Brutt-Griffler 2002). It is not only linguistics that has served colonialism well; other disciplines, such as anthropology, have also had their history marred by their role in the colonial enterprise.

"To give a proper name to languages requires a certain kind of consciousness of language, an assumption that languages can be standardized entities and that they can have names" (Mannheim 1991: 8). It is a linguistic consciousness that seems to be an outcome of formal Western education, a consciousness which is not necessarily a part of the social awareness of most peoples with limited or no formal education. Such peoples refer to what they speak as "human language." A language without a name would thus not be an oddity, it would have been the norm. The problem is akin to the virtual impossibility of discussing ethnicity other than in terms or labels that are "tribal."

Literacy and language education are as much tools of social control as forms of social emancipation. Discourses about multilingualism designed to reverse the inequalities of the apartheid legacy in which only Afrikaans and English were regarded as official do not take into account the linguistic differences within each of the languages labeled an "African language." In African language communities, there are significant linguistic differences between the official "standard" version of the language and the version that is actually used and spoken—as is the case with most languages. What is peculiarly African, however, is that the difference between the "standard" and the language used in practice "constitutes a gulf rather than continuity, and there is little movement across the divide. A reified standard may be honored, but it is rarely valued, and language must be valued to prosper" (Ridge *et al.* 2001: 10).

The essence of the argument is this: because African languages were not constructed and standardized taking into account the communicative practices of the users, there is a very sharp disjuncture between language praxis and standard forms of the languages. Notions of a "standard," particularly in written form, originated in the grammatical descriptions of the nineteenth century. In the case of African languages, however, the magnitude of the disjuncture is so great that there are potentially adverse effects for mother tongue education. Standard African languages are rarely used as primary languages in the homes and playgrounds in African communities, particularly in urban areas. A majority of students enter primary school speaking non-standardized versions of the official

African languages and urban argots which draw heavily and freely on English, Afrikaans, and "non-official" African languages. The extent to which they draw on Afrikaans and English, however, varies depending on the social status and gender of the speaker. Women's speech draws more heavily on English as a marker of femininity, social class, and urbanity while male speech relies more heavily on Afrikaans, which is a marker of male urbanity (Cook 2002).

The African languages listed in the South African Constitution and those frequently cited in the literature on African sociolinguistics reinforce the boundaries which were arbitrarily drawn by missionaries and subsequently awarded academic credibility through grammatical descriptions of Zulu, Xhosa, Tswana, and other "indigenous" South African languages. The framers of the South African Constitution have, unwittingly, perpetrated the misclassification of old and given it renewed credibility. The legacy of misclassification will be felt well into the twenty-first century unless serious sociolinguistic and political efforts are made to contain the mistakes of history.

Misclassification overlooks the great diversity within each of the distinct language labels, as can be easily illustrated through the case of one of the languages officially recognized in the South African Constitution: Xhosa. As with many other languages, Xhosa has several spoken varieties. It is said to be made up of such varieties as Ngqika, Thembu, Hlubi, Bhaca, Bomvana, Mpondo, Mpondomise, and others (Satyo 2000). Speakers of Hlubi and Bhaca from the Eastern Cape may experience problems with the standard Xhosa represented in textbooks. The written representation of African speech forms has historically run parallel to, but rarely intersected with, the daily language practices of most speakers of those languages. In fact, there seems to be a deliberate effort on the part of some speakers, particularly the youth, to distance themselves from the standard (Satyo 2001), which is rarely anybody's mother tongue.

There is such great diversity within some of the African language "boxes" that no dialect has successfully served as a standard. This should not be construed as an argument against the role of standard languages. Rather, it is an argument against the processes which formed the basis of the standardization of these languages in the first place. The selection of a specific dialect to serve as the basis of the standard language, the conventional procedure in most communities (Pennycook 1994), has been unsuccessful in the case of most African languages. The problem is so acute that it undermines any serious effort toward mother tongue education. For example, non-standard Zulu is so radically different from what is characterized as "Zulu" in urban settings that speakers who sociolinguistically feel affiliated with Zulu ethnically, or are administratively classified as "Zulu," may feel alienated, and their linguistic creativity may be stifled by the language assigned to them as their "mother tongue." The situation is not peculiar to Zulu. Cook (2002) provides evidence which suggests that most students from Tswana-speaking homes usually require remedial instruction in the form of the language assigned to them. This state of affairs results from the fact that the "mother tongue" assigned to students for educational purposes may not correspond with sociolinguistic reality—it may not be the language in which the learners are most proficient. The speakers are multilingual and multidialectal, proficient in non-standard versions of their languages and urban argots, but not in the reified and historically dated standard African language. For example, the standard Setswana taught in schools, which forms the written basis of most language teaching materials, has remained largely unchanged since 1937.

The notion of "mother tongue" may mean very different things when used for institutional purposes than when used in the real world. It is a relative concept depending on the discursive context and on whether one is talking institutionally or from the perspective of the language users. Because of the disjuncture between speaker and institutional constructions of mother tongue, mother tongue education may fail to realize its desired goals because the speakers are acquired by their mother tongues instead of the opposite! As a result of misclassification, mother tongue education may cognitively disadvantage the very people it is expected to benefit, as students are deprived of the necessary educational support they would have received had the full implications that they were learning in a non-home code been taken into account.

In language research, the discrepancy between classification of mother tongue based on speaker criteria and classification based on institutional criteria has not been the central concern of debates about the native speaker (Davies 1999). It is necessary to ask hard questions about underlying conceptions of mother tongue, particularly in social domains such as education. Shifting images of mother tongue should not be political icons in whose direction we have to reverently and invariably genuflect.

In the South African Constitution, languages created in historically dubious circumstances by missionaries and their African linguistic apprentices are accorded the status of uncontested judicial facts and become permanent sociolinguistic fixtures of the way the African landscape is imagined. The image is that of a landscape composed of many language boxes and linguistic "things," separate and distinct. This image runs counter to the lived and living experiences of most ordinary users of African speech forms. According to Satyo (2001), the language used by Xhosa youth in urban centers in South Africa is strongly influenced by Kwaito, a type of music popular with urban youth, somewhat akin to Hip Hop in the US. The speech of urban Xhosa youth is a form of language which reflects compelling evidence of innovative strategies for harmonizing resources from different languages as these youth build a pan-ethnic, urban identity. These pan-ethnic African speech forms sharply contrast with standardized African languages in terms of the images which the forms seek to convey. The speech transcends physical locality and is used to evoke a sense of urban space; thus the speech forms are even used in rural areas by speakers emphasizing and foregrounding an urban identity, as aptly captured in the title of Cook's recent chapter, "Urban language in a rural setting" (2002). Cook demonstrates empirically how people who wish to project an urban identity, or who emulate styles associated with urban life, do so through language forms associated with urbanity. It is speech which is thought of not as "a language," but as linguistic forms with a "range of expressive inventories that not only enable people to communicate with each other, but allow people to communicate something about themselves to the world" (Cook 2002: 110).

The pan-ethnic, urban, hybridized linguistic forms contain lexical items which are an "embodiment" of linguistic information drawn from different languages. These pan-ethnic varieties are excellent examples of "lexical pastiche" which try to capture the nuances of social relationships by exploiting the social, historical, and political associations of words (Myers-Scotton 1993; Childs 1997; Satyo 2001). For example:

1   *Tsotsitaal* is a combination of *utsotsi*, Xhosa for "criminal," as in most other Bantu languages, and *taal* from Afrikaans, referring to a language. Thus, *tsotsitaal* literally refers to "speaking the language of criminals."

2   *Imkasi* means "Black township"; the word is a recycled form of the Afrikaans word *lokasie*, with a Xhosa prefix.

3   *Abantwana ijive* refers to treating girls like children (unlike boys who are taken seriously), from Xhosa *abantwana*, which means "children," and *ijive*, meaning lacking in seriousness, probably from the English word *jive*, itself thought to be derived from West African Wolof, *jev*, entering English through the speech of American slaves. The implication of *abantwana ijive* is that all one can do with girls is engage in trivial matters.

Such linguistic forms and the processes that generate these forms reflect language harmonization developing organically from the grassroots, with neither respect for nor allegiance to typological distinctions characteristic of most linguistically inclined discourses about African speech. But the phenomenon is not peculiar to Southern Africa; linguists have drawn attention to its existence in other parts of Africa, for example in Central Africa. Goyvaerts (1996) presents language data from this region reflecting words comprised of constituents from four different languages: Swahili, Lingala, English, and French—e.g. *Mi iouink ki ndozala* (I am on my way to the market); *mi*, from Swahili *mimi*, *gouink*, from English *go/going*, *ki*, from French *qui*, and *ndozala*, from Lingala *zando*, market.

The version of multilingualism implicit in the South African Constitution is one best described as plural monolingualism: a variant and an extension of monolingualism. Instead of South Africans being encouraged to be multilingual, the policy could actually end up making each citizen merely competent in his/her own language. That is, since all the country's languages are officially recognized, all one need do is become competent in the standard version of his/her own language. The South African language policy should have specified only two or three African languages as official languages, a decision which would have been relatively easy to arrive at through a reconceptualization of "language." However, to propose official status for nine so-called "indigenous" African languages is to reaffirm the separateness of Black South African ethnic groups through language. It is a false separation, linguistically and ethnically, whereby the present South African government is, paradoxically, proposing a policy which the apartheid South African government could not successfully implement. After the destruction of mixed areas, the most well-known being Sophiatown in Johannesburg and District Six in Cape Town, the apartheid government went to extraordinary—but ultimately unsuccessful—lengths to keep each language group to itself.

> The concentration of these languages in industrialized areas led to an inevitable mixing of people who spoke different Bantu languages in churches, work places, social gatherings, and other situations. The folly of trying to keep the same people separate was exposed as a shameful fiasco. In industrialized areas there was nothing to be gained for the Africans in creating tribal laagers [exclusive spaces]. Apartheid succeeded only in separating blacks from whites, because an overwhelming majority of whites wanted that separation. The honesty of the Afrikaner provided a convenient scapegoat for what the English-speaking [citizen] tacitly approved of and supported.
>
> (Maake 1994: 113)

The problem of the implementability of the South African national language policy (its "inelegance, contradiction and messiness") is a direct consequence of the very nature of the languages it seeks to promote. The policy itself is, in effect, based on an inaccurate analysis of the prevailing sociolinguistic condition. Contrary to views of local and international scholars alike (e.g. Desai 1994; Smitherman 2000), who welcome the national language policy, I contend that what should be welcomed is the very problem posed by implementation because this forces us to consider the sociolinguistic realities which any language policy needs to take into account. I would suggest that a productive way out of this political, linguistic, and intellectual impasse is to institute a program to *disinvent* African languages, hence reconceptualizing the notions of language and ethnicity on which the South African language policy is founded. Notions about language and ethnicity in the South African Constitution are founded on "boxed" notions of language and ethnicity ultimately traceable to eighteenth-century German Romanticist ideas which treated territory, constructions of race, and conceptualizations of language as identical and indivisible. According to German Romanticism, language and identity/ethnicity were indistinguishable, with language considered to be the most powerful index of social identity. According to the indivisibility of language, race, and territory, you would, for instance, be said to speak Zulu if you were Zulu ethnically. That is, because you were affiliated with Zulu or inherited Zulu ethnically, you were, as a result, considered to be a speaker of Zulu. The possibility of someone who feels affiliated with Zulu ethnically, but who does not speak Zulu, is a contradiction within the framework of language, ethnicity, and race embodied in German Romanticist thought.

The disinvention proposal calls attention to the importance of reflecting on our tools of analysis and on the significant realization that linguists and non-linguists may be using terms differently. For example, one possible way of conceptualizing African speech forms is to think of them as constituting a continuum "stretching across Africa from the Atlantic to the Indian Ocean" (LePage and Tabouret-Keller 1985). The notion of a language continuum does not deny that there are differences among language forms at the extreme ends of the continuum, for example Yoruba on the West Coast and Xhosa in the South. However, a conceptualization of African speech forms as comprising a continuum suggests that the notion of "African lingua franca" may be best envisaged not as a

> single language but as a multilayered and partially connected chain, that offers a choice of varieties and registers in the speakers' immediate environment, and a steadily diminishing set of options to be employed in more distant interactions, albeit a set that is always liable to be reconnected more densely to a new environment by rapid secondary learning, or by the development of new languages.
>
> (Fardon and Furniss 1994: 4)

The perspective of imagining African languages as "multilayered and interconnected chains" is radically different from that which forms the basis of early missionary thought, and it is a perspective that can be supported empirically. For example, the relationship between Zulu and Xhosa is one not only of mutual intelligibility but also of interconnectedness. Words which are regarded as non-standard and are thus excluded from standard Xhosa appear in hlonipha and isikhwetha. Hlonipha and isikhwetha are special types of registers associated, respectively, with married women and young men in Xhosa. Hlonipha is a language variety used by recently married women, and isikhwetha is the type of language variety typically used by young men during circumcision. Similarly, words which are stigmatized as part of standard Zulu are acceptable when they enter Xhosa lexical usage through the specialized varieties of hlonipha and isikhweta (Satyo 1998).

The missionaries created languages which were describable as mutually exclusive boxes as opposed to interconnected patterns. In fact, the very notion of languages as discrete units, or "boxes," is a product of European positivism reinforced by literacy and standardization (Romaine 1984). Discussions about African vernaculars are as much about specific ways of imagining the African sociolinguistic landscape as they are about description. In this regard, it is only now that the full implication of the work of missionaries is beginning to dawn on us.

In countries in which the vast majority of the people are not literate, in the Western sense of the term, consciousness of languages as discrete boxes is likely to be alien. The "misinvention" of African languages had clear political consequences and implied particular forms of social relations, not only between Africans and Europeans, but also among Africans themselves. Hofmeyer argues that Africans actively took advantage of the presence of missionaries to articulate their dissatisfaction with existing political systems:

> Both among commoners and within the royal caste itself . . . there existed cause for dissatisfaction against the ruling lineage. The dissatisfaction was expressed by entering into a loose association with missionaries. For commoners, the mission and its schools which used a lot of Sesotho remained a source of attraction.
>
> (Hofmeyer 1993: 48)

The discourse which the missionaries created in the process of specifying and inventing African languages was designed to limit what could be said "about," "to," and "discussed with" Africans (Mühlähauser 1996). The construction of African languages was designed to restrict not only the universe of discourse entered into by Europeans with Africans but also the participation of Africans in the colonial world. (The extent of this construction of African languages has been ably outlined by Jeater [1994].) The major objective of missionary linguistics was to comprehend African cosmology in the missionaries' own terms, and only terms that could facilitate that process were included in the vernacular language. The missionaries were passing judgment on the societies in which they were operating. For example, Jeater demonstrates that Africans who preferred to find alternative sources of income, rather than work in the missionaries' translation endeavors, were defined as "lazy" and "dishonest" because they did not make themselves readily available for exploitation as cheap colonial labor.

The linguistic inventions of the missionary era were structured in such a way as to encourage Africans to internalize European epistemology about themselves, creating a new view about their current affairs and superimposing new values on their past. In this process, the educated African elite became alienated from their home communities and the languages of those communities—hence the danger of presuming that through vernacular use and the promotion of indigenous African languages a common sense of belonging can be created, democratic practices enhanced and imperialism counteracted. Indeed the opposite occurs: the promotion of African languages that were "cobbled together" and invented during the colonial era continues the separation of the people on the basis of language, facilitates the divide-and-rule tactics of old and serves contemporary neoimperialist interests. Thus the framers of the South African Constitution, by using linguistic labels from the past they are seeking to challenge, are, in fact, legitimating that past. It is therefore appropriate to sound a cautionary note.

> Times of rapid change place great pressure on language. The new must find expression and an articulated social presence must be negotiated

for it. However, the commanders of the new social space are often heirs both, unwittingly, to the discourses which maintained the old, and to those which prepared the way for their political success. The discourses which maintained the old embody the values of an order which has not yet gone and which may yet stage a comeback.

(Ridge 2001: 16)

It is not only that the current language policy of the South African Constitution reinforces the attitudes and practices of the missionary past. More significantly, in the context of this chapter, it reflects a present-day sociolinguistic orthodoxy. Consider the case of code-switching. Most sociolinguistic research on code-switching is premised on the assumption that speakers code-switch naturally from the different languages which they control. So, for example, a speaker who mixes English, Afrikaans, and African languages is assumed to have the ability to use English, Afrikaans, and African languages in their "unmixed" forms as separate codes. It is a logical inference, but unfortunately it is inaccurate and cannot be supported by the evidence from the sociolinguistic situation of urban African settings. In these urban centers the "mixed" forms are themselves the linguistic norm, the starting point in the process of language socialization for most people, and at times the only version of language for everyday encounters. Most people only encounter the "unmixed" speech as part of the formal process of education. The uneducated speakers may never have encountered the languages in their "unmixed" state. Thus the speakers cannot be said to have the capacity to speak languages which they do not control, may never have controlled, and are unlikely to get exposed to unless they get formally educated! It is relatively easy to understand the conceptual mistake made by the analysts of code-switching. Because they themselves may control English, Afrikaans, and African languages as separate codes, they assume that the speakers using the "mixed" forms are combining these three languages. What the analysts are overlooking is that their sociolinguistic autobiographies are very different from those of the people they are analyzing.

Because the sociolinguistic evidence suggests that mixtures resulting from the interconnected nature of language are indeed a defining part of the sociolinguistic situation, it is therefore possible that we are placing emphasis on and studying the wrong phenomenon. The area which needs urgent analysis is one in which attempts at linguistic "unmixing" or "uncoupling" take place. The metaphors we need to create are those which can capture the faltering nature of linguistic "uncoupling," particularly in mother tongue education, which is generally premised upon assumptions about discrete codes. "Uncoupling" refers to a process whereby a speaker expunges words by manipulating phonological rules that are supposedly not part of the language the speaker is using. For example:

1   Standard Swati: Indvodza iye edolobheni ekuseni. (The man has gone to town).

2   Standard Xhosa: Indoda iye edolobheni kusasa. (The man has gone to town).

3   Standard Zulu: Indoda iye edolobheni ekuseni. (The man has gone to town).

All three sentences mean "the man has gone to town." A child ethnically classified as Swati who produces the utterance *Indoda iye edolobheni kusasa* will be regarded as speaking incorrect siSwati, i.e. not speaking "pure" siSwati (as standard African languages are increasingly being referred to, even in educational circles). She is pronouncing *indoda* as in Standard Xhosa and Zulu instead of *indvodza*. Similarly, a Zulu child who says: *Indoda iye edolobheni kusasa* will be said to be speaking incorrect Zulu because she says *kusasa* instead of *ekuseni*. The child's Zulu would thus be classified as incorrect even though it is correct Standard Xhosa!

The metaphor that most accurately applies to the African situation is not self-enclosed partitions, but "frontiers." The main strength of the "frontier" metaphor is that it resists notions of barriers and works on the basis of interconnectedness, unlike the underlying construct forming the basis of notions about language in the South African Constitution. Conceiving of language as interconnected patterns enables me to talk about the number of languages a speaker controls. It is more prudent to talk about language repertoires or workable portfolios (Fardon and Furniss 1994). Language as "frontier" is more sensitive to the dynamics of social interaction. Frequency of interaction could lead to speakers becoming more like one another in their repertoire, in the repertoires they draw upon, and in the social meanings they attach to each selection from their repertoire.

Conceptions of language as interconnected patterns and scrambled systems seek to break, to rupture, the present from the overwhelming hold of the past. However, these conceptions are not legitimated by the South African Constitution, itself *par excellence* a residue of the past in contemporary form. The traces of the past in that Constitution are not unusual because all constitutions retain traces of their history in the way they are formulated. The language provision formulated in the South African Constitution is written in what Ridge calls "apocalyptic discourse." Such discourse "is deeply encoded and captures the end of history. This is a discourse that reflects a shift away from clear directions formulated with an awareness of context to exalted ideals as if beyond the claims of history—a shift away from actual to apocalyptic discourse" (Ridge 2000: 47).

The Constitutional discourse describing the Pan South African Language Board (PANSALB) is an excellent example of "apocalyptic discourse." The triumphalist tone used in relation to PANSALB is in sharp conflict with the discourse temperament in other sections of the chapter delineating Founding Provisions of the Constitution. PANSALB is placed in a difficult position in which it is given responsibilities it cannot reasonably be expected to meet. It is expected to "ensure respect for all languages commonly used by communities in

South Africa"—an open-ended list which cites eight languages over the fifteen already specified, and as if that were not enough, all languages used for religious purposes—three are mentioned. PANSALB is charged, at the highest level, with a task which is difficult, if not impossible, to achieve.

The other responsibilities placed upon PANSALB make very little sense in the real world. For example, Richterweld Nama is the only existing Khoi language. There are fewer than ten people who are speakers of San language. There are about 70,000 speakers of Italian and less than 800 speakers of Telegu. However, it is the latter that is mentioned in the Constitution. An apocalyptic discourse, which sets forth a perfect, ideal condition without suggesting any practical ways in which the historical processes can be realized, is a paradox. What is required is an articulation with the real world, not an apocalyptic vision, not proposals based on historical accident or concepts inapplicable to the African situation, but locally specific solutions. Such locally specific solutions may be constructed, I suggest, through the notion of *disinvention*.

Disinvention does not mean a return to arcane forms of African language speak. It is a serious effort to capture current language practices, which are generally pan-ethnic in nature—hence, which cut across conceptualizations about language/society/ethnicity affiliation implicit in the South African Constitution. Disinvention is a prerequisite to capturing the role and forms of African languages as interconnected patterns and moves away from notions of languages as boxes or discrete items. This can be realized through detailed descriptions of current language practices. These descriptions would be useful not only for disinventing African speech forms, hence constraining the legacy of nineteenth-century positivism, but also for facilitating the new roles created for African language speech forms by the Constitution.

The advantages of disinvention would not be limited to the Constitutional arena, but would extend to education as well. Most learners of African languages, mother tongue and second languages alike, find themselves confronted with a sharp divide between the official language, as embodied in current written texts, and the speech used in the everyday drama of life, moment by moment, situation by situation. One of the serious drawbacks apparent in any serious engagement with local speech communities is the limited amount of material for fostering literacy in the so-called African languages. A shift away from African languages as discrete boxes to interconnected hybridized forms would make it possible to produce a set of materials based on the same orthographic system. An orthographic commons would serve not only South Africa but also Southern Africa.

The disinvention project foregrounds the importance of retaining distinctions between standardized "indigenous" languages, non-standardized languages, and urban argots. The distinction can be made along a number of lines. The first one is historical. "Indigenous" languages were to some extent the creation and invention of missionaries using and interpreting data from their African apprentices. Non-standard and urban hybrids are more contemporary linguistic forms, the result, in part, of mass movements. "Indigenous" languages are currently standardized while local languages are not.

It is through the use of non-standardized and urban argots that some of the creativity and dramas of everyday life in the African sociolinguistic landscape are articulated. The non-standard speech forms also vary by gender and reflect and re-create the social histories and biographies of their users. Illustrative examples are provided in conversations recorded and analyzed by Cook (2002: 110–12). The excerpt from Transcript 1 is taken from a conversation between several working-class men in their thirties who are socializing and flirting with the women. The excerpt from Transcript 2 captures a conversational moment between young women. The conversational excerpts reflect a fair amount of "mixing" in both conventional and unconventional ways.

Excerpt from Transcript 1

Speaker #1 Hei Popompo! Abuti Popompo, abuti Popompo! Ga waa apara bine . . . bruku. (Hey Popompo! Brother Popompo, brother Popompo! You're not wearing underwear).

Speaker #3 Eish! Ga ke itsoore kajeno koo bereka yang waitse? (Hey! I don't know how I'll manage today, you know?)

Speaker #2 Wena o betere o . . . otjela mo naming mare o ntsoore o patagantse. (You're fine . . . you're living well but you keep saying you're struggling.)

Speaker #4 Aye ga gona sepe. (No, there's nothing like that.)

Speaker #1 Ko . . . go na le nama mos. (But there is meat.)

Speaker #3 Hei. (Hey.)

Speaker #5 Motjitji, go na le nama? (Motjitji, is there meat?)

Speaker #1 A?e, teng nama, monna. (The meat is there, man.)

Speaker #2 Bo bo bo bo Cleophus. (Cleophus and . . .)

Speaker #3 Ke tswa ko teng. (I just came from there.)

Speaker #2 Ko Cleophus? (From Cleophus's place?)

Speaker #3 Ee. (Yes.)

Speaker #1 Noo, o maaka, wena manga. (No, you're lying, you're lying.)

Speaker #2 Ko'ore goo fa wa shashara, waa ba Dolphina. (Because if you're lying . . . Dolphina.)

The non-standard Setswana of the men draws heavily on Afrikaans and African languages (e.g. Zulu). Interestingly, Afrikaans is often regarded as the language of "the oppressor." Yet an analysis of the language of urban male youth, such as those involved in the conversational interaction above, shows that Afrikaans, the language of "the oppressor," is subtly exploited as a marker of urbanity.

Excerpt from Transcript 2

Wendy E? e, le sa bua ka batho bao tu,batho ba ba sa existeng. E? e a re bueng ka batho. (No, don't talk about those people, people who don't exist. No, let's talk about real people.)

Masengo Nna, waiste ke eng? Ka re bathing ke mo rata gore . . . (Me, you know what? I say, you guys, I really like him . . .)

Wendy Ka re ga se go soGelwa lebatho ga re tswa contesting phakela, iyo. (I'm saying I was provoked by people when we came from the contest in the morning, yo!)

Dineo E? esa e bua eo.Waitsore keeng tsala ya me? Ke nako e eke buang ka yona, ga ke jouke bathing. O ko s'petlele. Ga se go robeng fela looto. (No, don't say that. You know what it is, my friend? It's that time, I'm talking about. I'm not kidding. He's in the hospital. He broke his leg.)

Wendy Ka re ka soGelwa tsheng'wa ke batho, ba mpolel'la gore, bampole'la gore ka a ba spitlela mare ke tawa. Thlabane suo fer, ke hirile fo Phokeng mare ka ba spitela. (I'm saying I'm being provoked and laughed at by people, they told me, they told . . . I ignore them, but I came from Thlabane so far, I'm renting in Phokeng, but I reject them.)

Dineo Ba re nn'a ke pila. Leshambola le le tshwanang le nna e be ba tloo re nna ke pila, huu, waitse ba mborile waitse. (They said I'm not beautiful. Looking like I look, how can they say I'm not beautiful, when, you know they bore me.)

In the women's conversational excerpt, the salient aspects of the mixing are English words such as *joke, contest, exist*. If one looks at the entire conversation, it can be seen that some words occur quite frequently, such as the modification of *bore* to *mborile*. The Afrikaans speech forms can be grouped into two categories: conventional borrowings, such as *s'petlele* (hospital), and more stylized code-switching, such as *suo ver* (so far). As in the excerpt from Transcript 1, words drawn from other African languages (*pila, leshammbola*) appear as well, but are not used as frequently.

Differences between standard and non-standard language systems are also evident at a syntactic level with an increased use of non-standard syntactic features even in the written standard. Consider the noun class system in Xhosa. According to descriptions of Xhosa, concordial agreement (between a noun and its assigned prefix) is the core of Xhosa. Descriptions of Xhosa dating to the earliest grammar by Casalis (1841) present the rule of concordial agreement as categorical, but in language practice the rule is variable. The difference between the noun–prefix agreement system in actual use and the idealized descriptions of standard/standardized Xhosa can be illustrated by the sentences below from the writing of educated Xhosa users (cited in Satyo 1998). (The s in parentheses after each noun indicates the noun class to which the noun belongs.)

1   Ulwimi (11) lithi lincede (5) ke nomtu ukuba azi ukuba yena ngowasiphi na isiwe—You can identify a person's nationality by the language he/she speaks.

2　Ungumtu ngokuba ekwazi ukutheba ulwimi (11) lakubo . . . (5) livelise (5) nempucko yomntu okanye abantu abo batheba elo (5) lwimi (11)—He/she is human because he/she speaks a language . . . his/her language will also reflect the culture of those people.

3　Ulwimi (11) lwesixhosa jikele labluke (5) kwaphela kwiilwimi ezininzi—Generally Xhosa differs markedly from other languages.

4　Abantu banolwimi (11) labo—People have their own languages.

Conclusion

The question of the specification of separate languages has always been an arbitrary procedure. In any event, disinvention is not an argument against such specification. It is an argument for mapping the landscape differently. The crucial issue here is which group decides on the arbitrary selection. In Southern Africa, at least, it was an outsider group—missionaries and colonial institutions—which decided with reference to their own convenience and without any consultation with the speakers of the languages being specified. In this respect, Zulu, Xhosa, Shona, and other Southern African "languages" are analogous to the artificial borders imposed by colonial powers in disregard of ethnic and sociocultural identities. The major objective of disinvention is to undo history, or at the very *least*, to contain it by disinventing languages so that when they are reconstructed they correspond more closely to actual linguistic boundaries. Ultimately, the *disinvention* project seeks not to do away with the concept of separate languages, but to recognize that languages are socially constructed and so can be socially deconstructed and reconstituted.

By reconstituting language, the disinvention project will be confronting the increasingly powerful movement toward language "purity" in South Africa in which standard African languages are equated with moral purity. Speakers of urban argots and non-standard African languages are regarded as morally irresponsible and corrupt. These speakers are morally suspect because they demonstrate that the so-called "impure" languages are indeed the norm of ordinary use.

South African media are likely to prove to be one of the most powerful agents through which disinvention takes place. Radio, television, popular magazines, and other forms of media are reconstituting and disinventing African languages. *Laduma*, a comic book on love, life, and sex, combines a wide range of languages, including Zulu, Xhosa, and English, to effectively communicate its message (Baleta 1996). Programs on South African television draw heavily on the pan-ethnic urban hybrid used in the real-life experiences of speakers, as is evident in popular programs such as *Simunye Grooves* (*simunye*, Swati for "We are one"), *Gabon Motho*, *Suburban Bliss*, *Going Up*, *Generations*, and *Egoli* (gold). In a very real sense, the media are demonstrating the powerful role of urban hybrids and argots as linguae francae. When officially sanctioned as media of instruction in teaching/learning, these linguae francae may resolve the educational problems which standard African languages are now causing in South African schools. Not only does this urban, hybridized speech reflect the sociolinguistic practices of students; local teachers are also expert in this lingua franca.

The past and its legacy in South Africa, as in other societies in transition, cannot be changed by using the same modes of thought which produced it. Change requires new thought and new ways, linguistically, of conceptualizing the problem. As Brink puts it:

> The past cannot be corrected by bringing to it the procedures and mechanisms and mind-sets that originally produced our very perception of it. After all, it is not the past as such that has produced the present or poses the conditions for the future . . . but the way we think about it. Or even more pertinently, the way in which we deal with it in language.
>
> (Brink 1998: 23)

References

Anderson, B. (1983) *Imagined Communities: Reflections on the Origin and Spread of Nationalism*, London: Verso.

Baleta, A. (1996) "At last—sex education project that reaches teens," *Cape Argus*, 30, November.

Bhabha, H.K. (ed.) (1990) *Nation and Narration*, London and New York: Routledge.

Brutt-Griffler, J. (2002) *World English: A Study of Its Development*, Clevedon: Multilingual Matters.

Campbell-Makini, Z.M. (2000) "The language of schooling: deconstructing myths about African languages," in S. Makoni and N. Kamwangamalu (eds) *Language and Institutions in Africa*, Cape Town: Center for Advanced Studies of African Society, 111–31.

Casalis, E. (1841) *Études sur la langue SeChuana*, Paris: Imprimerie Royale.

Childs, G.T. (1997) "The status of Isicamatho, an Nguni-based urban variety of Soweto," in A. Spears and D. Winford (eds) *The Structure and Status of Pidgins and Creoles*, Amsterdam and Philadelphia, PA: John Benjamins, 341–70.

Chimhundu, H. (1992) "Early missionaries and the ethno-linguistic factor during the invention of tribalism in Zimbabwe," *Journal of African History*, 33: 255–64.

Cook, S. (2002) "Urban language in a rural setting, the case of Phokeng, South Africa," in G. Gmelch and W. Zenner (eds) *Urban Life Readings in the Anthropology of the City*, Prospect Heights, IL: Waveland Press, 106–13.

Davies, A. (1999) *An Introduction to Applied Linguistics: From Practice to Theory*, Edinburgh: Edinburgh University Press.

Desai, Z. (1994) "Praat or speak but don't theta: on language rights in South Africa," *Language and Education*, 8 (1 and 2): 21–37.

Fardon, R. and Furniss, G. (1994) *African Languages, Development and the State*, London and New York: Routledge.

Gilroy, P. (1987) *There Ain't No Black in the Union Jack: The Cultural Politics of Race and Nation*, Chicago, IL: University of Chicago Press.

Goyvaerts, D. (1996) "Kibalele: form and function of a secret language in Bukuvu (Zaire)," *Journal of Pragmatics*, 25: 125–43.

Harries, P. (1995) "Discovering languages: the historical origins of standard Tsonga in Southern Africa," in R. Mesthrie (ed.) *Language and Social History: Studies in South African Sociolinguistics*, Cape Town and Johannesburg: David Philips, 154–72.

Hofmeyer, I. (1994) "We spend our years as a tale that is told: oral historical narrative in a South African chiefdom," Johannesburg, South Africa: Witwatersrand University Press, 633–53.

Hornberger, N. (2002) "Multilingual language policies and the continua of biliteracy: an ecological approach," *Language Policy*, 1 (1): 27–51.

Jeater, D. (1994) "'The way you tell them': ideology and development policy," paper delivered at Paradigms Lost, Paradigms Regained, University of Witwatersrand.

LePage, R. and Tabouret-Keller, A. (1985) *Acts of Identity*, Cambridge: Cambridge University Press.

Maake, N. (1994) "Dismantling the Tower of Babel: in search of a new language policy for a post-apartheid South Africa," in R. Fardon and G. Furniss (eds) *African Languages, Development and the State*, London and New York: Routledge, 111–22.

Makoni, S. (1998a) "In the beginning was the missionaries' word: the European Invention of African Languages," in K. Prah (ed.) *Between Distinction and Extinction*, Cape Town: Centre for Advanced Studies of African Society.

—— (1998b) "African languages as European scripts: The shaping of communal memory," in S. Nuttall and C. Cotzee (eds) *Negotiating the Past: The Making of Memory in South Africa*, Cape Town: Oxford University Press, 242–8.

Makoni, S. and Kamwangamalu, N. (eds) (2000) *Language and Institutions in Africa*, Cape Town: Centre for Advanced Studies of African Society.

Mannheim, B. (1991) *The Language of the Inka since the European Invasion*, Austin, TX: University of Texas Press.

Mühlähauser, P. (1996) *Linguistic Ecology: Language Change and Linguistic Imperialism in the Pacific Region*, London and New York: Routledge.

Myers-Scotton (1993) *Dueling Languages: Grammatical Structures in Codeswitching*, Oxford: Clarendon Press.

Nuttal, S. and Cotzee, C. (eds) (1998) *Negotiating the Past: The Making of Memory in South Africa*, Cape Town: Oxford University Press.

Pennycook, A. (1994) *The Cultural Politics of English as an International Language*, London: Longman.

Phillipson, R. (1992) *Linguistic Imperialism*, Oxford: Oxford University Press.

Prah, K. (ed.) (1998) *Between Distinction and Extinction: The Harmonization of African Languages*, Johannesburg: Witwatersrand University Press.

Ranger, T. (1985) *The Invention of Tribalism in Zimbabwe*, Gweru: Mambo Press.

Ridge, S.G. (2000) "Language policy and democratic practice," in S. Makoni and N. Kamwangamalu (eds) *Language and Institutions in Africa*, Cape Town: Centre for Advanced Studies of African Society, 45–65.

—— (2001) "Discourse constraints on language policy in South Africa," in E. Ridge, S.G. Ridge, and S. Makoni (eds) *Freedom and Discipline: Essays in Applied Linguistics from Southern Africa*. New Delhi: Bahri Publishers, 15–30.

Ridge, E., Ridge, S.G., and Makoni, S. (eds) (2001) *Freedom and Discipline: Essays in Applied Linguistics from Southern Africa*, New Delhi: Bahri Publishers.

Romaine, S. (1984) *The Language of Children and Adolescents: The Acquisition of Communicative Competence*, Oxford: Blackwell.

Satyo, S. (1998) "Soft harmonization and cross-fertilizing vocabularies: the case of Nguni languages," in K. Prah (ed.) *Between Distinction and Extinction: the Harmonization and Standardization of African Languages*, Johannesburg: Witwatersrand University Press, 213–29.

—— (2000) Foreword in S. Makoni and N. Kamwangamalu (eds) *Language and Institutions in Africa*, Cape Town: Centre for Advanced Studies of African Society.

—— (2001) "Kwaito-speak: a language variety created by the youth for the youth," in E. Ridge, S.G. Ridge, and S. Makoni (eds) *Freedom and Discipline: Essays in Applied Linguistics from Southern Africa*, New Delhi: Bahri Publishers, 139–48. ˙

Smitherman, G. (2000) "Language and democracy in the United States and South Africa," in S. Makoni and N. Kamwangamalu (eds) *Languages and Institutions in Africa*, Cape Town: Centre for Advanced Studies of African Society, 65–92.

Southern Rhodesia (1929) *Report of the Director of Native Development for the Year 1929*, Salisbury, Southern Rhodesia: Government Printing House.

Part 3

INCLUSION AND EXCLUSION
THROUGH LANGUAGE

8

Linguistic profiling

John Baugh

Mr. Darden: "The second voice that you heard sounded like the voice of a Black man; is that correct?"

California v. Orenthal James Simpson

This chapter consolidates a long-standing tradition in dialectology and sociolinguistics: the study of linguistic discrimination based on speech or writing. The concept of "linguistic profiling" is introduced here as the auditory equivalent of visual "racial profiling." We ultimately argue that linguistic profiling is more finely tuned to diversity among Americans than are dissatisfactory racial classifications that have been used in the courts and for controversial social and educational policies based on race. Matters of fairness, which Americans value, lie at the core of linguistic profiling. As with racial profiling, linguistic profiling can have devastating consequences for those US residents who are perceived to speak with an undesirable accent or dialect.

At the very outset I acknowledge that accents vary substantially in terms of prosody, phonetics, and phonology, while distinctive dialects exhibit unique grammatical properties that are shared by other speakers of the same dialect, but which may be unfamiliar to, unused by, or unknown to speakers of other dialects of the same language. As such, our language, be it speech or writing, tells others much about us as we perform linguistic tasks throughout our daily lives. Perceptions of intelligence, or the lack of it, are often deeply interwoven with perceptions about language, or specific dialects and accents within a particular language.

This discussion traces different trends, including discriminatory linguistic profiling, preferential linguistic profiling, which might include profiles in linguistic adoration, and the legal paradox resulting from linguistic profiling in America. Tentative policy implications with global ramifications are introduced in the conclusion of this chapter. More narrowly, within a US context, I hope this analysis may be of value for improving linguistic acceptance throughout the Republic, and, in so doing, that it may be particularly beneficial to educators, diplomats, legal scholars, jurists, and legislators who must ultimately determine the (il)legality of linguistic profiling.

Discriminatory linguistic profiling

Racial identification based on speech captured public attention during the O.J. Simpson trial. Simpson's African American attorney, Mr. Cochran, objected forcefully to the assertion that one can deduce racial identity from speech (*California v. Orenthal James Simpson*):

Mr. Darden When you heard that voice, you thought that that was the voice of a young white male, didn't you?
Mr. Cochran Object to the form of that question, your Honor.
Judge Ito Overruled.
Mr. Cochran Speculation, conclusion.
Judge Ito Overruled.
Mr. Cochran How can he tell if it was a white man, your Honor?
Judge Ito[1] Counsel, overruled.

In 1999, in the case of *Clifford v. Kentucky*, the Supreme Court of Kentucky enlisted linguistic profiling to convict an African American appellant who was overheard by a white police officer. Thus far this case affirms the legality of racial identification based on speech by a lay witness. The case, for obvious reasons, is obscure when compared to the global visibility of the Simpson trial, but the practice of linguistic profiling was no less acute.

> Smith testified that he saw Birkenhauer enter the apartment. He then heard four different voices, the first of which he recognized as being that of Birkenhauer. He then heard the voice of another male, the voice of a female, and, then later, a fourth voice which "sounded as if it was of a male Black." Smith testified that he had been a police officer for thirteen years and had spoken to Black males on numerous occasions; that based on that experience, he believed that the last voice which he heard was that of a Black male. Appellant is a Black male; Vanover is a white male.

Smith then testified as follows:

Q Based on that [Smith's experience], as best you can recall, I just want you to tell me what you can recall of the conversation you heard between Detective Birkenhauer, just tell the jury what the male Black said, or the person you believed to be a male Black.
A That would have been the fourth and final voice on the tape. Detective Birkenhauer stated that he would take the "75" now and asked how long it would be, something along those lines, before he could get back with the additional drugs. What was believed to be a male Black responded, fifteen or twenty minutes or so, I didn't bring it with me, I left it at my house, you

know what I am saying, I didn't want to have it on me. Detective Birken-hauer said, I'll take the "75" now, and we will hook up later.

On cross-examination, the following colloquy occurred between Smith and defense counsel:

Q Okay. Well, how does a Black man sound?
A Uh, some male Blacks have a, a different sound of, of their voice. Just as if I have a different sound of my voice as Detective Birkenhauer does. I sound different than you.
Q Okay, can you demonstrate that for the jury?
A I don't think that would be a fair and accurate description of the, you know, of the way the man sounds.
Q So not all male Blacks sound alike?
A That's correct, yes.
Q Okay. In fact, some of them sound like whites, don't they?
A Yes.
Q Do all whites sound alike?
A No sir.
Q Okay. Do some white people sound like Blacks when they're talking?
A Possibly, yes.

In his ruling opinion, Justice Cooper of the Supreme Court of Kentucky noted that "an opinion that an overheard voice was that of a particular nationality or race has never before been addressed in this jurisdiction." Citing the case of *People v. Sanchez* (1985), Justice Cooper noted that "a lay eyewitness to a fatal shooting was permitted to testify that immediately prior to the shooting, he over-heard the victim and the killer arguing in Spanish, and that the killer was speaking with a Dominican, rather than a Puerto Rican, accent."

In support of the preceding ruling, the New York Superior Court noted that:

> It is clear that lay witnesses can often detect the distinctive accent related to particular ethnic or geographic groups. Thus, a lay witness, depend-ing upon his experience, could distinguish between a Yiddish accent and an Italian accent, or between a Russian and an English accent, or between a Spanish and a French accent. In addition, within broad cat-egories, certain more specific accents, characteristic of [a] particular region, may be ascertained. For example, the lay witness may be able to reliably identify the "Brooklyn" accent, as distinguished from the "Boston" accent, or the "Southern" accent from the "Cockney" accent. Human experience has taught us to discern the variations in the mode of speech of different individuals.

Returning to the Kentucky case in question, Justice Cooper observed that: No one suggests that it was improper for Officer Smith to identify one of the voices he heard as being that of a female. We perceive no reason why a witness could not likewise identify a voice as being that of a particular race or nationality, so long as the witness is personally familiar with the general characteristics, accents, or speech patterns of the race or nationality in question, i.e. so long as the opinion is "rationally" based on the perception of the witness.

Whereas "racial profiling" is based on visual cues that result in the confirmation or speculation of the racial background of an individual, or individuals, "linguistic profiling" is based upon auditory cues that may include racial identification, but which can also be used to identify other linguistic subgroups within a given speech community. The legal distinction and disagreement lie between Justice Cooper's assertions that lay people can indeed confirm the race or nationality of an individual based on his or her speech and those of Mr. Simpson's attorney who claimed—quite forcefully—that basing racial identification on speech is overtly racist and should not be permitted in a court of law. We shall return to this legal paradox briefly.

My earliest work on African American Vernacular English (AAVE) focused substantially on "style-shifting" among African Americans. During years of fieldwork I observed that a majority of African American adults would adjust their speech to fit their immediate social circumstances (Baugh 1983). Dillard (1972) and Labov (1972) made similar independent observations, noting that adult African Americans tended to use AAVE less frequently than did younger African Americans. By contrast, my research, which included observations of the same adults in a broad range of speaking circumstances, demonstrated considerable linguistic elasticity.

Similar forms of "linguistic accommodation" have been noted in other speech communities as well, suggesting that my observations in the African American community readily extend to other speakers who adjust their manner of speaking to fit the situation (Weinreich 1953; Blom and Gumperz 1972; Ervin-Tripp 1972; Goffman 1972; Hymes 1974; Giles and Powesland 1975; Trudgill 1986; Hazen 1998; Schilling-Estes and Wolfram 1999). This is not to suggest that AAVE speakers "sound white" when speaking in formal situations and "sound black" in colloquial circumstances. Rather, the preceding court rulings seem not to take "style-shifting" or "linguistic accommodation" into account, thereby calling the veracity of Justice Cooper's ruling into question.

I first became aware of "linguistic profiling" through deeply personal circumstances, as have some of my peers who are also African American professionals with advanced graduate degrees. Two anecdotes illustrate the point. In 1988 I was honored to accept a fellowship at the Stanford Center for Advanced Study in the Behavioral Sciences (CASBS), and I was trying to relocate my family to Palo Alto for a year. I moved to Palo Alto first in search of accommodations that would serve my entire family. Any reader who has ever tried to rent a home or apartment knows the experience of scouring the classified advertisements and then calling to make an appointment.

During all calls to prospective landlords, I explained my circumstances, as a visiting professor at CASBS, always employing my "professional voice," which I am told "sounds white." No prospective landlord ever asked me about my "race," but in four instances I was abruptly denied access to housing upon arrival for my scheduled appointment. Although I suspected that these refusals were directly the result of my race, which was confirmed through visual racial profiling, my standard English fluency was (and is) such that I escaped "linguistic profiling" because I sounded white.

Anita Henderson describes nearly identical circumstances in her search for an apartment in Philadelphia:

> I went to a large apartment complex in Philadelphia to inquire about apartments. I was steered to the most expensive apartment in the building and told that this was the only apartment available for the following month and that no other apartments would be coming available. However, the next day, using my very best Standard American English on the phone and inquiring about apartments at the same complex, I discovered that, miraculously, several less expensive apartments were immediately available, and I was more than welcome to come and see them.
>
> (Henderson 2001: 2–3)

In my particular case I was unable to prove that I had escaped auditory "linguistic profiling," only to eventually be snared by visual "racial profiling," but Henderson's experience incontrovertibly confirms "racial profiling." Her ensuing telephone call to the same apartment complex escaped linguistic profiling. She further observes, "Having guessed the nature of our face-to-face interaction, I knew I should 'sound white' in order to obtain the truth about the actual availability of apartments." She was ultimately able to rent "the apartment I wanted with no subsequent attempts on the part of the apartment building management to explain the mysterious availability of apartments" (Henderson 2001: 6).

As African American linguists with considerable professional training and extensive speech dexterity, our experiences are still relatively rare; that is, in the sense that we possess the ability to "sound white" if we choose to do so. Many of our fellow African Americans either cannot or will not attempt to adopt standard English under similar circumstances, thereby making them vulnerable to the kind of linguistic profiling described by Kentucky's Justice Cooper. I am not suggesting that speakers of AAVE must embrace Standard English if it is not their personal desire to do so. Rather, because of our professional circumstances, Henderson and I have been able to confirm the practice of linguistic profiling against Blacks.

Linguistic stereotypes have long been studied by linguists. Preston (1993), Lippi-Green (1997), and Cukor-Avila (2000) each provide independent evidence of "accent discrimination" or "dialect discrimination" against speakers of various regional, racial, and ethnic accents (or dialects) throughout the United States. Cukor-Avila (2000) confirms this practice in the workplace, noting that prospective employers are concerned with the linguistic impressions conveyed by their employees.

Because of the manner in which this first came to my attention, however, I have devoted most of my research on this topic to forms of housing discrimination, which has been documented extensively by the National Fair Housing Alliance (NFHA) in different regions of the country. Without the benefit of detailed linguistic analyses, "testers" who work for NFHA routinely seek to determine the existence of linguistic profiling associated with various forms of housing discrimination. Horwitz (1999) describes the situation as follows:

> Testers for the nonprofit group (i.e. the Fair Housing Council of Greater Washington) called more than 60 insurance offices and sought information about renters' insurance. In 150 cases, responses to Black and Latino callers were compared with responses to white callers, and 45 percent revealed discrimination.

My own research on this topic, produced in collaboration with phoneticians,[2] confirms Justice Cooper's observation. Through modified versions of matched guise studies that were adapted to compare standard English, AAVE, and Chicano English, over 80 percent of listeners were able to correctly identify the dialect spoken based on hearing the single word, "Hello." (See Purnell *et al.*: 1999.) Since many Americans routinely answer the telephone by saying "Hello," these results further confirm the potential for linguistic profiling, even when such racial or ethnic identification (or speculation) is not overtly used for discriminatory purposes.

Shanna Smith, executive director of the National Fair House Alliance, notes, "It is such an effective way of not doing business with people of color. It is subtle, not in your face, not slamming down the phone. But not following up by calling back or mailing material is just as malicious as saying, 'I won't give you insurance because you're Black or Mexican'" (Horwitz 1999: B 01). It is this "subtle" quality, combined with the fact that linguistic profiling can take place over the telephone, or through written correspondence, that has made it difficult to prosecute in the courts.

Ironically, in most of the cases of housing discrimination that have come to my attention, either as a consultant or as an expert witness, defendants have routinely denied the identical accent or linguistic detection skills that Justice Cooper confirmed through his ruling and subsequent conviction. That is to say, when confronted with evidence that suggests that linguistic profiling was used to deny housing, or insurance, or mortgages, to members of minority groups, defendants often retreat to Mr. Cochran's assertion that one cannot draw any racial or ethnic inference based on speech that is heard over the telephone, or, in Mr. Cochran's case, through an intercom system.

The NFHA recognized that many prospective home buyers or renters were simply unaware of the illegality of linguistic profiling, and they produced a series of advertisements to alert African American and Latino/a populations to be wary of these subdued forms of discrimination, as illustrated in Figures 8.1 and 8.2.

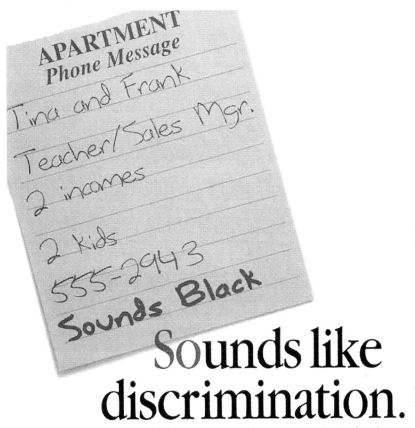

Figure 8.1 Sounds Black

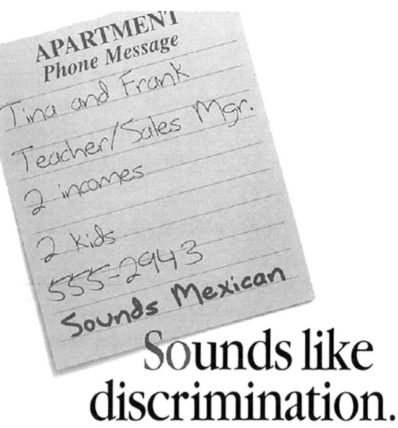

Sounds like discrimination.

What matters is how you look on paper – not how you sound over the phone.
Judging you by your national origin or race instead of your qualifications
is discrimination. It's unfair, it's painful... and it's against the law.
The best way to stop housing discrimination is to report it.

FAIR HOUSING IS THE LAW!

If you suspect unfair housing practices, contact
HUD or your local Fair Housing Center.

EQUAL HOUSING
OPPORTUNITY

U.S. Department of Housing and Urban Development • 1-800-669-9777 • TDD 1-800-927-9275

Figure 8.2 Sounds Mexican

Although my remarks thus far have been focused on People of Color, linguistic profiling trawls through much deeper demographic waters than visual profiling which is constrained to navigation by race alone. Perhaps the most insidious cases are those where accent is employed as a surrogate for race in attempts to maintain overt discrimination, say, through illegal redlining or employment discrimination. Whites who speak with "undesirable" accents may fall victim to linguistic profiling just as readily as members of minority groups. Cukor-Avila's (2000) research confirms the existence of linguistic prejudice against various white dialects, along with regional preferences that defy simplistic racial attribution.

Preferential linguistic profiling

Thus far some of the negative consequences of linguistic profiling have been pronounced, but there is a positive side to the coin of this realm. Language, dialects, and accents also serve to bind Americans, reminding us of the ancestors who left distant lands to seek their freedom and fortune here.

Before turning completely to the sunny side of linguistic profiling, I would be remiss if I did not acknowledge the death of hundreds of indigenous American languages that resulted from colonization and the ensuing attacks on Native Americans. The legacy of Native American linguistic mortality is etched deeply in our collective past because the spread of English came at the expense of America's primordial languages. Ever the optimist in search of a silver linguistic lining, I am heartened by indigenous people's efforts to revive their heritage languages throughout the continental US, Alaska, and Hawaii. In my opinion these are positive cultural developments resulting from a positive interpretation of linguistic profiling, to which I now turn.

Just as linguistic diversity has been used to accentuate differences among us, it also unites us into the bundles of linguistic enclaves that reinforce our heritage and pride in our ancestry. That heritage is multiethnic by definition. When we are able to converse with people who share linguistic backgrounds similar to our own, most of us feel most comfortable and at ease. These same linguistic sensitivities alert us to differences among us that come into play when we see others of "our own linguistic kind," be they speakers of English or languages other than English. The unique American linguistic hybrids that blend English with other languages from throughout the world may also fall under the microscope of linguistic profiling. Such linguistic hybrids serve to evoke solidarity among their speakers at the very same time that they may be the objects of linguistic bigotry beyond their vernacular sanctuary.

Whereas racial differences and controversies over affirmative action have tended to divide us, the recognition that most of our ancestors came from lands where English was foreign gives us a common historical bond that has the potential to help reunite Americans. Those readers who are US citizens whose ancestors had the luxury of immigrating to America of their own volition typically take considerable pride in the accomplishments of their ancestors, as do those of us whose ancestors were enslaved. Yet most of our ancestors, in freedom or in bondage, were once mocked for their speech, and linguistic profiling spread to greet each wave of immigrants who struggled to master "good" English.

JOHN BAUGH

A strong honorific sense of ancestral pride is certainly not unique to America, but the American multiethnic tapestry includes a tremendous linguistic repository of global languages that are derived from every continent on earth. While some other nations may likewise boast of considerable linguistic diversity, the dominance of the US culture and economy has evoked the full continuum from scorn to envy among those who are not citizens of our extraordinary Republic. Inclusive linguistic profiling is exercised daily as Americans choose those with whom they like to associate most. For some these personal choices are highly diverse, for others they remain narrow. Although "inclusiveness" tends to evoke positive connotations, I use it here as a neutral heuristic concept that concedes that one person's linguistic pride can easily serve as another person's source of linguistic displeasure.

Profiles in linguistic adoration

There are many noteworthy examples of linguistic adoration, if not linguistic envy, that produce another form of linguistic profiling. It results from forms of linguistic admiration of "beautiful speech" or other positive linguistic attributes that we might feel are somehow lacking in ourselves. Two examples readily come to mind, including French and British accents. Many Americans find both accents appealing, if not somewhat intimidating. At this point I resort to a greater degree of speculation in an effort to provide a comprehensive picture of linguistic profiling in America because I have only conducted preliminary pilot research to date. However, the data suggest that a wide range of socially stratified British dialects hold considerable prestige in America. Whether it is the speech of Queen Elizabeth or that of Mick Jagger, many Americans hold a British accent in higher regard than they do most American accents.

A French accent is viewed somewhat differently, or at least it seems so. Whereas American English cannot deny its British ancestry, positive interpretations of French culture, and a shared historical ethos of equality, liberty, and fraternity, tend to yield favorable linguistic stereotypes. I seek not to imply that there is universal love by Americans for either British or French accents; linguistic resentment often lies beneath the surface of linguistic envy and adoration. Nevertheless, hostile reactions to a British accent pale when compared to the hostile reception that greeted Ebonics's global debut (Baugh 1999, 2000; Smitherman 2000).

Another brief anecdote illustrates the point at hand. By remarkable coincidence, several of my linguistic colleagues at Stanford are originally from England, and faculty meetings are striking in a US context because of the extensive use of British English. I once made an informal observation to a group of students that I believed speakers of British English were loath to adopt American English for any number of reasons, not the least of which being that so many Americans admire British speech and strongly associate upper-class British English with high levels of intelligence. If one must suffer from a linguistic

164

stereotype, I would argue that being perceived as highly intelligent is not a social detriment in American society.

British intelligence notwithstanding, one young woman in the group disagreed with my offhand observation. Her experience demonstrates that despite the general American adoration of British English, there is at least one social context where this variety of English is not welcome. She pointed out that she was from England and had arrived in the US speaking a highly educated variety of British English, which she had learned at an exclusive school for young women in London. When she arrived in New York, encountering a wide range of Americans from diverse backgrounds, she found that many of her new-found peers mocked her speech, and so she not only embraced American English, she even chose to adopt AAVE over Standard American English. She was the first Black graduate student that I ever taught who was a native of England, and, to date, she has been the only speaker of British English to inform me that she had abandoned her native dialect to escape linguistic chastisement. While her case represents an exception to the general American adoration for British accents, it fits squarely within the context of Black American adolescents criticizing their peers for "talking" or "sounding white."

The legal paradox of linguistic profiling

Returning to discriminatory linguistic profiling, Judge Cooper would have us believe that lay citizens who are "rational" witnesses can confirm legal identification which connects linguistic behavior with racial background. As a dialectologist and linguist I find this position to be inherently problematic. The testimony cited in Judge Cooper's court asserts that some Blacks sound white, and vice versa. Be that as it may, Judge Cooper sent the appellant to jail on the basis of linguistic profiling that was used to obtain a conviction.

The other side of the paradox lies in the area of linguistic profiling when it is employed in racially motivated criminal discrimination. As previously observed, such acts are alleged to have exclusionary intent at their core, and defendants in such cases typically claim to lack the capacity for linguistic or racial identification that Judge Cooper affirmed by his ruling. Stated another way, Judge Cooper accepted the fact that many lay people can draw racial inference from speech, whereas many defendants in housing discrimination cases or insurance redlining deny that they can make any such racial determination, say, during a telephone conversation.

Linguistic profiling is either legal, or it is not. Under current legal statutes the US Supreme Court has yet to rule on linguistic profiling, *per se*, and it will be interesting to see how the Supreme Court rules on this matter should the issue ever come before that body. Supreme Court Justice Clarence Thomas observed during his confirmation hearings before the US Senate that he pursued an undergraduate major in English because many of his elementary school teachers told him that he spoke a language other than English. This was a lighthearted moment in the proceedings, and his comments evoked laughter, if not empathy, from Senators and an American public who readily acknowledged that AAVE and his skills as a jurist were in open conflict in a profession that demands considerable Standard English proficiency. No one suggested, as I do now, that young Clarence Thomas was the object of uninformed linguistic profiling within an educational system that made African American students of his generation feel a sense of linguistic inferiority and, by extension, a sense of linguistic shame. (See Baugh 2000; Lanehart 2002.)

Conclusion

I have intentionally focused on the US in this discussion, resisting the temptation to discuss new research from South Africa that shows evidence of linguistic profiling there. Nor have I made biblical reference to shibboleths, or trotted out well-worn examples from Shaw's *Pygmalion*, or similar Greek plays that preceded it. Each example confirms global linguistic profiling in human antiquity. On the baisis of our keen auditory skills as a species, I believe that linguistic profiling will exist as long as human language exists. The challenge to Americans and our fellow citizens elsewhere is to have wisdom, patience, and sufficient tolerance of others whose linguistic backgrounds differ substantially from our own. To do so would accentuate the benefits of preferential linguistic profiling, while discarding the tradition of discriminatory linguistic profiling that fans the embers of racial discord.

Acknowledgments

Previous research on similar topics has been supported by funding from the Ford Foundation, the Office of Educational Research and Improvement, the United States Department of State, and the Center for Applied Language Studies and Services in Africa at the University of Cape Town, South Africa. I am grateful to Shanna Smith and Robyn Webb-Williams of the National Fair Housing Alliance, which produced the advertisements that appear herein as Figures 8.1 and 8.2. I gratefully acknowledge the advice, guidance, and insights of Charla Larrimore Baugh, Anita Henderson, Janet Hales, Hesham Alim, Dennis Preston, Tom Purnell, Doug Young, Rajend Mesthrie, Kay McCormick, and Connie Eble. All limitations herein are my own.

Notes

1 Judge Lance Ito became the object of linguistic profiling when former Senator Alfonse D'Amato openly mocked his speech during a radio talk show. The Senator adopted a stereotypical Asian accent that was attributed to Judge Ito. The linguistic portrayal was a cartoon with inescapable racist overtones, for which the Senator publicly apologized.

2 Linguists are strongly encouraged to consult Purnell *et al.* (1999) for detailed discus-

sion of a series of experiments which were conducted pertaining to phonetic properties of dialect perception of three American English dialects: African American Vernacular English, Chicano English, and Standard American English.

References

Baugh, J. (1983) *Black Street Speech: Its History, Structure, and Survival*, Austin, TX: University of Texas Press.

—— (1999) *Out of the Mouths of Slaves: African American Language and Educational Malpractice*, Austin, TX: University of Texas Press.

—— (2000) *Beyond Ebonics: Linguistic Pride and Racial Prejudice*, New York: Oxford University Press.

Blom, J.P. and Gumperz, J.J. (1972) "Social meaning in linguistic structures: code-switching in Norway," in J.J. Gumperz and D. Hymes (eds) *Directions in Sociolinguistics: The Ethnography of Communication*, New York: Holt, Rinehart, and Winston, 407–34.

California v. Orenthal James Simpson (1995), Los Angeles District Court.

Clifford v. Kentucky (1999) 7 SW 3d 371, Supreme Court of Kentucky.

Cukor-Avila, P. (2000) "Linguistic diversity in the workplace: how regional accent affects employment decisions," paper presented at the 2000 NWAV Conference, East Lansing, Michigan State University.

Dillard, J.L. (1972) *Black English: Its History and Usage in the United States*, New York: Random House.

Ervin-Tripp, S. (1972) "On sociolinguistic rules: alternation and co-occurrence," in J.J. Gumperz and D. Hymes (eds) *Directions in Sociolinguistics: The Ethnography of Communication*, New York: Holt, Rinehart, and Winston, 213–50.

Giles, H. and Powesland, P. (1975) *Speech Styles and Social Evaluation*, New York: Academic Press.

Goffman, E. (1972) "The neglected situation," in P.P. Giglioli (ed.) *Language in Social Context*, New York: Penguin, 61–6.

Hazen, K. (1998) "The birth of a variant: evidence for a tripartite, negative past *be* paradigm," *Language Variation and Change*, 10: 221–43.

Henderson, A. (2001) "Put your money where your mouth is: hiring managers' attitudes toward African-American Vernacular English," PhD dissertation, University of Pennsylvania.

Horowitz, S. (1999) "Minority renters face insurance bias," *Washington Post*, September 29, p. B-01.

Hymes, D. (1974) *Foundations in Sociolinguistics*, Philadelphia, PA: University of Pennsylvania Press.

Labov, W. (1972) *Language in the Inner-City: Studies in the Black English Vernacular*, Philadelphia, PA: University of Pennsylvania Press.

Lanehart, S. (2002) *Sista, Speak! Black Women Kinfolk Talk about Language and Literacy*, Austin, TX: University of Texas Press.

Lippi-Green, R. (1997) *English with an Accent: Language, Ideology, and Discrimination in the United States*, London: Routledge.

People v. Sanchez (1985) 129 Misc. 2d 91, 492, NYS 2d 683, New York Supreme Court.

Preston, D. (ed.) (1993) *American Dialect Research*, Philadelphia, PA: John Benjamins.

Purnell, T., Idsardi, W., and Baugh, J. (1999) "Perceptual and phonetic experiments on

American English dialect identification," *Journal of Language and Social Psychology*, 18: 10–30.

Schilling-Estes, N. and Wolfram, W. (1999) "Alternative models of dialect death: dissipation vs. concentration," *Language*, 75: 486–521.

Smitherman, G. (2000) *Talkin That Talk: Language, Culture and Education in African America*, New York and London: Routledge.

Trudgill, P. (1986) *Dialects in Contact*, Oxford: Blackwell.

Weinreich, U. (1953) *Languages in Contact*, The Hague: Mouton.

9

"Whassup, homeboy?" Joining the African Diaspora: Black English as a symbolic site of identification and language learning

Awad El Karim M. Ibrahim

Herein lie buried many things which if read with patience may show the strange meaning of being black here in the dawning of the Twentieth Century. This meaning is not without interest to you, Gentle Reader; for the problem of the Twentieth [and the Twenty-First?] Century is [still] the problem of the color-line.

(DuBois 1903: 13)

When I imagine the terror of Africans on board slave ships, on auction blocks, inhabiting the unfamiliar architecture of plantations, I consider that this terror extended beyond fear of punishment, that it resided also in the anguish of hearing a language they could not comprehend. I imagine them hearing spoken English as the oppressor's language, yet I imagine them realizing that this language would need to be possessed, taken, claimed as a space of resistance. I imagine that the moment they realized the oppressor's language, seized and spoken by the tongues of the colonized, could be a space of bonding was joyous. In [their] mouths, English was altered, transformed, and became a different speech. The power of this speech is not simply that it enables resistance, but that it also forges a space for alternative cultural production and alternative epistemologies—crucial to creating a counter-hegemonic worldview.

(hooks 1994: 168)

"This is the oppressor's language," Adrienne Rich announced, "yet I need to talk to you" (cited in hooks 1994: 167). Or, as the youths in the present research announced: You who altered, transformed, and rendered English a Black English, we also want to talk to you. This chapter is about desire, investment,

169

identity, identification, and their impact on language learning. It is also about how the act of language learning, namely learning English as a Second Language (ESL), is turned into a symbolic act of politics and resistance, an act which forms and simultaneously performs a subject formation project where Blackness is central. This chapter, in short, is about the process of *becoming Black*, that is, the interrelationship between race, culture, identity, and language learning. I contend that a group of French-speaking immigrant and refugee Continental African youth attending an urban Franco-Ontarian high school in Southwestern Ontario, Canada, enters *a social imaginary*—a discursive space in which they are already imagined, constructed, and thus treated as Blacks by hegemonic discourses and groups. This imaginary is directly implicated in whom they identify with (Black North Americans), which in turn influences what and how they linguistically and culturally learn. They learn Black Stylized English (BSE), a subcategory of Black English, which they access in Hip Hop cultural and linguistic styles. I conclude that Black English becomes as much a site of language learning as it is a symbolic space of identification, bonding, investment, and desire.

I intend to show that Continental African youth are joining the African Diaspora, specifically in North America, by becoming part of it. In recent years, Continental Africans have been crossing the Atlantic Ocean to North America *en masse* (Ibrahim 1998). This, one may argue, is on the one hand an act of defiance of the history of colonialism, imperialism, and the middle passage (Asante 1990; Chideya 2000; Ibrahim 2000d). On the other hand, however, this journey to North America necessitates a new dialogue (or dialogic relation) between Continental and Diasporic Africans. Thanks, in part, to the praxis of Afrocentrism (Asante 1990), to music, literary, and other symbolic cultural exchanges (Gilroy 1991), and to African and African American Studies programs, this new dialogue is underway. Part of it is enhanced, ironically, by tourism and immigration (as well as involuntary displacement). Indeed, in the face of history, Diasporic Africans in North America, for example, are making the journey back to Africa and Continental Africans are making the journey to North America.

Before joining the African Diaspora, Continental Africans have to first confront the history of the present (Foucault 1980)—where their bodies are already read as "Black"—with a modernist colonial/imperial outlook (Willinsky 1998). They have to translate, negotiate, and answer the following questions (which are also the questions I shall explore in this chapter): What does "being" Black really mean in North America? If one is "becoming" Black, what does this call for, entail, and thus produce? In other words, how do socially constructed persons transform themselves from a nationality—say, Djiboutian—to a color? And above all, how is language central or fundamental to this transformation? Two additional questions also pose themselves. First, why would Continental African youth *need* and *want* to learn, appropriate, reproduce, and re-perform Diasporic African *symbolic systems* of dress, walk, and talk? Second, what does it mean for a

170

Black ESL learner to acquire Black English as a Second Language (BESL)? At a time when North American Blackness is governed by how it is negatively located in a race-conscious society (e.g. West 1993; Ibrahim 1999, 2000a, 2000b, 2000c; Wright 2000), what symbolic, cultural, pedagogical, and identity investments would learners have in locating themselves politically and racially at the margin of representation?

By *symbolic system*, I am referring to a set of norms, rules, and regulations that are expressly operating together to create an entity, form, mode, structure, or what Foucault (1984) calls discourse—an ensemble of discursive frameworks or formations. They are symbolic, Bourdieu argues, because they are misrecognized or barely visible, yet they constitute the deep infrastructures of any material system (1991: 163–4). Significantly, they are constituents of and at the same time constitute these infrastructures. Stated differently, they need a system (authorized or not)—what Bourdieu (1991) calls *champ* or field—in order to exist and function. However, they also constitute the grounds upon which this system depends and indeed where the system expresses itself. I have an identity, for example, but my identity would not exist outside the *linguistic field* where it expresses itself.

The symbolic, Bourdieu warns, contrary to its conventional everyday use, is not in opposition to the material (1991). Very easily, in fact, a symbolic field or capital can be converted into the material. The French language in Canada, for instance, may represent *symbolic capital*; learning it can be the key to accessing *material capital*—a job, business, and so on. My point is that language is a symbolic system, with its infrastructures, history, and grammar (in its broad semiological sense). However, it is also directly implicated in our everyday material life. As a matter of fact, language is where we express our feelings, who we are or what we have become, and where we invest our desires. It is where power is expressed. Language, therefore, is not only a medium of communication; it is also within and through language that we form and perform our social identity and negotiate history and historical social relations.

In this chapter, I first distinguish between "being" and "becoming." Then I discuss my study, its contentions and propositions, methodology, site, and subjects. I offer examples of African youth speech in order to demonstrate the interplay between subject formation, identification, and BESL learning. I also offer youth narratives on their desires and on the impact of identification and becoming Black. I conclude with a discussion of the need to deconstruct this imperial and panoptic gaze, which limits, as we shall see, African youth life possibilities.

Theorizing the performed: being or becoming?

Central to the theoretical framework for this project is the Kristevan (1974) notion *sujet en procès* or subject in progress or being as a continuous act of becoming. It is a notion which assumes not fixity, but performativity (Butler 1999)—not "being" in a thetic and static sense, but being which is never complete—and for this project, it assumes a being that is becoming Black. The process of becoming Black was, on the one hand, marked by an identification with and a desire for North American Blackness, and on the other, it was as much about gender, race, and age as it was about language and cultural performance. For example, although both young women and young men verbalized a strong identification with Blackness during interviews, the situation was different when it came to the intensity of bodily performance. Whereas all male students articulated and performed a strong identification with and a complete appropriation of Hip Hop and Rap through their dress, posture, walk, and talk, female students tended to be more diverse. The younger girls (twelve to fourteen years old) had the same linguistic and cultural practice and performance as the boys in their appropriation of Rap and Hip Hop, but the older girls tended to be more culturally eclectic. For example, they combined Hip Hop with "traditional" dress without any sense of contradiction—hence creating a "third space" (Ibrahim 2000a, 2000c).

Being is here being distinguished from *becoming*. The former is an accumulated memory, an understanding, a conception and an experience, upon which individuals interact with the world around them, whereas the latter is the process of building this memory of experience. As a Continental African, for example, I was not considered "Black" in Africa; other terms served to patch together my identity, such as *tall*, *Sudanese*, and *basketball player*. In other words, as Stuart Hall (1997) would argue, my Blackness was not marked, it was outside the shadow of the Other—North American whiteness. However, as a refugee in North America, my perception of self was altered in direct response to the social processes of racism and the historical representation of Blackness whereby the antecedent signifiers became secondary to my Blackness, and I retranslated my being: I became Black.

A significant incident in my understanding of what it means to "be" Black in North America occurred on May 16, 1999. That day I was officially declared "Black" by a white policeman who stopped me in Toronto, Canada, for no reason other than "We are looking for a dark man with a dark bag," as he uttered it. When I questioned him about my "darkness," he said, "We are looking for a Black man with a dark bag." There is no need to mention that my bag was actually light blue and that I metamorphosed from "dark" to "Black." Later I reflected that some people either cannot see or have a "color problem." I cite this experience here for two reasons. First, to frame the overall social context where my research subjects circulate and form their identities; that is, to further our understanding of the everyday racism, human degradation, and general annihilation of Black people in North America. And second, to acknowledge how the present researcher is implicated in the research and the questions I am asking.

Research subjects, method, and site

This project constitutes part of a larger, critical ethnographic research project[1] I conducted at Marie-Victorin (Ibrahim 1998) between January and June 1996, which made use of my newly developed methodological approach, *ethnography of performance*. The research looks at the lives of a group of Continental Franco-phone African youth and the formation of their social identity in an urban, French-language high school in Southwestern Ontario, Canada. In addition to their gendered and racialized experience, their youth and refugee status was vital in their *moments of identification*, that is, where and how they saw themselves reflected in the mirror of their society (Bhabha 1994). Stated differently, once in North America, I contend, these youth were faced with a social imaginary (Anderson 1983; Hobsbawm and Ranger 1983) in which they were already "Blacks." As such, they were subjected to the everyday racism, exclusion, and marginalization similar to that experienced by their US Black counterparts. This imaginary was directly implicated in how and with whom they identified, which, in turn, influenced what they learned, linguistically and culturally. What they did learn is Black Stylized English (BSE), which they accessed in and through Black popular culture. They learned BSE by taking up and repositioning Rap as a linguistic and musical genre and, in different ways, by acquiring and rearticu-lating a Hip Hop cultural identity.

BSE is Black Stylized English, a subcategory of "Black English," or what Smitherman now refers to as African American Language (AAL) (Smitherman 2000a) or Black Talk (Smitherman 2000b). AAL has its own grammar, morphol-ogy, and syntax. BSE, on the other hand, refers to ways of speaking that do not depend on full mastery of AAL. It banks more on ritual expessions such as *whas-sup*, *whadup*, *whassup my nigga*, *yo*, and *yo*, *homeboy*, which are performed habitually and recurrently in Rap. These linguistic rituals are more an expression of poli-tics, moments of identification, and desire than they are manifestations of full competence in the language *per se*. BSE is a way of saying, "I too am Black," or "I too desire and identify with Blackness."

By Black popular culture I am referring to African American films, news-papers, and magazines, and more importantly African American music, in this research, particularly Hip Hop music. Hip Hop culture is also a way of dressing, walking, and talking (see also Walcott 1995). The dress refers to the myriad shades and shapes of the latest *fly gear*: high-top sneakers, bicycle shorts, chunky jewelry, baggy pants, and polka-dotted tops (Rose 1991: 227). The hairstyles, which include high-fade designs, dreadlocks, corkscrews, and braids are also part of this Hip Hop fashion. The *walk* usually means moving the fingers simultane-ously with the head and the rest of the body while walking. The *talk*, however, is BSE. By adopting these behaviors, African youth enter the realm of becoming Black. As an identity configuration, the latter is deployed to talk about the *subject-formation project* (i.e. the process and the space within which subjectivity is formed) that is produced in and simultaneously produced by the process of

173

language learning—Black English as a Second Language (BESL) learning in this case. More concretely, becoming Black meant learning BESL, as I will show below; yet the very process of BESL learning produced the epiphenomenon of becoming Black.

Continental African youth find themselves in a racially conscious society that, wittingly or unwittingly, and through fused social mechanisms, such as racist representations, asks them to racially fit somewhere. To "fit somewhere" signifies choosing or becoming aware of one's own being, which is partially reflected in one's language practices. Choosing is a question of agency, which itself is governed and disciplined by social conditions. For example, to be Black in a racially conscious society, like the Euro-Canadian and US societies, means that one is expected to act and talk Black and so be the marginalized Other (Hall 1991; hooks 1992). Under such disciplinary social conditions, Continental African youth express their moments of identification in relation to African American culture and language, thus becoming Black. That they take up Rap and Hip Hop and speak BSE is by no means a coincidence. On the contrary, these actions are articulations of the youth's desire to belong to a location, a politics, a memory, and a history.

The site of the research was a small Franco-Ontarian intermediate and high school (seventh to thirteenth grades), Marie-Victorin (MV). MV had a school population of approximately 400 students from various ethnic, racial, cultural, religious, and linguistic backgrounds. Although it is a French-language school, the language spoken by students in the school corridors and hallways was predominantly English. Arabic, Somali, and Farsi were also spoken. The school had twenty-seven teachers, all of whom were white, and its archives show that up until the 1990s, the students were also almost all white, except for a few students of African and Middle Eastern descent.

For over six months, I attended classes at MV, talked to students, and observed curricular and extracurricular activities two or three times per week. Because of previous involvement in a two-year project at the same school, I was well acquainted with MV and its population at the time of my research, especially its African students, with whom I had developed a good communicative relationship.

Being the only Black adult—with the exception of one counselor—and being a displaced subject, a refugee, and an African, had given me a certain familiarity with the students' experiences. I was able to connect with different age and gender groups through a range of activities, initially "hanging out" with the students and later playing various sports with some of them. Eventually, I became the basketball team's coach, a team dominated by Continental Africans and a small but active group of Haitian students. I was also approached by these students for guidance and academic help. Because of my deep involvement in the student culture, at times my status as researcher was forgotten, and the line between the students and myself became blurred. Clearly, we shared a *safe space* of comfort that allowed us to open up and speak freely. On many occasions, students felt safe enough to speak about sensitive issues—such as how they were abused and maltreated by teachers and school administration—issues so sensitive that the students requested that no one know, hear, or read them.

The students sought my academic help, including help with languages (French and English, especially writing), and I sought their help in the confirmation of my research findings. I frequently asked them about my ethnographic observations, either during interviews or in informal settings such as basketball practice. Although they did not have access to any of my published texts, they knew my findings.

Given their postcolonial educational history, most African youth, in fact, come to Franco-Ontarian schools already possessing a highly valued symbolic capital: *le français parisien* (Parisian French). They are part of a growing Continental Francophone African population in Franco-Ontarian schools, which I refer to as *Noirs franco-ontariens* (Black Franco-Ontarians). Their numbers have grown exponentially since the beginning of the 1990s. The participants in the study varied in terms of length of stay in Canada (from one to six years), in legal status (some were immigrants, but the majority were refugees), and in gender, class, age, and linguistic and national background. They came from places as diverse as the Democratic Republic of Congo (formerly Zaïre), Djibouti, Gabon, Senegal, Somalia, South Africa, and Togo. Without exception, all of the African students in MV were at least trilingual—English, French, and an indigenous African language—with various postcolonial histories of language learning and degrees of fluency in each language.

With their permission, as well as that of their parents and the school administration, I chose ten boys and six girls for extensive ethnographic observation inside and outside of the school, and I interviewed all sixteen. Of the ten boys, six were Somali speakers (from Somalia and Djibouti), one was Ethiopian, two were Senegalese, and one was from Togo. Their ages ranged from sixteen to twenty. The six girls were all Somali speakers (also from Somalia and Djibouti), ages fourteen to eighteen. The students chose the language in which their interview was conducted (English or French), and I translated the French-language interviews into English. The only Black counselor and the former Black teacher were also interviewed.

Becoming tri-or multilingual: sites and sides of BESL learning

Since these youth find themselves in a context where English is the medium of everyday interaction, they would usually want to learn English rapidly. Popular culture, especially television, friendship, and peer pressure were the three mechanisms that hastened the speed of learning. The African students felt particular peer pressure in their early days at the school, when they were denigrated for not speaking English. Franco-Ontarian students, Heller has explained, use English in their everyday interaction, especially outside of class (1992, 1994). If

African students want to participate in school activities, they have no option but to learn English. Once it is learned, English becomes as much a source of pride as a medium of communication. Mastery of English allows African students to make friends and fully participate in North American public life.

Making friends, and even learning English, is influenced by the popular imaginary, the dominant source being television. I asked students in all of the interviews "Où est-ce que vous avez appris votre anglais?" ("Where did you learn English?"). "Télévision," they all responded. However, within this *télévision*, a particular representation—Black popular culture—seems to interpellate (Althusser 1971) African youths' identity and identification. Because these youth at first have few African Canadian and/or African American friends, they access Black cultural identities and Black linguistic practices through Black popular culture, especially Rap, music videos, television programs, and Black film. When I queried Najat (14, F, Djibouti)[2] she responded:

Najat I don't know, I saw *Waiting to Exhale* and I saw what else I saw, I saw *Swimmer*, and I saw *Jumanji*; so wicked, all the movies. I went to *Waiting to Exhale* wid my boyfriend and I was like "men are rude" [laughs].
Awad Oh believe me, I know, I know.
Najat And den he [her boyfriend] was like "no, women are rude." I was like we're like fighting you know and joking around. I was like, and de whole time like [laughs], and den when de woman burns the car, I was like "go girl!" You know and all the women are like "go girl!" you know? And den de men like khhh. I'm like "I'm gonna go get me a pop corn" [laughs].

(Individual interview, English)

Besides showing the influence of Black English in the use of *de, den, dat*, and *wicked* as opposed to, respectively, *the, then, that*, and *really really good*, Najat's answer shows that youth bring agency and social subjectivities to the reading of a text. These subjectivities, importantly, are embedded in history, culture, and memory. The two performed subjectivities that interpellate Najat's reading of *Waiting to Exhale* were her race and gender identities. Najat identified with Blackness, embodied in the female character; and with the Black woman in burning her husband's car and clothes.

Another example (a videotaped moment) in a different context demonstrates the impact of Black popular culture on African students' lives and identities. Just before a focus group interview I had with the boys, *Electric Circus*, a local television music and dance program that plays exclusively Black music began. "Silence!" one boy exclaimed in French. The boys started to listen attentively to the music and watched the different fashions of the young people on the program. After the show, the boys' code switched between French, English, and Somali as they exchanged observations about the best music, the best dance, and the cutest girl. Hip Hop music and the corresponding dress were at the top of their list.

These moments of identification point to the process of identity formation, which is, in turn, implicated in the linguistic norm to be internalized. The Western hegemonic representations of Blackness, Hall (1990) shows, are mostly negative and tend to work alongside historical and subconscious memories that facilitate their interpretations by members of the dominant groups. Once African youth encounter these negative representations, they look for Black cultural and representational forms as sites for positive identification (Kelly 1998). An important aspect of identification is that it works over a period of time and at the subconscious level. In the following excerpt, Omer (18, M, Ethiopia) addresses the myriad ways in which African youth are influenced by Black representations.

> Black Canadian youth are influenced by the Afro-Americans. You watch for hours, you listen to Black music, you watch Black comedy, *Mr. T.*,[3] the *Rap City*, there you will see singers who dress in particular ways. You see, so.
>
> (Individual interview, French)

Mukhi (19, M, Djibouti) explored identification by arguing that:

> We identify ourselves more with the Blacks of America[s]. But, this is normal, this is genetic. We can't, since we live in Canada, we can't identify ourselves with whites or country music you know [laughs]. We are going to identify ourselves, on the contrary, with people of our color, who have our life style you know.
>
> (Group interview, French)

Mukhi invokes biology and genetic connection as a way of relating to Blackness, and his identification with it is clearly stated. For Mukhi and all the students I spoke to, this identification is certainly connected to their inability to relate to dominant groups, the public spaces they occupy and their cultural forms and norms. Alternatively, Black popular culture emerged as a site not only for identification, but also as a space for language learning.

"A'ait, Q7 in the House!"

Rap was an influential site for language learning. On many occasions, the boys performed typical gangsta Rap language and style, using linguistic as well as bodily performance, including name-calling. What follows are just two of the many occasions on which students articulated their identification with Black America through the re/citation of Rap and Hip Hop linguistic styles.

Sam One two, one two, mic check. A'ait [aayet], a'ait, a'ait.
Juma This is the rapper, you know wha 'm meaning? You know wha 'm saying?

177

Sam Mic mic mic; mic check. A'ait you wonna test it? Ah, I've the micro-
phone you know; a'ait.

Sam [laughs] I don't Rap man, c'mon give me a break. [laughs] Yo! A'ait
a'ait you know, we just about to finish de tape and al dat. Respect to
my main man [pointing to me]. So, you know, you know wha 'm mean,
''m just represen'in Q7. One love to Q7 you know wha 'm mean and
all my friends back to Q7. Stop the tapin boy!

Jamal Kim Juma, live! Put the lights on. Wordap. [Students talking in
Somali] Peace out, wardap, where de book. Jamal 'am outa here.

Shapir Yo, this is Shapir. I am trying to say peace to all my niggas, all my
bitches from a background that everybody in the house. So, yo, chill
out and this is how we gonna kick it. Bye and with that pie. All right,
peace yo.

Sam A'ait this is Sam represen'in AQA [. . .] where it's born, represen'in
you know wha 'm mean? I wonna say whassup to all my niggas, you
know, peace and one love. You know wha 'm mean, Q7 represen'in for
ever. Peace! [Rap music]

Jamal [as a DJ] Crank it man, coming up. [Rap music]

(Group interview, English)

Of interest in these excerpts is the use of Black Stylized English, particularly the
language of Rap: "Respect for my main man," "represen'in Q7," "kick the free
style," "peace out, wardap," "'am outa here," "I am trying to say peace to all
my niggas, all my bitches," "so, yo chill out and this is how we gonna kick it," "I
wonna say whassup to all my niggas," "peace and one love."

The fact that Rap was more prevalent in the boys' narratives than in the girls'
raises the question of the role of gender in the process of identification and
learning. When Shapir offers "peace to all" his "niggas" and all his "bitches," he
is re/appropriating the word "nigger" as an appellation which is common in
Rap and Hip Hop culture as a term of endearment for one's friends. However,
Shapir also uses the sexist language that is so commonly found in Rap (Rose
1991). The sexism in Hip Hop language has been challenged by female rappers
such as Queen Latifah and Salt N Pepa. This language was also critiqued by the
female—and male—students in this study. For example, Samira (16, F, Djibouti)
expressed her dismay at the sexist language found in some Rap lyrics and Hip
Hop circles:

Okay, Hip Hop, yes I know that everyone likes Hip Hop. They dress in a
certain way, no? The songs go well. But they are really, really, they have
expressions like "fuck bitches," etc. Sorry, but there is representation.

(Group interview, French)

Here Samira is addressing the impact that these expressions might have on the
way society at large relates to and perceives the Black female body, which in

turn influences how it is represented both inside and outside of Rap/Hip Hop culture. Hassan (17, M, Djibouti) also expressed his disapproval of this abusive language: "Occasionally, Rap has an inappropriate language for the life in which we live, a world of violence and all that" (Individual interview, French).

In Rap, the artist/performer starts a performance by "checking the mic": "One two, one two, mic check." Then the rapper either recites an already composed lyric or otherwise "kicks a free style," displaying the spontaneity that characterizes Rap. Next in the public performance, the rapper introduces him/herself with a true or made-up name—"Yo, this is Shapir"—and thanks her or his "main man" (best friend), who often introduces the rapper to the audience. Specific to gangsta Rap, one represents not only oneself but a web of geophysical and metaphorical spaces and collectivities that are demarcated by people and territorial spaces: "Represen'in Q7"; "A'ait, this is Sam represen'in AQA." At the end of the performance, when the recitation or freestyle is completed, again one thanks the "main man" and "gives peace out" or "shad out" (shout out) to the people.

The boys were clearly influenced by Rap lyrics, syntax, and morphology (in their broader semiological sense) and especially by gangsta Rap. Depending on their age, the girls, on the other hand, were ambivalent about gangsta Rap. Boys and girls used the same three strategies in learning ESL and BSE from music: listening, reading, and reciting. Jamal, in the excerpt cited above, was listening to the tunes and lyrics while reading and following the written text. Acting as a DJ, he then repeated not only the performer's words and expressions but also his accent. For their part, the girls used similar strategies. During a picnic organized by a group of males and females, the girls listened to music while following the written text and reciting it (complete with accents) along with the singer. The girls' choice of music (e.g. Whitney Houston, Toni Braxton) differed in that it was softer than that chosen by the boys and contained mostly romantic themes.

For the most part, the older girls/women (sixteen to eighteen) tended to be more eclectic in how they related to Rap and Hip Hop. Their eclecticism was evident in how they dressed and in the language they engaged and learned. Their dress was either elegant middle class, or partially Hip Hop, or traditional. Their learned language was what Nourbese Philip (1991) calls plain Canadian English. The younger girls (twelve to fourteen), on the other hand, like the boys, dressed totally in Hip Hop style and performed BSE.

Both the older and the younger girls incorporated features of Black English in their speech. Three patterns occurred frequently:

1   copula absence, e.g. "They so cool";
2   negative concord, e.g. "If somebody just dies or if I decide to shoot somebody, you know, he is not doing nothing";
3   aspectual *be*, e.g. "I be saying dis dat you know?"; "He be like 'Oh, elle va être bien' [she's going to be fine]".

179

These Black English markers reflect the influence of Black Talk on the girls' speech and performances of the girls' identity, location, and desire, which they apparently align with Blackness.

Performing acts of desire

I have identified Rap and Hip Hop as influential sites in African students' processes of becoming Black, which in turn affected what and how they learned. Their narratives also significantly show that the youth were fully cognizant of their identification with Blackness and the impact of race on their choices. In the following conversation, Mukhi reflected on the impact of Rap on his life and the lives of others around him:

Awad But do you listen to Rap for example? I noticed that there are a number of students who listen to Rap eh? Is . . .
Sam It is not just us who listen to Rap, everybody listens to Rap. It is new.
Awad But do you think that that influences how you speak, how . . .
Mukhi *How we dress, how we speak, how we behave* [italics added].

(Group interview, English)

The linguistic patterns and dress codes that Mukhi addresses are accessed and learned by African youths through Black popular culture. As I already noted, these patterns do not require mastery and fluency. Indeed, they are performative acts of desire and identification. As Amani (16, F, Somalia) contended:

We have to wonder why we try to really follow the model of the Americans who are Blacks? *Because when you search for yourself, search for identification, you search for someone who reflects you, with whom you have something in common* [italics added].

(Group interview, French)

Hassan concurred with Amani:

Hassan Yes, yes, African students are influenced by Rap and Hip Hop because they want to, yes, they are influenced probably a bit more because it is the desire to belong maybe.
Awad Belong to what?
Hassan To a group, belong to a society, to have a model/fashion [he used the term *un modèle*]. You know, the desire to mark oneself, the desire to make, how do I say it? To be part of a Rap society, you see. It is like getting into rock and roll or heavy metal.

(Individual interview, French)

One invests where one sees oneself mirrored. Such an investment includes linguistic as well as cultural behavioral patterns. In an individual interview, Hassan told me it would be unrealistic to expect to see Blackness allied with rock and roll or heavy metal since they are socially constructed as "white" music. On the other hand, he argued emphatically that African youth would have every reason to invest in basketball—constructed as a Black sport—but not hockey, for example.

Populating the word: possessing desires, desiring to be

> The word in language is half someone else's. It becomes "one's own" only when the speaker populates it with his own intention, his own accent, when he appropriates the word, adapting it to his own semantic and expressive intention. Prior to this moment of appropriation, the word does not exist in a neutral and impersonal language (it is not, after all, out of a dictionary that a speaker gets his words!) but rather it exists in other people's mouths, in other people's concrete contexts, serving other people's intentions: it is from there that one must take the word and make it one's own.
>
> (Bakhtin 1981: 142)

The desire on the part of African youth, particularly the boys, to invest in basketball is analogous to their desire to learn BESL. Learning is hence neither aimless nor neutral, nor does it occur without the politics of identity. As I have shown, a second-language learner can have a marginalized linguistic norm as a target, depending on who is learning what, why, and how. I have also discussed how these youth were becoming Blacks, which meant learning BESL. Becoming Black, I have argued, was an identity signifier produced by and producing the very process of BESL. To become Black is to become an ethnographer who translates and searches around in an effort to understand what it means to be Black in North America, for example. In becoming Black, the African youth were interpellated by Black popular cultural forms, Rap, and Hip Hop, as sites of identification. Gender, however, was as important as race and age in determining what was being chosen and translated.

Choosing the margin, then, is simultaneously an act of investment, an expression of desire, and a deliberate counterhegemonic undertaking. Choosing Rap must be read as a special act of resistance. In its historical origin, Rap was formed as a voice for voicelessness and performed as a prophetic language that addresses silence, the silenced, and the state of being silenced. To be sure, Rap has diversified over the decades since its creative inception. Yet several Rap artists (e.g. KRS-One, Common, Mos Def) continue the tradition of exploring the hopes and the human, political, historical, and cultural experience of the *Black Atlantic* (Gilroy 1993). As Jamal argued,

> Black Americans created Rap to express themselves; how do I say it? Their ideas, their problems, [and] if we could integrate ourselves into it,

it is because rappers speak about or they have the same problems we have.

(Individual interview, French)

Becoming Black—or entering already pronounced regimes of Blackness—meant joining the exiled category of Blackness; exiled because of the history of colonialism, the middle passage, and slavery. The exiled is a *Black Atlantic* which does not know passport and purposely works against national borders (Gilroy 1993). It does this through music, language, cinematic, literal, and other symbolic cultural exchanges. Learning BESL by African youth was indeed an act which reflected the significance and importance of the tradition of symbolic exchanges that took place between Africans in the Americas, in Europe and on the Continent. BESL learning was the space where the word, as Bakhtin argued, was appropriated and populated by the speaker's semantic and expressive intention. The latter was as much an expression of desire and investment as of struggle for identity and identification. The populated word, significantly, was not neutral before it was appropriated, nor was learning it neutral.

Importantly, in learning BESL, African youth did not neglect or negate their mother tongues. Indeed, African languages were prominent in the students' everyday speech. Their daily interaction was almost exclusively in their mother tongues and, except for academic terms, they studied in their mother tongues. These languages, especially the Somali language, were also used in theatrical plays. The code-switching between their mother tongues, French, school English, and BESL is not only a fact of life, but also the norm, inside and outside the school (Ibrahim 1998). The following excerpt is only one example among many others where this code-switching is put into practice. It was tape-recorded during dinner time in a student's house. We were sitting on the floor around a big plate eating with our bare hands—African style. In the excerpt, I am interested more in the code-switching than in the coherence of the content. The text was transcribed as heard. I used standard transcription for English, italics for French, and underlining for Somali. Here <u>wallahi bellahi</u> is Somali borrowed from Arabic, meaning "I swear to God."

A male voice Alors ferme la, voilà ferme!
Sam <u>Wallahi</u>, I don't believe you man, <u>wallahi bellahi.</u>
A male voice Ça doit être 50 piece man. Wardap!
Juma Yo, *toi* XX [noise, laughs].
Sam [laughs] Juma man . . .!
Juma Yo, yo, Bogey *c'est moi.* Watch the music! *C'est le même mot qu'on avait . . .*
 Where are you going? Sit down! . . .
Sam *Je reviens* man XX, you know. It's from Mecca you know? Reprezin'
 you know, Mecca a'ait? You ask [laughs]. [Inaudible Somali]. You
 know wha'm mean?

(Group interview, French and English)

182

In the same sentence, one finds French, "plain English" (Philip 1991), Somali, and BESL. And, significantly, mastery of BESL was accomplished additively since part of the African youths' desire "to be" was in relation to their African languages. As one male student put it, "Here, we live in Canada, you see! We are [still] going to keep our culture [in another context, he said "language"], but at the same time there are new technologies, new musics." Another said, " I don't find it embarrassing to speak my language and dress in Boubou [an East African dress]." For these youth, African languages were fundamental to the expression of their linguistic, national, and historical allegiance and kinship, and to the creation of safe spaces of comfort, bonding, and familiarity. In the school, students used these languages with ease, both in public and private spheres, and invoked them as both a medium of communication and an indicator of history, nationality, and identity. In so doing, these Francophone African youth in Southwestern Ontario, Canada, understood that this is how history continues, how languages are guaranteed to last and with them ourselves and our humanity.

Notes

1. *Critical ethnographic research* (Simon and Dippo 1986) is a set of activities situated within a project that seeks and works its way toward social transformation. This project is political as well as pedagogical, and who the researcher is and what his racial, gender, and class embodiments are necessarily govern the research questions and findings. This project is, as Simon and Dippo might say, "an activity determined both by real and present conditions, *and* certain conditions still to come which it is trying to bring into being" (1986: 196). The assumption underpinning my project was based on the assertion that Canadian society is "inequitably structured and dominated by a hegemonic culture that suppresses a consideration and understanding of why things are the way they are and what must be done for things to be otherwise" (1986: 196).
2. Each student's name—all names are pseudonyms—is followed by age, gender (F = female, M = male), and country of origin. Each excerpt quoted from the transcripts is followed by the type of interview (individual or group) and the language in which it was conducted. The following transcription conventions were used:
    underlined text English spoken within French speech or French spoken within English speech
    [ ] Explanation or description of speaker's actions
    [. . .] Text omitted
    XX Inaudible voice
3   "Mr. T." is an MC of a local Canadian Rap music TV program, called Rap City, which airs mostly American Rap lyrics.

References

Althusser, L. (1971) *Lenin and Philosophy*, London: New Left Books.
Anderson, B. (1983) *Imagined Communities: Reflections on the Origin and Spread of Nationalism*, London: Verso.
Asante, M.K. (1990) *Kemet, Afrocentricity and Knowledge*, Trenton, NJ: Africa World.
Bakhtin, M.M. (1981) *The Dialogic Imagination: Four Essays* (M. Holquist and C. Emerson, trans.), Austin, TX: University of Texas Press.

Barthes, R. (1983) *Elements of Semiology*, New York: Hill and Wang. (Original work published in 1967.)

Bhabha, H. (1994) *The Location of Culture*, London and New York: Routledge.

Bourdieu, P. (1991) *Language and Symbolic Power* (G. Raymond and M. Adamson, trans.), London: Polity Press.

Butler, J. (1999) *Gender Trouble: Feminism and the Subversion of Identity*, New York: Routledge. (Original work published in 1990.)

Chideya, F. (2000) *The Color of our Future: Race for the 21st Century*, New York: William Morrow.

DuBois, W.E.B. (1903) *The Souls of Black Folk*, New York: Penguin.

Foucault, M. (1980) *Power/knowledge: Selected Interviews and Other Writings*, New York: Pantheon.

—— (1984) *The Foucault Reader*, New York: Pantheon Books.

Gilroy, P. (1991) *There Ain't No Black in the Union Jack: The Cultural Politics of Race and Nation*, Chicago, IL: University of Chicago Press.

—— (1993) *The Black Atlantic: Modernity and Double Consciousness*, London and New York: Routledge.

Hall, S. (1990) "Cultural identity and diaspora," in J. Rutherford (ed.) *Identity, Community, Culture, Difference*, London: Lawrence and Wishart, 222–37.

—— (1991) "Ethnicity: identity and difference," *Radical America*, 13 (4): 9–20.

—— (1997) *Representation: Cultural Representation and Signifying Practices*, London: Sage, in association with the Open University.

Heller, M. (1992) "The politics of codeswitching and language choice," *Journal of Multilingual and Multicultural Development*, 13: (1 and 2): 123–42.

—— (1994) *Crosswords: Language, Education and Ethnicity in French Ontario*, Berlin and New York: Mouton de Gruyter.

Hobsbawm, E. and Ranger, T. (eds) (1983) *The Invention of Tradition*, Cambridge: Cambridge University Press.

hooks, bell (1990) *Yearning: Race, Gender, and Cultural Politics*, Toronto: Between the Lines.

—— (1992) *Black Looks*, Boston, MA: South End Press.

—— (1994) *Teaching to Transgress: Education as the Practice of Freedom*, London and New York: Routledge.

Ibrahim, A. (1998) 'Hey, whassup homeboy?' becoming Black: race, language, culture, and the politics of identity: African students in a Franco-Ontarian high school," unpublished PhD dissertation, OISE: University of Toronto.

—— (1999) "Becoming Black: Rap and Hip-Hop, race, gender, identity, and the politics of ESL learning," *TESOL Quarterly*, 33 (3): 349–69.

—— (2000a) "'Hey, ain't I Black too?': the politics of becoming Black," in R. Walcott (ed.) *Rude: Contemporary Black Canadian Cultural Criticism*, Toronto: Insomniac Press, 109–36.

—— (2000b) "Whassup homeboy?" Black/popular culture and the politics of 'Curriculum Studies': devising an anti-racism perspective," in G.J. Dei and A. Calliste (eds) *Power, Knowledge and Anti-Racism Education*, Halifax: Fernwood Publishing, 57–72.

—— (2000c) "Trans-framing identity: race, language, culture, and the politics of translation," *Trans/forms: Insurgent Voices in Education*, 5 (2): 120–35.

—— (2000d) "Being or becoming? Race, language, culture, identity, and the African experience of becoming Black (in North America)," paper presented at the Crossroads in Cultural Studies international conference, Birmingham, UK, June 21–5.

Kelly, J. (1998) *Under the Gaze: Learning to Be Black in White Society*, Halifax, NS: Fernwood Publishing.

Kristeva, J. (1974) *La révolution du langage poétique* [*Revolution in Poetic Language*], Paris: Lautreament et Mallarmé.

Philip, M.N. (1991) *Harriet's Daughter*, Toronto: The Women's Press.

Rose, T. (1991) "Fear of a Black planet": Rap music and Black cultural politics in the 1990s," *Journal of Negro Education*, 60 (3): 276–90.

Simon, R.I. and Dippo, D. (1986) "On critical ethnography work," *Anthropology and Education Quarterly*, 17: 195–202.

Smitherman, G. (2000a) *Talkin That Talk: Language, Culture and Education in African America*, London and New York: Routledge.

—— (2000b) *Black Talk: Words and Phrases from the Hood to the Amen Corner*, Boston and New York: Houghton Mifflin.

Walcott, R. (1995) "Performing the postmodern: Black Atlantic Rap and identity in North America," unpublished PhD dissertation, OISE: University of Toronto.

West, C. (1993) *Race Matters*, Boston: Beacon.

Willinsky, J. (1998), *Learning to Divide the World: Education at Empire's End*, Minneapolis, MN: University of Minnesota Press.

Wright, H.K. (2000) "Why write back to the new missionaries? Addressing the exclusion of (Black) others from discourses of empowerment," in G.J. Dei and A. Calliste (eds) *Power, Knowledge and Anti-Racism Education*, Halifax: Fernwood Publishing, 122–40.

10

US and South African teachers' developing perspectives on language and literacy: changing domestic and international roles of linguistic gate-keepers

Arnetha F. Ball

Globalization, technological advances, and the increasing numbers of students in classrooms worldwide who speak a first language other than a "standard" English make multicultural and multilingual education an imperative in the twenty-first century. US demographers predict that by 2020, 46 percent of the US school population will be students of color. In South Africa, students of color comprise well over 50 percent of the school population. Reports on educational achievement in both countries confirm that a large number of these students attend schools in poor, underresourced areas and that many of them are failing to achieve at their full potential. Clearly, an important goal of multicultural and multilingual education globally must be to prepare teachers to work effectively with students from culturally and linguistically diverse backgrounds. The research reported here was designed to explore the application of language studies to this educational context.

This cross-national comparative study is based on an innovative teacher education course implemented over a three-year period in the US and South Africa in an effort to help teachers become better prepared to teach culturally and linguistically diverse students. Using data collected from over 100 US and South African pre-service and in-service teachers, this research investigates the evolving perspectives of teachers as they prepare to face challenging situations in diverse schools. The research involves discourse and text analyses of narrative essays, literacy autobiographies, journals, interviews, small-group discussions, and videotapes of teaching collected from the teachers enrolled in the course. These data illustrate the teachers' changing ideologies concerning theoretical principles and teaching practices. The teachers' literacy histories and reflective writings provide glimpses into the worlds of their early literacy experiences and their evolving ideologies about literacy practices in their classrooms. Additionally, this research investigates the concept of teachers as linguistic gate-keepers—a practice that is evident when we look at historical changes in official and unofficial language policies in the US and South Africa and at classroom practices in US and South African schools. Teachers operate with a body of assumptions and beliefs, which constitute their language ideology. This language ideology may reflect—or resist—their national language policy. Through case studies and an analysis of teachers' written texts, I demonstrate how teachers' perspectives on literacy can change over time as a result of their participation in a strategically designed teacher education program and how, as these perspectives change, their class-room practices as linguistic gate-keepers can begin to change as well.

This chapter has three parts. The first part discusses linguistic gate-keeping and similarities and differences in the educational policies and practices histori-cally adopted in US and South African schools designed for students of African descent. The second part presents the program of study that was designed to facilitate teachers' interest in and commitment to teaching students from diverse backgrounds in general and students of African heritage in particular. In the third part I provide a discussion of the dual approach—survey and discourse analysis—used in the analysis of the teachers' texts and consider its usefulness within a broader context. In the midst of current discussions about the improve-ment of teacher education programs, little has been done to explore the use of linguistic and discourse analyses to gauge the effectiveness of programs designed to prepare teachers for changing school demographics. Using this dual approach, I explore how teachers' developing ideologies are facilitated when intellectual activity is coupled with interactive participation in carefully designed classroom activities. Further, I explore how those developing ideologies are revealed in the teachers' changing voices and in their practices as linguistic gate-keepers.

Linguistic gate-keeping and US and South African education

South Africa and the US share some striking similarities in their histories of the education of marginalized people of color. These two countries have shared many of the same ideologies about language policies and the mechanisms used to implement those policies. The primary ideology of South Africa and the US in past years was manifested in apartheid and segregation which resulted in sep-arate and unequal systems of education that deliberately miseducated Blacks in an attempt to lower their aspirations and prepare them for a subordinate role in society. Both countries share a history of racial disparities in the quality of schools, in educational access, and in the preparation of teachers of Black stu-dents (Johnson 1941; Margo 1990; Hartshorne 1992; Fultz 1995; Rist 1996).

In comparison to the system of education designed for whites, the quality of schools for Blacks, teacher qualifications, class size, school facilities, funding, and accessibility of schooling can historically be characterized as unequal and frequently neglected. In the US, Goodenow and White argue that the "main end of Southern industrialists, Northern philanthropists, and educational reformers was to force Blacks into a workable scheme of social organization that would permit the structuring of a caste economy least removed from slavery" (1981: 27). Following the abolition of slavery in the US, the goal of the school was to help fit Blacks into that caste scheme. In South Africa, a similar plan was implemented. In both countries the goal of the white power structure was to prepare Blacks as industrially trained workers; few Blacks were trained as professionals. It was felt that vocational education would achieve this desired end. Manual training was used to keep Blacks in their "place," not to offer them advancement (Goodenow and White 1981: 125–6). In South Africa, Bantu Education was instituted to create Blacks who would be functionally illiterate and economically shackled. The schools were organized to teach them the "master's language" and to provide them with a limited vocabulary. In both countries, the educational system provided Blacks with elementary-level literacy and trained them in discipline and the skills of manual labor in order to instill in them feelings of inferiority—e.g. a curriculum of carpentry for boys, dressmaking, cooking, and laundering for girls, and gardening for both.

John Samuel, Director of Education for the African National Congress (ANC) in 1991, noted the deliberate undereducation of Black South African children in the areas of math, science, and language (Novicki 1991). He indicated that as late as 1990, of the 200,000 students in high school, only twelve Black children obtained an A-grade pass in mathematics. He also noted the "huge disparities" between levels of training and educational development yielding vast disparities between numbers of white and Black graduates who are trained and skilled (Novicki 1991). The ANC noted that apartheid and Bantu education had left thousands of young Blacks lacking decent education, skills, and work habits to participate constructively in the South African economy following the end of apartheid. In 1989, the Black pass rate on country-wide matriculation exams (the equivalent of a high school diploma in the US) was only 40 percent; in 1990 it was only 36 percent. The white pass rate exceeded 95 percent in both years. Former South African Prime Minister Hendrik Verwoerd, the ideological architect of apartheid, envisioned as one of his cornerstones a separate, completely different, and inferior educational system for Blacks. Bantu education was that cornerstone. In a statement to Parliament in 1954 Verwoerd declared that the natives would be taught from childhood to realize that equality with Europeans is not for them (Tygesen 1991). In 1950, slightly over one third of Black children went to elementary school. Although today the figure is nearly 80 percent, the drop-out rate for Blacks at secondary level is extremely high. Another disheartening statistic is the low number of Blacks who are able to go on to a university. Of approximately 82,000 Blacks who were interested in attending a university, only about 17,000, or 21 percent, had the qualifications for admission to college.

In the US, early American slave masters worked to keep slaves in their menial positions (Webber 1978). They believed that without literacy education, African slaves and their descendants would be doomed to powerlessness, and true free-dom would forever evade them (Harris 1992: 278). In practice, in segregated schools in the 1930s and long thereafter, Blacks rarely ever received equal educa-tional appropriations or facilities (Southern Education Reporting Service 1961). Furthermore, rather than the more classical curriculum for whites, emphasis was placed on domestic and industrial education for Blacks. Expectations for Black and white schools were very different. By 1940, Black schools were ill equipped, their terms shorter, teachers poorly trained, and their instructional curricula in-ferior compared to those of their white counterparts. In fourteen Southern states in 1929, the average number of students assigned to a white teacher was thirty-one; for Blacks, it was forty-four (Goodenow and White 1981: 63; Waters 1989). Even as late as 1990, the educational situation for Blacks in poor, urban, and inner-city communities had not significantly changed.

In South Africa, one out of every four Black children drop out of school within the first two years, and one out of every five Black children has no access to school. In the US in 1860, proportionately twenty-seven times more white than Black children went to school. In 1910, only about 60 percent of Black stu-dents ages six to fourteen attended schools in sixteen Southern states. In some Southern states, that proportion ran as low as 33 percent (Woodson 1930: 187).

In both countries, there has historically been a deprivation of adequate facili-ties and well-trained teachers to serve the educational needs of Black students. For the first half of the twentieth century, the bulk of African American children in school attended impoverished, small, short-term schools with pronounced inadequacies in every phase of the educational program (Moss 1994). In prac-tice, even today, students attending predominantly Black schools rarely receive educational appropriations or facilities equal to those of whites. Furthermore, rather than the more classical college preparatory curriculum offered to a large number of whites, emphasis is placed on low-level, skills-based education and discipline in predominantly Black schools. The disparity in funding for the edu-cation of white versus Black children is disheartening. In 1900, $2 was spent on every Black child in the US as compared to $3 for every white child. In 1930, $7 was spent for whites and still only $2 for Blacks. In 1935–6, the expenditure for white students averaged $37.87 per child, while expenditure for Black students was $13.09 per child (Franklin and Moss 1994: 406). Even today, these dispari-ties continue.

Significant disparities in the South African government's spending per pupil ranged from textbook allocations, to school facilities, to quantity and quality of teachers. The teacher–pupil ratio is about one to fifteen for whites and about one to forty for Blacks. During the 1970s, government spending was eighteen times more for white than Black students. Although the ratio had dropped to about 4.6 to one by 1987–8, spending for Black students still was not on par with that of whites. Black teachers have historically been underpaid in South Africa (and in the US), and they are subject to frequent misadministration (Hartshorne 1992; Fultz 1995; Rist 1996). The Department of Education and

Training (DET), the department responsible for oversight of Black education, recorded a shortage of 5,531 primary teachers and 1,350 secondary school teachers in 1988 (Mncwabe 1993). In the 1930s, the government was spending more than forty times as much per white pupil as they spent per Black pupil (Kallaway 1984). In 1980, five times as much was being spent on the education of whites as on the education of colored students (Finnegan 1986), and the discrepancy was even greater for Black students.

The story of Black people and their experiences with education in Africa and the Americas is deeply laden with struggle, oppression, and adversity. However, one of the most notable things about this story is the perseverance of Black people in striving to attain quality education for the livelihood and prosperity of future generations. Within this context, teachers as linguistic gate-keepers historically adopted roles as implementers of national language policies designed to hold Blacks back. As teachers in both countries assumed this role, they overtly or covertly sent messages to their students that their home and community ways of expressing their ideas were not welcome within the educational context. They also implemented programs of instruction geared toward subtractive bi-and multilingualism, with the message that the students' home and community forms and expressions must be exterminated, or at least subjugated, if students were to succeed in educational settings and within the broader societal context. There have been numerous efforts across national boundaries not only to denigrate the heritage languages of people of African descent, but also to eliminate the vestiges of these languages so as to leave these populations feeling that they have no history worth maintaining—to strip them of language that could serve as a unifying force among these people of shared heritage. Linguistic gate-keeping can be investigated from the perspective of applying language studies to the educational context. An investigation of related studies from this perspective reveals that the literature on classroom discourse is extensive. It includes studies on ethnography of communication (Hymes 1972; Cazden 1988), sociology (Mehan 1979), sociolinguistics (Hymes 1974), and the analysis of interactional processes. This body of research can serve as a foundation from which other studies can expand our current understandings of classroom practices.

Research on classroom discourse

Sociolinguists, working in the tradition of ethnography of communication, focus on classroom communicative or interactional competence as an end in itself or as a means to accomplish educational objectives. The term "communicative competence" was used by Hymes (1972, 1974) to describe the complex ways in which speakers interpret rules of participation across speech communities. Gumperz and Hymes (1972) used the idea of communicative competence to question the "standard" language bias in schools and to deepen our understanding of the complexities of language used in classrooms as a tool in the social transmission of knowledge. From their perspective, difference is conceived of as linguistic variability, not inferiority. According to these researchers, the failure of schools to incorporate variability and an appreciation for difference into the language and learning environment may account for minority students' failure.

Sociolinguistic research on classroom discourse is commonly limited to understanding classroom interactional dynamics, without an examination of the influences and competencies from outside of school and their relationship to classroom interactional processes or academic success. In addition, traditional definitions of communicative competence in research on classroom discourse usually refer to the demands of instructional encounters that are teacher-directed, thus assuming communicative competence to be solely the students' responsibility, rather than active co-construction of communication between students and teachers. This research sometimes views non-mainstream students as being linguistically mismatched and does not examine the ways in which classroom language practices may act as a social filter that denies students' access to educational opportunities and their resultant economic advantages. We must begin to assume that the linguistic conflict that goes on in classrooms is not simply a mismatch between home and school language. Rather, it may be a more active exclusion of students' home language and literacy practices, which applies directly to the study of linguistic gate-keeping in educational contexts.

Much of sociolinguistic research on classroom discourse has focused on normative discourse and participation patterns (Mehan 1979; Cazden 1988) and teacher and student script patterns (Gutierrez et al. 1995). Research on classroom discourse from both sociolinguistic and ethnography of communication perspectives has focused primarily on analysis of lessons and participation patterns (Philips 1972; Sinclair and Coulthard 1975; Mehan 1979). Assuming that prior intentions and expectations of teachers and students influence the interaction, researchers have examined the interaction between teachers and students in a classroom with diverse language speakers, and how teachers and students reveal their expectations and construct rules for participation.

Building on these prior studies, this chapter draws primarily on discourse and text analyses to investigate teachers' changing perspectives over time as revealed through their oral and written narratives and other texts they produced. The analysis of narrative has unique relevance to investigations in social science research in general (Mitchell 1981; Lightfoot 1983, 1988; Mishler 1986, 1995) and to research on teaching in particular (Bolster 1983; Bruner 1985, 1986; Connelly and Clandinin 1985a, 1985b, 1990). The narratives and other texts that these teachers created in my course yielded powerful disclosures about their changing ideologies and their conceptualizations of literacy. They also yielded powerful disclosures about how teachers' participation in a course can facilitate changes in their roles as linguistic gate-keepers within their worlds of teaching. The various texts created over time by the teachers in this study, along with the videotapes of their teaching and follow-up audiotaped discussions, serve as a window into the developing perspectives these teachers held about literacy and learning in multicultural settings.

The study

This research was designed to investigate how teachers' evolving ideologies on literacy can be influenced by their exposure to theoretical principles and teaching strategies within a teacher education program, and how, as their ideologies on literacy change through their participation in a strategically designed teacher education program, their classroom practices as linguistic gate-keepers change as well. To address these questions, I collected the oral and written texts of over 100 US and South African teachers who participated in a one-semester course that I taught over a three-year period. The oral and written texts were written by these teachers to reflect their developing perspectives on literacy and teaching. The data included the teachers' narrative essays of their own literacy experiences, transcripts of classroom discussions, journal entries, written reflections in response to course readings and experiences, and their reflective writing about their teacher research projects. I hypothesized that, as teachers are exposed to strategically designed readings and activities within a teacher education program, their perspectives on literacy and their classroom practices with diverse student populations would be affected in positive ways.

Methodology

The US and South African teachers in this study were exposed to a course which I designed to give them opportunities to consider the role and function of literacies in their lives and in the lives of others and to consider how literacies could be used strategically to teach diverse students more effectively. I proposed that, through considering these issues, teachers' perspectives concerning language use in the classroom would broaden and their practices of linguistic gate-keeping would also be impacted. The course introduced developing teachers to a range of theoretical frameworks that undergird effective teaching of literacies to diverse students and provided the participants a safe environment where they could question their preconceived ideologies about language, literacy, and classroom practices associated with different ideologies.

Throughout the course, teachers were required to read and reflect on a number of short theoretical texts on topics of diversity, language, literacy, and teacher practice. In one of these texts, Au (1994: 30) rejects a transmission model of school literacy, which focuses heavily on teacher-centered instruction and low-level skills such as decoding, spelling, and grammar. Instead, she emphasizes a constructivist ideology, which places meaning-making and socially useful literacy at the center of all teaching and learning. Au proposes that literacy classrooms should be redefined to highlight instructional practices that involve an active process of meaning-making and literacy instruction that makes students' background experiences central along with culturally responsive instruction, multicultural literature, and the development of critical literacy (1994: 34). Teachers in the course also considered extracts from Richard-Amato and Snow's *The Multicultural Classroom* (1992), a text written explicitly to mainstream US educators faced with "language minority students" (a situation directly relevant to that of many South African teachers in multilingual classrooms). These texts drew teachers' attention to cultural considerations and pedagogical approaches for area content teachers working with culturally and linguistically diverse students. Teachers also considered Hudelson's (1994) perspective on literacy development in second-language children and ways to facilitate the language development of low-literacy learners. Additional readings included the works of Vygotsky (1978), Bakhtin (1981), Giroux (1988), and McElroy-Johnson (1993). The text by McElroy-Johnson cautioned teachers that it would be difficult for them to assist students in developing a voice if they had not yet developed a voice of their own, while Giroux challenged teachers to become "Transformative Intellectuals." Giroux speaks of his concern with harnessing the language of critique to a language of possibility in order to develop alternative teaching practices that are capable of shattering the logic of domination both within and outside of our schools (1988).

Reading the works of Giroux and others served to ignite thoughtful discussions in our course—not only about re-creating teacher education programs, but also about re-creating teachers' own classrooms so they become committed to articulating a language that can contribute to examining the realm of education as a new public sphere, one that seeks to

> recapture the idea of critical democracy as a social movement for individual freedom and social justice—that defines student teachers as intellectuals who will establish public spaces where students can debate, appropriate, and learn the knowledge and skills necessary to achieve that individual freedom and social justice.
>
> (Giroux 1988: 167)

These readings provided opportunities for teachers to consider models of teaching that were very different from those aligned with the practices of linguistic gate-keeping.

As most teachers enter teacher education programs, they bring with them very limited perspectives on what literacy is, what it means for a person to be literate, and ways that they can strategically use language and literacies to more effectively teach students from diverse backgrounds. Linked to these limited views is the fact that many of these teachers have also given very little thought to teaching students who are different from themselves or who have had different literacy histories from their own. These limited perspectives oftentimes play themselves out in subtle and overt practices of linguistic gate-keeping where teachers unconsciously (and sometimes consciously) convey messages to multicultural and multilingual students that their home and community ways of expressing their ideas are not welcome in educational contexts. They also implement programs of instruction geared toward subtractive bi- and multilingualism

193

with the message that students' home and community forms and expressions must change if they are to succeed within the educational context. My prediction was that through engagement with strategically designed course readings and activities (activities that included in-class exchanges concerning the education of students of color in general and African and African American students specifically, teacher research projects, and teaching in actual classrooms), teachers enrolled in my course would begin to give serious consideration to the possibility of using language and literacies in strategic ways to teach diverse students. One indicator of these serious considerations would be the teachers' expressions of broadening perspectives about the definitions and uses of literacies in the oral and written texts they produced for the course.

Near the beginning of the course and prior to any engagement with literacy theory, all 100 teachers were asked to write their own definitions of a literate person. They were asked to write the same definition as they approached the culmination of the course. The teachers produced literacy histories and reflective writings, including autobiographies of their literacy experiences. A subset of the teachers' written work was analyzed to determine emerging themes and linguistic indicators of the teachers' literacy perspectives and practices. (Although I do not discuss them in this chapter, I also conducted interviews with the teachers and videotaped a subset of the teachers as they worked with linguistically diverse students.)

Analysis of data

The data were analyzed on two levels:

1   a macro-analysis of the changing perspectives of the 100 US and South African teachers about what it means for a person to be literate. Their written definitions of literacy were categorized, tallied, and summarized (see Figures 10.1 and 10.2.);
2   a micro-analysis of the literacy histories and reflective writings of a smaller subset of the 100 teachers to determine emerging themes and linguistic indicators that reflected their perspectives and practices.

Findings

Figures 10.1 and 10.2 are summaries of the 100 US and South African teachers' definitions of literacy. As mentioned, at the beginning of the course and before any exposure to literacy theories, all 100 teachers were asked to write their own definitions of what it means to be a literate person. At the end of the course, they were again asked to provide their definitions of literacy.

As can be seen from Figure 10.1, among the US and South African teachers the highest number of definitions of a literate person, before their exposure to the course, was "the ability of individuals to communicate using reading, writing

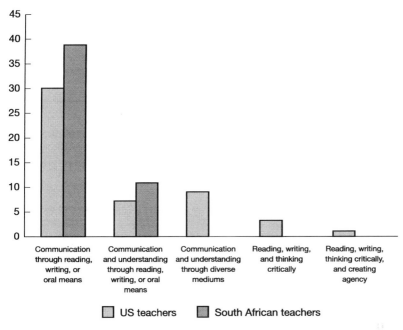

Figure 10.1 Teachers' initial definitions of literacy

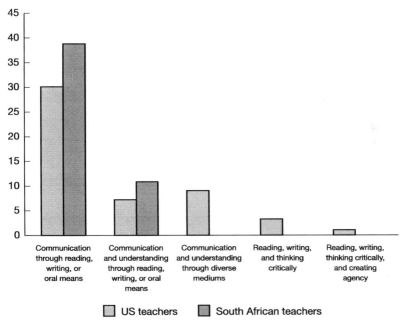

Figure 10.2 Teachers' post definitions of literacy

and oral language." Few teachers defined a literate person as one who used other media to communicate effectively. Only one of the US teachers conceptualized the complexities of literacies to include such factors as critical agency in one's life. Clearly, the majority of these teachers viewed literacies in simplistic, limited terms. In their initial definitions, the majority of the teachers who regarded literacy simplistically as "using reading, writing and oral language" embraced ideologies of the "autonomous model" of literacy in which literacy is conceptualized in simplistic technical terms, treating it as independent of social context (Street 1993a, 1993b). From this perspective, reading and writing become technological forms to be mastered by repetition and drill, in which the issues of meaning and social context are secondary at best. This practice is particularly debilitating for diverse students and is pervasive in novice teachers' views of literacy. It is reflective of their limited perspectives about the use of literacies to facilitate successful teaching and learning. It is also reflective of the limited perspectives generally held by teachers who adhere to the old paradigms of segregation in the US and apartheid in South Africa during which teachers generally assumed the role of linguistic gate-keepers, sending messages to marginalized students of color that their home and community languages, forms, and expressions must be exterminated or subjugated if they were to succeed in educational settings and broader societal contexts.

Figure 10.2 represents the teachers' evolving definitions of literacy after their exposure to the course activities and theoretical perspectives. Reading the US teachers' literacy definitions, I noted that many of them were very interested in the notion of critical literacy by the end of the course. A comparison of Figures 10.1 and 10.2 reveals that only a few of the preexisting US teachers' definitions mentioned critical thinking in contrast to the large number of postcourse definitions that addressed it. The same trend is apparent with the South African teachers although not as strong. None of the South African teachers mentioned critical thinking in their preexisting definitions, whereas many of the post definitions mentioned it. Several of the teachers indicated their desire to assist their students in acquiring a voice of their own, and they expressed the belief that critical literacy was an important tool for helping students to do this. Two similarities between the US and South African teachers' post definitions were that both groups' responses suggested that their definitions of literacy had broadened and that course activities had greatly expanded their conceptualizations of literacy. These expanded perspectives on literacy were commonly held by teachers who had resisted the role of linguistic gate-keepers during and after the periods of US segregation and South African apartheid.

One goal of the course was to facilitate teachers' considerations about how literacies can be used in strategic ways to more effectively teach content area materials to all students, including those from culturally and linguistically diverse backgrounds. Another goal of the course was to investigate whether teachers' tendencies toward linguistic gate-keeping might decrease owing to their participation in this course. The results of the macro-level analysis of the data suggest that these teachers were beginning to broaden their understanding of the many different ways that an individual can be considered literate and the different ways of expressing that literacy. Certainly, Figures 10.1 and 10.2 give evidence of the teachers' changing perspectives concerning literacies over time; however, it is not clear from these data whether the teachers' engagements with the readings and activities in the course facilitated the development of reflective, committed epistemologies of practice in teaching diverse students.

In my readings of the teachers' reflective writings, I noted that they discussed more explicitly how their perceptions of literacy had changed and how, as these perceptions changed, so did their considerations about teaching diverse students. Their rejection of ideologies consistent with linguistic gate-keeping began to emerge as well. By the end of the course, many of the teachers were using phrases like "expansion of home resources," "appreciation of community discourses," and "respect" for students' ways of expressing ideas in their expanded definitions and reflective writings which had not appeared in their initial definitions. Whereas the teachers initially thought of literacy as simply being able to read and write or as a "skill," many of their later perspectives on literacy referred to "an understanding," "an appreciation," and a desire to promote literacy as "an active thinking process." Furthermore, in their reflective writings, many of the teachers discussed action plans and strategies that they would use in their classrooms to teach diverse populations. I was therefore motivated to consider the use of text analysis to examine the teachers' extended writing as a means for investigating the research questions. I propose that this analysis could be used as a tool for gauging the success of teacher education programs in developing teachers who have more inclusive ideologies toward the languages and literacies of linguistically diverse, poor, and marginalized students. Specifically, I propose that discourse analysis could be used in addition to the analysis above as a tool for investigating how teachers' evolving ideologies can be influenced by their exposure to theoretical principles and teaching strategies within a teacher education program.

Discourse analysis

All of the teachers asserted that they had gained a broader understanding of and appreciation and respect for conceptualizations of what it means to be literate. Some of them also began to articulate changing ideologies that impacted their teaching practices. As I looked for indicators of changing ideologies on the part of these teachers, the articulation of specific action plans and strategies that these teachers intended to implement in their classrooms was important—since a commitment to change would need to be accompanied by a decisive choice on their part that involved them in a definite course of action.

In the section that follows, I share the voices that emerged from the literacy histories and reflective writings of three teachers in my course as they discuss their evolving perspectives on literacy and action plans for their current and future teaching. These teachers' shared personal autobiographies of their own literacy experiences, and reflections on the readings and activities that they encountered during the course that helped to alter their philosophies on literacy and their thoughts about their future teaching. Like many other teachers in the course, these three teachers shared reports on how encounters with theoretical readings and course activities were used as a vehicle (or catalyst) that helped them to contemplate the challenges of teaching different students. The eventual implementation of these teachers' action plans for their future teaching were confirmed by follow-up interviews and classroom visitations three years after their participation in the course.

In working with the teachers' discourse, I conducted a content analysis of their texts, searching for emerging themes and overarching ideas from the teachers' personal histories and their reflective writings. I also analyzed these texts for indicators at the word, phrase, and discourse level that revealed the teachers' evolving ideological stances. Building on the narrative research that focuses on teaching (Bolster 1983; Bruner 1985, 1986; Connelly and Clandinin 1985a, 1985b, 1990), in the following discussion I share excerpts from these teachers' narratives, which exhibit powerful disclosures about how they conceptualized their roles as teachers and learners. The various texts the teachers created over the course of the term serve as windows into their developing ideas, and provide snapshots of their reflections on their changing perspectives.

Sharing autobiographies of early literacy experiences

One American and two South African teachers in my teacher education course were selected as the focus of this analysis. These particular teachers were selected because they provide a representative sample of the wide range of perspectives expressed by the transitioning group of teachers. One South African teacher, Irene, was a female in her mid-twenties who had been considered a "coloured" in apartheid South Africa. The other South African teacher, Linda, was a female in her mid-twenties who came from a Black African language-speaking background. The third teacher, Niko, was also a female in her mid-twenties; she came from an Asian American background. All three teachers were from working- or middle-class backgrounds. I trace these teachers' discourses and show evidence of their developing ideologies and plans for practice through their personal narratives, reflections on the course readings, and their discussions of how their participation in course activities influenced their teaching practices.

Irene and Linda attended a teacher education program that was offered at a major university located in the Western Cape Province of South Africa. Although the university offered a traditional teacher education program, these teachers were enrolled in a course for current teachers seeking certification in a Further Diploma in Education program. This teacher education program was designed to prepare teachers to teach in multilingual and multicultural schools.

Irene was an early-career teacher who lived and taught in an area of the city designated for "coloureds" during apartheid. In her autobiography, Irene shares the following about her early literacy experience.

> My childhood was always centered around my mom and the school she taught at, the same school I am teaching at. She was always busy with this play or that stage production . . . I remember memorizing songs and scripts. It wasn't long before I was going to Speech and Drama . . . and ballet . . . In retrospect I realise that my mom introduced me to a wide variety of literacy (interpretation of music, movement, character scripts, drama) before I entered the schooling system. I continued these activities till I was a first year university student. I realise now that, through the activities that my mom insisted on, I was well-versed in interpretation and critical thought of the abstract. Now I realise that this background has quite a bit to do with who I am and how I think about things. My mom gave me quite a head start . . . I must also admit that at the time I did not appreciate having to go to speech and drama, and ballet every alternate day. When other children were outside playing I was going to this class or that. I could never understand why this was? It is only now that I fully understand and appreciate what my parents were trying to do, even though their methods were slightly undemocratic. Still I only benefited from these experiences.

Niko, the Asian American student from a middle-class community in the Midwestern United States, described her early literacy experiences, noting that "I was always taught in a positive atmosphere . . . I had a positive experience of empathetic and understanding teachers who sincerely desired to help make my learning environment an enjoyable and productive place."

In contrast to the early literacy experiences of Niko and Irene, Linda tells the story of a different route to becoming a teacher. She shares:

> I started my schooling at ——— Lower Primary School in Guguletu. My teacher was Miss ———. We started learning to write by writing cursive and copying patterns . . . After that we were told to draw an egg with a tail to make an "a" . . . When writing "m" we . . . were told to write a half moon and then close it . . . When writing "I," we were told to write a man wearing a hat, with no arms and legs . . . When reading we had to repeat after the teacher even if we were saying things that we did not understand. What I liked most at school was to do recital and singing. I remember when I first learned the Lord's Prayer. When I was doing Grade 1, we didn't know what the words were, but we had to sing them in English anyway. There was a part that we sang like this: "Hallow there, give us Lo our Daddy Bre." We were not corrected. We just sang that until I realized that it was not correct in the church. Most of the

time we were taught to memorize without meanings, especially when we were doing our English and Afrikaans lessons. What made learning then not to be fun was the use of corporal punishment. I remember one day when I was in Grade 5, we were being taught Geography and Maps and the teacher pointed to Dar Es Salaam. Instead of saying that, I said Datsotsala. I was so scared and shaky. Because I said it incorrectly, I was beaten so badly. As a result I hated Geography. Otherwise I had fun when I learned, even though my problem was with the punishment.

All three teachers recount early life experiences that were filled with literacy-related activities. Irene recounts early literacy experiences that engaged her in a wide variety of interpretative literacy activities which began well before she entered the schooling system, while Niko recalls being educated in a positive atmosphere with teachers who were empathetic and understanding. Linda attended school in a Black South African township where teachers were rigid and quite strict. However, she concludes, "I had fun when I learned." These early literacy experiences helped to lay the foundations for their perceptions about language and literacy, about what it meant to be a teacher, as well as their later decisions to become teachers.

Each participant in my course engaged in this activity—of reflecting on their own autobiographies of early literacy experiences—in order to bring to a metacognitive level of awareness those experiences that helped to influence their own literacy attitudes and their preconceived notions about what it meant to be a teacher. Indicators that these students' levels of metacognitive awareness were increasing included the use of statements that began with words and phrases like "I remember one day . . .," "Now I realize that . . .," "In retrospect I realize that . . .," "I could never understand why . . .," and "It is only now that I fully understand and appreciate . . ." As these teachers' metacognitive levels increased, many began to question and challenge some of their long-held perspectives that they may not have been consciously aware of earlier. This autobiographical activity served as a readiness exercise that prepared teachers to consider new and different perspectives, attitudes, and visions for language and literacy, inclusion, and teaching practices in their classrooms.

Opportunities for reflection, introspection, and critique

Following their experiences of sharing and reflecting on their personal literacy histories, the teachers were exposed to assigned readings that were carefully selected to broaden their previously held views on literacy and classroom practice. In essence, exposure to these theoretical readings and practical strategies, coupled with reflective writing and authentic teaching experiences, served as the catalyst to motivate transformative activity and planning.

After reading Freire's *Pedagogy of the Oppressed* (1993), Irene wrote the following in her reflective journal:

> I feel that these should be the 4 corner-stones of my teaching. Inevitably these have to be relevant to my learners because of common back-ground that has its basis in our common/shared oppression. What especially interests me in this respect is Freire's Pedagogy of the op-pressed. In order for learners to succeed their [current] situations must be understood . . . Anti-racist and moral education/personal opinion . . . These theories can facilitate this. Critical analysis and personal opin-ion . . . Here the theory is very important. I work from the premise of an oppressed child, who has no voice, emotionally, socially, or intellectu-ally. My aim then is to bring my learners to an understanding of where we find ourselves and then to bring them to an understanding of the past. From there, I want to move them to a full potential of the future.

After reading McElroy-Johnson (1993) and articles on critical reading and criti-cal thinking in the course, Irene wrote in her reflective journal that she wants her students to be independent thinkers and to develop their own voice. She expressed what she wants for her students in her classroom:

> I don't want little robots, [I want] to allow my kiddies to talk, to have the space to experiment, to grow, to think for themselves, to pose ques-tions, then to seek more questions, to look at themselves, to help themselves, to speak out for themselves. I want to free my kiddies from what has been, to allow them to be whatever they want to be. I want my students to develop their voice because I, through a series of lec-tures in this course, am now once again believing in my own voice.

During our class, Niko was an active participant. Although she seldom volun-teered extended comments during large-class discussions, she noted the benefits of participating in small-group activities. In her journal writing she noted:

> Although it was difficult at first, once we got over the hump of feeling inadequate about speaking up, the students in our small-group discus-sions were challenged there in ways that reading and writing cannot challenge you. Sometimes we were paired up with the person next to us and discussed passages, issues or situations . . . On the whole, these exercises were positive learning experiences.

Niko's reflections on her reading assignments revealed an openness to new ideas:

> The article by Delpit [1988] was an extremely powerful article that chal-lenged me personally and opened my eyes to the reality and possible

201

struggles that I will potentially have in the future . . . Delpit's conclusion that, "it is impossible to create a model for the good teacher without taking issues of culture and community context into account" [p. 37] is very relevant. I never realized to what extent this idea holds true until reading the examples of how interpretations of authority and empowerment were interpreted by blacks as opposed to whites. My thoughts about teaching in the inner-city have forced me to consider and think about how it is that I want to approach teaching and how my concept of effective teaching may have to be altered.

Niko was a student who not only participated in the class-assigned activities, but was also engaged in her own tutoring and peer counseling activities. As she struggled to integrate the new course theories and best practices that she was learning about into her actual teaching activities, she expressed her developing perspectives in her journal writing:

> As teachers, although we will have been educated as to "how to teach," we can never really learn without experiences, circumstances that provide for different variations of what works. We need to take heed to the possibilities that the problems may reside in ourselves and not in the student. In any case, the responsibility to teach them [not only accept them] is the ideal that we need to instill in ourselves . . . As I thought about how my readings inform my teaching, the idea that grabbed me most intensely was the idea that we need to "turn ourselves inside out, giving up our own sense of who we are, and being willing to see ourselves in the unflattering light of another's angry gaze" [p. 46]. More than applying this to teaching, this is something that should be applied to any and every situation. To understand our own power and not be afraid to expose our vulnerabilities and raise questions of discrimination is essential to almost every situation.

Linda also indicated that she had learned a great deal from the course readings:

> In reading Vygotsky, I began to realize that the child's cultural development appears twice: first in social plane and then on the psychological plane. The child needs assistance for her development in learning. As the child is engaged in verbal interaction, she develops the higher thinking abilities of awareness, abstraction and control. I've also learned that a child should be given an opportunity to learn by himself—not guided. He can be guided so as to be independent in the future. Vygotsky states that what the child can do in co-operation today he can do it alone tomorrow. He said that in order for the child to be operating within her zone of proximal development, a child must be engaged in an instructional activity that is too difficult for her to

perform and her performances should be supported by an adult . . . The teacher's role in supporting learning within the zone of proximal development is to mediate the child's learning by providing support through social interaction. What the teacher does depends on feedback from the child while they are engaged in learning. The support that the teacher gives should range from explicit to vague hints. These are important facts I've learned from this article . . . Also, Au said that instead of telling the pupils to write a letter required by the syllabus, we should let them write letters to their pen-pals. That will bring a willingness to write freely. After reading these articles, I think that rather than giving pupils "topics" chosen by me, I will let them write about their own topics so as to enable them to write more freely. I will use these ideas in my teaching by changing my strategies for learning how my pupils learn, by allowing the pupils to use their mother-tongue as the base so as to make them proficient in reading and learning English, by letting pupils bring their experiences into the classroom so that each and every one should be able to learn from others, and by bringing into my classroom the students' home learning environment by putting charts on the walls, and pictures and certain information relevant for education so as to make the classroom have that learning atmosphere.

These reflections reveal that each of these teachers was affected by their reading in profound, yet different, ways. These three teachers' reflections reveal that they benefited from the opportunities provided for reflection, critique of course readings, and introspection. In her reflections on the readings, Linda notes that Vygotsky makes a good point when he states that, on the one hand, children need assistance for their development in learning, but on the other hand, they should be given an opportunity to learn by themselves sometimes so they can be independent in the future. From Au she determines that it would be a good idea to bring the students' home learning environment into the classroom and let students choose their own topics for writing. In her critiques of the course readings, Niko notes that the article by Delpit (1988) was an extremely powerful and relevant one that challenged her personally and opened her eyes to the realities and possible struggles that she will potentially encounter in her future teaching.

Each of the teachers began to take an introspective stance as they considered these readings. Irene concludes that Freire's ideologies would be useful in the implementation of anti-racist and moral education and that they would help to facilitate critical analysis and personal opinion in her classroom. As she contemplates the emergence of her own voice as a result of this course, she determines that she does not want her students to be little robots. Rather, she wants to allow them to talk, to have the space to experiment, to grow, to think for themselves, to pose questions, to look at themselves, to help themselves, to speak out for themselves, and to develop their own voice. Niko noted that as she thought about how these readings informed her teaching, the idea that grabbed her most intensely was the idea that, as teachers, we need to "turn ourselves inside out, giving up our own sense of who we are, and being willing to see ourselves in the unflattering light of another's angry gaze." Not only does she apply this to her teaching, but she also states that this is something that should be applied to any and every situation they encounter. As Linda contemplates the impact of the readings on her practice, she determines to implement several changes, including bringing the students' home learning environment into the classroom, allowing the students to use their mother-tongue in their learning, and encouraging the students to learn from each other.

Some linguistic indicators that these teachers' reflective and introspective activity were increasing included the use of statements that began with phrases like "I feel that these should be the corner-stones of my teaching," "My aim then is to bring my learners to an understanding of . . .," "I want to move them to a full potential of the future," "[This] was an extremely powerful article that challenged me personally and opened my eyes," "I never realized to what extent this idea holds true," "My thoughts about teaching in the inner-city have forced me to consider and think about . . .," "We need to take heed to the possibilities that the problems may reside in ourselves and not in the student," and "In reading [this article], I began to realize that . . ." As these teachers engaged in reflective introspection, they turned their "eye of critique" inward. And as they looked at themselves and their teaching practices, an abundant use of personal pronouns appeared in their texts—including increased uses of "me," "I," "my," "my own," and the self-inclusive "we" and "ourselves"—as indicators of an increased sense of personal involvement. It is evident that each of these teachers was beginning to take on a stance in opposition to linguistic gate-keeping. They were beginning to realize that it was their responsibility as teachers to aid in the rebuilding of the minds and hearts of the children who perhaps had once been told that they were inferior or unable to succeed. They were beginning to move toward liberating their students linguistically "helping them not to be robots," but to find their own voices.

Personal voice in teachers' final reflections

After many classroom hours spent in discussions, reading theoretical information, working with diverse students, and implementing practical strategies, bridges were formed between old perspectives and new information. Below, the teachers in this study provide final reflections on their expanded definitions of literacy, on the links that have been forged between theory and practice, on their continuing commitment to teaching, and on their emerging thoughts about literacy and teaching in diverse classrooms.

Irene's definition of literacy evolved from one that included the ability to "critically analyze, critically discuss, communicate visually, verbally, and via script," to one that "also takes into consideration the cultural background of the students." For Irene, the concept of literacy evolved to include "the ability to voice out your thoughts orally and . . . to interpret what your surroundings or environment look like. Knowing and realizing the imbalances of the society." Irene stated that this growth in her view of literacy was directly correlated with her attendance in this course, and now she feels that she "needs to make a stand for what she believes literacy is." When asked to write an essay about her most meaningful learning experience, Irene talked about this course as her most memorable learning experience. She wrote:

> Ironically my most important learning did not come about when I was an early learner but rather when I became an educator. It has not been a single event, but rather a series of events. It did not occur in the past but rather the present. What I am currently experiencing in this course is my most memorable learning experience. This whole course is having such a profound experience on me; it is changing me socially, emotionally and intellectually. I've learned that despite "the system," I can and want to change my teaching . . . since joining this course I was instilled with new ideas about my approach to tackle and develop literacy in my class. Yet, it frustrates me as well. I want to change and develop so fast, and yet, time pressures won't allow me to do all I want to do. I want more. I want to institute so much more, but time limits me. I say this is my most memorable learning experience because it has instilled in me the desire to keep learning, and I know that this will influence my little kiddies.

These statements illustrate that, for Irene, the course activities have had a phenomenal impact on her and have greatly helped her to gain the strength needed to voice her feelings and to go out and be an active agent of change for students of color in a system that desperately needs restructuring. Irene clearly indicates that she feels the course has armed her with the essentials she needs to go out into the system and "make waves." She confesses, "I know that as much as I don't want to make waves, waves are a part of the nature of events. Having recognized that I need to make a stand for what I believe literacy is, I am far more relaxed. The frustration has eased." Irene left my course with this commitment. As an early-career teacher, she went out into the South African school system determined to make the waves that were necessary to better the lives of her South African students. A few years later, I received the following letter from Irene:

> Dear Arnetha, It was such a wonderful surprise to hear from you. I have since moved from [my prior school appointment]. I left soon after our course ended. In finding my voice in your class, I also found my independence. My former school was a very safe environment, so safe that it would have stifled me eventually. That to me was too dangerous, I could not risk that . . . That year, I applied for another post and was

hired to bring transformation in the school . . . The school then was the last bastion of Apartheid. It certainly made for an extremely interesting ride. I was right there at the cutting edge of transformation . . . the children had been exposed to hate and prejudice . . . But through hard work, patience and lots of love we have brought the children together. It is wonderful to see them so close, when 7 months ago they would have nothing to do with each other. Similarly it has been a wonderful experience to see each child find their own voice. I am enjoying myself, but I must admit that it is quite stressful . . . [My school] is by no means an easy environment to work in, it is too fraught with prejudice and misunderstanding. I suppose that is to be expected since we are still trying to come to terms and understand all that has happened in this country, it still makes for an interesting learning experience. One thing is sure, I will never be quite the same after this experience. Thank you for your class! Regards and best wishes, Irene.

As she moved toward the end of the course, Irene shared her plans about how students should be treated in the classroom, that there should be, "Equality, mutual respect for all learners and their languages and culture." She also expressed her desire to create a multilingual and multicultural environment, "by respecting my learners, who they are and where they come from." Irene articulated that she felt that it was her responsibility as a teacher to go beyond simply standing at the front of the classroom and transferring knowledge from herself to the students. Irene felt that her role as a teacher is to be a "friend, confidant, counselor, social worker, mother, father, doctor and nurse." These statements illustrate how Irene is willing to move above and beyond the traditional South African role of teacher as linguistic gate-keeper to, as she put it, give all aspects of herself to her students.

As Niko talked and wrote about theory and her own teaching activities in the presence of her peers and supportive instructors, she began to challenge her preconceived notions about teaching diverse student populations and to stretch herself to consider new possibilities for her future teaching. As she contemplated theoretical issues related to teaching for diversity, and as she struggled to implement those theoretical notions in the context of her teaching projects and course activities, she voiced her changing perspectives in the language she used in classroom discussions, daily journals, and reflective essay writing. She writes:

At the beginning of this course, I defined a literate person as someone who has basic reading and writing skills in order to function in society. My revised version: A literate person is someone who can actively engage in reading materials such that critical thinking takes place along with active appreciation of new found knowledge. Where do I begin to comment in my growth as a result of this class? Even now as I write these words, there are so many unresolved dilemmas, contradictions, questions—and I am trying to live with the worries I've confronted as a student who is soon to be a teacher . . . I came into this course arrogant and self assured. Critical thinking had always been my forte; it has been my natural disposition to try and search for deeper meaning and deeper truths. I began with my personal essay about . . . what I wanted to do for the rest of my life. And in this way I began the course, with a love for literature, arrogance from acquired knowledge, and hope for a glorious future . . . Our class had engaging discussions on critical thinking, critical reading, communicating with students and lots of activities. And then I read an article that stated: "The life experiences of teachers stem from their beliefs and belief systems . . . these beliefs strongly affect the literacy practices a teacher may use . . ." I began to ask lots of questions . . . And from then on, my arrogance began to deflate. I began to realize my potential role within these students' lives. I was introduced to things I had never even considered. What if my students cannot read? How will they internalize this lack of skill? Who will they become as adults? How can I change this? How can I become the teacher I want to be? . . . I began trying to see through the student's eyes, trying to remember what it was like to be like them. The readings I have done for this class have elucidated cobwebs of half thoughts and have finished solutions that had begun in my head . . . In this way my thinking has evolved, going down various alleys of hypotheses, analyzing potential results, and choosing what to incorporate or not to incorporate from my new research into my future practice as a teacher . . . And one would think that exposure to such future scenarios of "what if" and "what to do next" would calm my anxieties. But . . . I am anxious about having been ignorant and insensitive to certain students . . . I am afraid to make the wrong moves just as I am excited to make the right one. But in the end, I take my future position . . . as a privilege to have the opportunity to help mold the wet clay that will one day become fine art . . . I do not see myself as an English teacher, but a teacher of life, an educator of human emotions, of human relationships, and human history. I believe the subject at question is not the literature, but the many diverse students that I will be teaching. It is their minds that I am exploring and trying to expand.

Niko's decision to engage interactively with the theory and activities that were planned for her in the course, to push the limits of her zone of comfort, to participate in the tutoring project, the face-to-face mentoring activities, as well as her own tutoring and peer counseling activities—these factors served as a catalyst that helped her to consider seriously the challenge of teaching diverse students which was displayed in (and revealed through) her developing discourse.

At the beginning of the course, Linda wrote that "A literate person is someone who has knowledge gained through education, oral [exchanges], and their social community." Her evolving definition of literacy included these points, but expanded to note that "Literacy occurs differently according to one's background. Children interpret certain issues according to their culture and their communities." In her final essay for the course, Linda, a student who came from a very strict, teacher-centered educational background, talks about the profound effect the course has had on her and how it influenced her to reject the traditional teacher role as linguistic gate-keeper:

> Dear Dr. Ball, Firstly I just want to thank you for coming here to S.A. I hope we will be seeing more of you. The few weeks that I have known you, I have changed totally. I feel as if I am a "born again teacher" meaning that my old thinking, methods and strategies of teaching have changed to new ones, more especially when I read the article by Au. I came here to this course with an unanswered question which is how do I deal with multi-lingualism in the classroom. You have answered them all. I never thought when teaching English to my pupils I should use their first language as the base. According to the old South African syllabus, the Head of the department did not allow us to do that. But now my perception has changed. And also after reading the article by Vygotsky, that has changed my perception about literacy. I used to dictate the work all the time. I told the students what assignments to go and do. But after I read this article, I told the students to give me some topics to write about. I guide them so they can become independent, to work without being guided . . . As a result of these articles you gave us I began to develop an interest in learning more about Teacher Research. My interest in teaching was crippled when I was retrenched [laid-off from work as an excess teacher] when I started teaching in 1988. I was teaching English Std 6, when I was told that English should be taught by an English speaker. Eventually, my case was taken up by the teachers' union. They wanted to take the matter to high court. The Department of Education threatened me by saying that, in the whole Republic of S.A., I would never be able to teach again. I dropped the charges, because I liked teaching. I still like it. After five months of not teaching I was employed. Since that incident in 1988, my self-esteem was taken away. My pride as a teacher was gone. I never had an interest in anything after that incident. I didn't want to improve my teacher's qualification since then, I felt "what was the point." I might be seen as useless again.Then I saw an advertisement for this course. I couldn't leave teaching because I know the children need me and I need them. That was the first step I took—to register for this course—after all I've gone through. So all in all, this course has brought back my confidence as a teacher. Because the course deals with problems I encounter in my classroom. I wish, Arnetha, may God be with me to get all the support I need to further my education for "dealing with the

ways of helping a learner." I will always remember you for the change you have done in my teaching career. May God be with you, and your family till we meet again. With Love, Linda

To this letter, Linda added the following specific plans for teaching in ways that are contrary to the role of "teacher as linguistic gate-keeper":

As the teacher, I would like my school to reach the top [highest] standard of learning. I would like to be the one who would motivate my pupils in seeing the importance of education. I would like to see my pupils achieve their goals in life, trying to reach them [internally]. They must let go of their bad habits, e.g. Gangsterism, dropping out early from school. I would like to be best example to them by acting as a good teacher not only in the classroom, but outside of the classroom as well. And I want the pupils to trust me, rely on me and on my part to dedicate my whole life to them . . . What I've learned as a teacher, is that I hold a child's future on my hands. I must make it a point that he becomes successful in his growing life. I might not be aware that I am the cause of dropouts in my school. For me to be successful in leading the child to the better future, I should know where he comes from and where he is going to. By "coming from" I mean his cultural and social background . . . Secondly, the child should be free to express his fears, expectations and goals so that I'll know where he's "heading to." As a teacher I think I should address the issues that make learning difficult for the child so that my teaching can be effective. For example, in one of my classes one student could not attend school regularly because she had to go and work in order to support her family, and that affected her studies. I called her mother and we discussed the problem and I suggested some other alternatives for making money. What was the surprise? The girl's progress improved not only by coming to school regularly, but also I think by seeing that the teacher is concerned about her. I show an interest in their lives, and I don't look down on them as they are seen in the location as "low people." I also want to instill a sense of pride in their culture, customs and language. I made them see the importance of their language first so that they can learn the second one after having mastered their first language. I told them, "I'm a Xhosa, I'm also not so good in English but I'm better than them, though I am still learning it. So let's learn it together." By doing that I'm trying to build up their confidence so that when they read in English no one laughs at each other if one pronounces the word wrongly. What has helped me a lot is this course. It has changed me so much. It's only now that I've noticed, that my students understand certain aspects according to the places where they come from. An example is when I was teaching "Discovery of Diamonds," I asked what is "urbanization" and I received different explanations, but not the correct ones. A good teacher does not only stick to the curriculum, she explores. One should take some of students' life experiences as part of learning. Sometimes seek their opinions on how they should be taught. Then, I'll make learning easier for them and fun . . . What I've experienced during my school days, most especially in high school, was that I wanted to leave school but I couldn't. All I could do was to become a teacher in order to make sure that the horrible things I encountered in school will never happen to any other child. I've learned not only to be a teacher, but to be everything that a child may need that would brighten up his future.

Discussion

In each case, these teachers have embarked upon the process of the development of a personal voice on issues related to the teaching and learning of their students. This development of personal voice is evident in the use of statements that began with words and phrases like "I can and want to change my teaching . . . since joining this course I was instilled with new ideas about my approach to tackle and develop literacy in my class," "In finding my voice in your class, I also found my independence," "Similarly it has been a wonderful experience to see each child find their own voice," "I began to realize my potential role within these students' lives," "I began trying to see through the student's eyes, trying to remember what it was like to be like them," "In this way my thinking has evolved," and "One thing is sure I will never be quite the same after this experience."

> Evidence of the development of teachers who began to actively resist the role of linguistic gate-keepers was clearly heard in the emerging voices of the teachers in my course. As Irene says: "This whole course is having such a profound experience on me; it is changing me socially, emotionally and intellectually. I've learned that despite 'the system,' I can and want to change my teaching . . . I know that as much as I don't want to make waves, waves are a part of the nature of events. Having recognized that I need to make a stand for what I believe literacy is, I am far more relaxed. The frustration has eased . . ."

Niko closes the course with these reflections that reveal her emerging voice:

> I came into this course arrogant and self assured . . . my arrogance began to deflate. I began to realize my potential role within these students' lives. I was introduced to things I had never even considered . . . How can I become the teacher I want to be? . . . I began trying to see through the student's eyes, trying to remember what it was like to be

like them . . . In this way my thinking has evolved . . . but, in the end, I take my future position . . . as a privilege to have the opportunity to help mold the wet clay that will one day become fine art . . . I believe the subject at question is not the literature [I teach] but the many diverse students that I will be teaching. It is their minds that I am exploring and trying to expand.

Linda closes the course with these words:

The few weeks that I have known you, I have changed totally. I feel as if I am a "born again teacher" meaning that my old thinking, methods and strategies of teaching have changed to new ones . . .

The voices of these teachers confirm that as teachers become metacognitively aware of a wide range of perspectives on literacies and teaching, many of them do, in fact, embark on a journey that moves them toward reflective, committed, and generative ideologies concerning language, literacies, and educational practice. These voices demonstrate some of the ways teachers use language to reveal their emerging personal philosophies and to reveal their rejection of the role of linguistic gate-keeper in the classroom. The rejection of this role becomes evident as they make conscious decisions to encourage their students to express their own opinions and voices, to become independent workers, critical thinkers, and students who are agents of change in a democratic global society.

Conclusion

When these teachers first entered my course, most of them freely admitted that they had given very little conscious consideration to issues of working as advocates for students from poor and marginalized backgrounds. During the course, teachers are confronted with the challenge of considering these issues through interpersonal and socially mediated forums, including individual and shared reflections on a range of related issues, written engagement with carefully designed prompts on these topics, and challenging discussions that cause them to consider these issues. Exposure to theoretical readings and practical activities take place during the course as a catalyst to engage teachers in oral and written conversations that can impact their thoughts and developing ideologies on these issues.

In this chapter, I have introduced rich examples from three teachers in the study that provide illustrations of how increased metacognitive levels, reflection, introspection, and critique can serve as a catalyst for generative thinking. Class discussions give way to the development of strategies that ultimately "explode" into generative plans of action. The teachers share insights about how these activities have impacted their development of commitment and the sense of empowerment they experience as they develop their own voices. According to

McElroy-Johnson (1993), teachers cannot help students to develop voice, unless they have a voice of their own. These teachers' stories, reflections, and insights reflect their development of voice as they contemplate becoming change agents in schools—a role very different from that of linguistic gate-keeper.

This chapter reported on a cross-national study that investigated the effectiveness of a course designed to facilitate the development of teachers committed to teaching culturally and linguistically diverse students. This work can help us to design teacher education programs that will prepare teachers of excellence for students in the African Diaspora.

In my analysis of the teachers' reflective writings, I noted how the teachers' perceptions of literacy changed and how, as these perceptions changed, so did their considerations about teaching diverse students. Not only was there an increase in expressions that indicated the development of metacognitive awareness, reflection, introspection, and critique, but there was also the articulation of specific action plans that served as an important indicator of developing voice and commitment—since commitment is defined as "the act of taking on the charge, obligation or trust to carry out some action or policy; to make a decisive moral choice that involves a person in a definite course of action" (Webster's Dictionary 1986).

In the midst of current discussions about the improvement of teacher education programs, little has been done to explore the use of linguistic and discourse analyses to gauge the effectiveness of programs designed to prepare teachers for changing school demographics. This study contributes to these discussions by presenting an analysis of teacher discourse as an investigative site. Using such an analysis, I explore how teachers' developing commitment is facilitated when intellectual activity is coupled with interactive participation in carefully designed classroom activities.

As a Black linguist, I bring an interpretation to observed practices steeped in my own cultural experience—practices that have been overlooked or not valued by researchers who bring Eurocentric perspectives and values. Through the use of descriptions, discourse analyses, and discussions of emerging themes in the writings of the teachers in this study, I demonstrate how the educational plans of teachers are influenced by their ideological stances and how, as these stances change through their participation in a strategically designed teacher education program, their classroom practices can change as well. Ultimately, through the implementation of such programs, linguistic gate-keeping in classrooms in South Africa and the US may become a thing of the past.

References

Au, K. (1994) "An expanded definition of literacy," in K. Au, *Literacy Instruction in Multicultural Settings*, New York: Harcourt Brace College Publishers, 20–34.

Bakhtin, M. (1981) *The Dialogic Imagination: Four Essays by M.M. Bakhtin* (ed. M. Holquist; trans. C. Emerson and M. Holquist), Austin, TX: University of Texas Press.

Bolster, A.S. (1983) "Toward a more effective model of research on teaching," *Harvard Educational Review*, 53: 294–308.

Bruner, J. (1985) "Narrative and paradigmatic modes of thought," in E. Eisner (ed.) *Learning and Teaching the Ways of Knowing*, Chicago, IL: National Society for the Study of Education, 97–115.

—— (1986) *Actual Minds, Possible Worlds*, Cambridge, MA: Harvard University Press.

Cazden, C. (1988) *Classroom Discourse: The Language of Teaching and Learning*, Portsmouth, NH: Heinemann.

Connelly, F.M. and Clandinin, D.J. (1985a) "Personal practical knowledge and the modes of knowing: relevance for teaching and learning," in E. Eisner (ed.) *Learning and Teaching the Ways of Knowing*, Chicago, IL: National Society for the Study of Education, 174–98.

—— (1985b) *Teachers as Curriculum Planners: Narratives of Experience*, New York: Teachers College Press.

—— (1990), "Stories of experience and narrative inquiry," *Educational Researcher*, 19 (5): 2–14.

Delpit, L. (1988) "The silenced dialogue: power and pedagogy in educating other people's children," *Harvard Educational Review*, 58 (3): 280–98.

Finnegan, W. (1986) *Crossing the Line*, New York: Harper and Row.

Franklin, J. and Moss, A. (1994) *From Slavery to Freedom*, 7th edition, New York: Alfred A. Knopf, Inc.

Freire, P. (1993) *Pedagogy of the Oppressed* (trans. M.B. Ramos), New York: Continuum.

Fultz, M. (1995) "African American teachers in the South, 1890–1940: powerlessness and the ironies of expectations and protest," *History of Education Quarterly*, 35 (4): 401–22.

Giroux, H. (1988) *Teachers as Intellectuals: Toward a Critical Pedagogy of Learning*, New York: Bergin and Garvey.

Goodenow, R. and White, A. (1981) *Education and the Rise of the New South*, Boston, MA: G.K. Hall and Co.

Gumperz, J. and Hymes, D. (eds) (1972) *Directions in Sociolinguistics: The Ethnography of Communication*, New York: Holt, Rinehart, and Winston.

Gutierrez, K., Larson, J., and Kreuter, B. (1995) "Cultural tensions in the scripted classroom: the value of the subjugated perspective," *Urban Education*, 29: 410–42.

Harris, V. (1992) "African-American conceptions of literacy: a historical perspective," *Theory into Practice*, 31 (4): 276–86.

Hartshorne, K. (1992). *Crisis and Challenge: Black Education 1910–1990*, Cape Town: Oxford University Press.

Hudelson, S. (1994) "Literacy development of second language children," in F. Genesee (ed.) *Educating Second Language Children: The Whole Child, the Whole Curriculum, the Whole Community*, New York: Cambridge University Press, 129–58.

Hymes, D. (1972) "Models of the interaction of language and social life," in J. Gumperz and D. Hymes (eds) *Directions in Sociolinguistics: The Ethnography of Communication*, New York: Holt, Rinehart, and Winston.

—— (1974) *Foundations in Sociolinguistics*, Philadelphia, PA: University of Pennsylvania Press.

Johnson, C.S. (1941) *Growing Up in the Black Belt: Negro Youth in the Rural South*, Washington, DC: American Council on Education.

Kallaway, P. (1984) *Apartheid and Education*, Johannesburg: Ravan Press.

Lightfoot, S.L. (1983) *The Good High School: Portraits of Character and Culture*, New York: Basic Books.

—— (1988) *Balm in Gilead: Journey of a Healer*, New York: Addison-Wesley.

McElroy-Johnson, B. (1993) "Teaching and practice: giving voice to the voiceless," *Harvard Educational Review*, 63 (1): 85–104.

Margo, R. (1990) *Race and Schooling in the South, 1880–1950: An Economic History*, Chicago, IL: University of Chicago Press.

Mehan, H. (1979) *Learning Lessons*, Cambridge, MA: Harvard University Press.

Mishler, E.G. (1986) "The analysis of interview-narratives," in T.R. Sarbin (ed.) *Narrative Psychology: The Storied Nature of Human Conduct*, New York: Praeger.

—— (1995) "Models of narrative analysis: a topology," *Journal of Narrative and Life History*, 5 (2), 87–123.

Mitchell, W.J.T. (1981) Foreword, in W.J.T. Mitchell (ed.) *On Narrative*, Chicago, IL: University of Chicago Press, vii–x.

Mncwabe, M. (1993) *Post-Apartheid Education*, London: University of America.

Moss, B. (ed.) (1994) *Literacy across Communities*, Cresskill, NJ: Hampton.

Novicki, M. (1991) "Interview: John Samuel: ending Apartheid education," *Africa Report*, May/June 1991, 18–22.

Phillips, S. (1972) "Participant structures and communicative competence: Warm Springs young adults in community and classroom," in C. Cazden, V. John, and D. Hymes (eds) *Functions of Language in the Classroom*, New York: Teachers College Press, 370–94.

Richard-Amato, P. and Snow, M. (eds) (1992) *The Multicultural Classroom: Readings for Content-area Teachers*, New York: Addison-Wesley.

Rist, R. (1996) "Color, class, and the realities of inequality," *Society*, 33 (3): 32–6.

Sinclair, J. and Coulthard, M. (1975) *Towards an Analysis of Discourse*, Oxford: Oxford University Press.

Southern Education Reporting Service (1961) *A Statistical Summary, State by State, of Segregation-Desegregation Activity Affecting Southern Schools from 1954 to Present, Together With Pertinent Data on Enrollment, Teachers, Colleges, Litigation, and Legislation*, Nashville, TN: SERS.

Street, B. (1993a) *Cross-cultural Approaches to Literacy*, Cambridge: Cambridge University Press.

—— (1993b) "The implications of the new literacy studies for the new South Africa," *Journal of Literacy Research*, 9 (2), Johannesburg: University of Witswaterstrand.

Tygesen, Peter (1991) "The ABC's of Apartheid," *Africa Report*, May/June 1991, 13–17.

Vygotsky, L. (1978) *Mind in Society: The Development of Higher Psychological Processes* (eds M. Cole, V. John-Steiner, S. Scribner, and E. Souberman), Cambridge, MA: Harvard University Press.

Waters, M. (1989) "An agenda for educating black teachers," *The Educational Forum*, 53 (3), 267–79.

Webber, T. (1978) *Deep Like the Rivers: Education in the Slave Quarter Community 1831–1865*, New York: W.W. Norton Company, Inc.

Webster's Third New International Dictionary Unabridged (1986), Springfield, MA: Merriam-Webster, Inc.

Woodson, C. (1930) *The Rural Negro*, New York: Russell and Russell.

Contributors

Hassana Alidou is Assistant Professor of Curriculum and Instruction and Coordinator of English as a Second Language and the International Program at Texas A & M University. She received her Bachelor's degree from the University of Niamey in Niger and holds a PhD in Linguistics and an Advanced Certificate in Gender Roles in International Development from the University of Illinois-Urbana. She has served as a visiting lecturer at several universities in Africa and Europe, and has fifteen years of work experience with international development agencies, including service as Technical Director of Bilingual Teacher Training Workshops sponsored by the German Foundation for International Development in Francophone Africa. Dr. Alidou's research and published articles focus on language and education policies, social justice, and postcolonial studies.

H. Samy Alim is a doctoral candidate in Educational Linguistics at Stanford University. He is also the developer and instructor of Stanford's linguistics course, "The Language of Hip Hop Culture," which focuses on discourse analysis. He is co-author of *Street Conscious Rap* with James G. Spady and Charles G. Lee (Philadelphia: Black History Museum Umum/Loh Publishers, 1999) and is current editor of *The Black Arts Quarterly*. Alim's dissertation research investigates stylistic variation and identity in schools and society from the dual perspective of quantitative sociolinguistics and linguistic anthropology.

Arnetha F. Ball is Associate Professor of Education at Stanford University, where she has taught for the past three years. Prior to that, she taught at the University of Michigan (1992–9) where she received an Outstanding Teaching Award in 1998. Her research interests focus on the oral and written literacies of culturally and linguistically diverse populations in South Africa and the US and on the development of successful pedagogies for teachers who work with students of African descent. Before entering the professoriate, she taught students at every educational level for over twenty-five years and was founder and Executive Director of Children's Creative Workshop, an early education center for students of color. She served as an Academic

Specialist for the United States Information Services Program in South Africa, taught in the Further Diploma in Education Program at the University of Cape Town and co-taught courses on multiliteracies and English methodologies in the teacher education program at Johannesburg College of Education. She has published widely, including numerous book chapters and journal articles in *Linguistics and Education, Applied Behavioral Science Review, Language Variation and Change,* and *Written Communication.* She is author of *Bakhtinian Perspectives on Language, Literacy and Learning* (with S. Freedman, New York: Cambridge University Press, in press) and *Literacies Unleashed: Reimagining the Possibilities for African American Students in the Composition Classroom* (with T. Lardner, Illinois: University of Illinois Press, in press). In 1997 Dr. Ball received the Richard Braddock Award (with Dr. Ted Lardner) for outstanding journal article of the year.

John Baugh is Professor of Education and Linguistics at Stanford University, where he joined the faculty in 1990 after having taught for ten years at the University of Texas. He is past President of the American Dialect Society and served as an inaugural member of the National Advisory Committee to the Social, Behavioral, and Economic Sciences Division of the National Science Foundation. His recent research on linguistic profiling has been featured on National Public Radio, *World News Tonight* (with Peter Jennings), *ABC 20/20 Downtown,* and the *Ananda Lewis Show.* His research studies the social stratification of linguistic diversity among low-income and language minority populations. His most recent books include *Out of the Mouths of Slaves: African American Language and Educational Malpractice* (Austin: University of Texas Press, 1999) and *Beyond Ebonics: Linguistic Pride and Racial Prejudice* (New York: Oxford University Press, 2000).

Awad El Karim M. Ibrahim is Assistant Professor in the Educational Foundations and Inquiry Program at Bowling Green State University. He previously taught at Bishop's University in Canada where he received the 2001 Teaching Award. He grew up in Sudan where he obtained his BA in French Linguistics. He holds Master's degrees from Canada's York University and Université de Montréal, and he received his PhD from the University of Toronto. He has published in a variety of academic journals, including the *TESOL Quarterly, Taboo,* and *Contact.* His research focuses on connections between race, language, culture, and identity politics. Dr. Ibrahim is author of the forthcoming book, *"Hey, Whassup, Homeboy? Becoming Black: Race, Language, Hip Hop Culture and the Politics of Identity in High School* (Toronto: University of Toronto Press, in press).

Sinfree Makoni is Associate Professor in Linguistics and Applied Language Studies at Pennsylvania State University. From 1999 to 2001 he was the DuBois-Mandela-Rodney Fellow at the University of Michigan, Ann Arbor. He is a native of Southern Africa, did his undergraduate work in Ghana and received his PhD in Applied Linguistics from the University of Edinburgh, Scotland. He has extensive professional experience in Southern Africa, including Associate Professor of Language and Literature at the University of Cape Town, South Africa. He is former President of the Southern African Applied Linguistics Association and an Executive Board member of the International Applied Linguistics Association. He has published widely in the areas of applied linguistics and language issues in health. Dr. Makoni's recent co-edited books include *Aging in Africa: Sociolinguistic and Anthropological Approaches* (with Koen Stroeken, London: Ashgate, 2002), *Freedom and Discipline: Essays in Applied Linguistics from Southern Africa* (with Stan and Elaine Ridge, Bahri, India, 2001), and *Language and Institutions in Africa* (with Nkonko Kamwangamalu, Cape Town: Centre for Advanced Studies of African Society, 2000).

Nkhelebeni Phaswana is Senior Lecturer in Linguistics at the University of Venda where he also served as Chair of African Languages and Linguistics. He grew up in Venda in South Africa's Northern Province and received the BA (Honors) and the BEd from the University of Venda and Master's degrees from South Africa's University of Stellenbosch and the University of Cape Town. He holds a PhD in English Language Studies from Michigan State University. He has presented papers at international conferences in and outside of South Africa, including Namibia, Eritrea, the US, and Canada. He is an established writer and past Chair of the Tshivenda Writers Association. He has published widely in his mother tongue, Tshivenda, including *Tshi do lilwa* (a novel, Johannesburg: Scorpion Publishers, 2001), *Ipfi sogani* (poetry, Pietersburg: NAM Publishers, 1987), *Tsimbe ya vhutshilo* (short stories, Johannesburg: MacMillan Boleswa, 1994), and *Kha ri shele mulenzhe* (a grammar textbook series, Johannesburg: Maskew Miller Longman, 1996). Some of Dr. Phaswana's literary works are required reading in South African primary and secondary schools.

Velma Pollard is a retired Senior Lecturer in Language Education at the University of the West Indies in Mona, Jamaica. Her major research interests are creole languages of the Anglophone Caribbean, the language of Caribbean literature and Caribbean women's writing, and she has published articles in these areas in local and international journals. Other publications include *From Jamaican Creole to Standard English: A Handbook for Teachers* (New York: Caribbean Research Center, Medgar Evers College [CUNY], 1994), and *Dread Talk: The Language of Rastafari* (Mona, Jamaica: University of the West Indies, 1994, 2000). An established writer, Pollard has published three collections of poetry, including *The Best Philosophers I Know Can't Read and Write* (London: Mango Publishing, 2001); a novel, *Homestretch* (Harlow: Longman, 1994); and short fiction, including the collection *Considering Woman* (London: The Woman's Press, 1989). Her novella, *Karl and Other Stories* (Harlow: Longman Group, UK, 1994), won the Casa de las Americas Prize in 1992.

Zaline M. Roy-Campbell is a researcher and scholar who has worked on language issues in different parts of Africa and the Caribbean. One of her primary interests is understanding ways in which the language of instruction can empower or disenfranchise students. She is author of *Empowerment through Language: The African Experience—Tanzania and Beyond* (Trenton, NJ: Africa World Press, 2001) and co-author of *Language Crisis in Tanzania: The Myth of English versus Education* (with Martha Qorro, Dar es Salaam, Tanzania: Mkuki ny Nyota, 1997*)*. She is currently an independent educational consultant based in Syracuse, New York.

Geneva Smitherman (aka Dr. G.) is University Distinguished Professor of English at Michigan State University, where she has been since 1989 after serving on the faculty of Harvard University and Wayne State University. She is also founder and Director of "My Brother's Keeper" Program, a male mentoring program for middle school students at Malcolm X Academy in the city of Detroit. From 1977 to 1979, she was the chief advocate and expert witness for the children in *King* (the "Black English" Federal court case in the US). She is internationally recognized for her research and publications in African American Studies and on African American Language/US Ebonics. Her current research focuses on Language Planning-Policy in South Africa. She has published several books and numerous articles, including the classic book, *Talkin and Testifyin: The Language of Black America* (Boston: Houghton Mifflin, 1977) and *Black Talk: Words and Phrases from the Hood to the Amen Corner* (Boston and New York: Houghton Mifflin, 1994, 2000). In 2001, she received the David H. Russell Research Award for her recent book, *Talkin That Talk: Language, Culture and Education in African America* (London: Routledge, 2000). Dr. Smitherman is a scholar-activist with a lifelong commitment to struggles for language rights.

Arthur K. Spears is Professor of Anthropology and a member of the doctoral faculty in Linguistics and Anthropology at the City University of New York. His research focuses on African American English, pidgin, and creole languages, including Haitian and other French creoles, language and education, and race and ideology. He is founder and the first editor of *Transforming Anthropology* (journal of the Association of Black Anthropologists). His publications include the ground-breaking article, "The Black English semi-auxiliary *come*" (published in *Language*, 1982), "African-American language use: ideology and so-called obscenity," published in *African-American English* (eds. Mufwene *et al.*, London: Routledge, 1998) and "Vers un modèle des systèmes temps—mode—aspect dans trois langues creoles" (*Etudes Créoles*, 1997). He has appeared on numerous radio and television programs, including the BBC's *The Story of English*, discussing creole languages, Black English/Ebonics, language and education, and controversial vocabulary such as the "N-word." Dr. Spears is editor of *Race and Ideology: Language, Symbolism, and Popular Culture* (Detroit: Wayne State University Press, 1999) and co-editor of *The Structure* *and Status of Pidgins and Creoles* (Amsterdam: John Benjamins, 1997) (with D. Winford).

Donald Winford is Professor of Linguistics at Ohio State University where he has taught for the past fourteen years. Prior to that, he taught at the University of the West Indies, Trinidad (1972–88). His primary research interests include sociolinguistics, particularly Variationist Theory, Contact, and Creole Linguistics, with focus on Caribbean creoles, and African American English. He has published widely, including journal articles in *Language, Linguistics, Lingua, Language in Society, American Speech,* and *the International Journal of the Sociology of Language.* His books include *Predication in Caribbean English Creoles* (Philadelphia: John Benjamins, 1993), *An Introduction to Contact Linguistics* (Oxford, Blackwell, in press), and co-edited volumes, including *Focus and Grammatical Relations in Creoles* (with Frank Byrne, Amsterdam: John Benjamins, 1993), *The Structure and Status of Pidgins and Creoles* (with Arthur Spears, Amsterdam: John Benjamins, 1997), and *Verb Phrase Patterns in Black English and Creoles* (with Walter Edwards, Detroit: Wayne State University Press, 1991). Dr. Winford is past President of the Society for Caribbean Linguistics (1998–2000) and current editor of *The Journal of Pidgin and Creole Languages.*

Index

Abrahams, R.D. 27, 32
Adorno, Theodor 62
Afolayan, A. 87
Africa: Francophone: alternative schools
106; educational policy and issues
105–10; emigration to Canada 170–1;
experimental bilingual schools 110–13;
ideology and historicity 24–7;
mainstream French schools 107–10;
multilingualism 2; reforming 113–15;
rural and urban differences 107;
structure of education 103–5;
African American English/Language: and
AAVE 22; African heritage 41;
common features of syntax and
phonology 46; cultural consciousness of
53–5; and liberation 40–2; stylistic
variation 42–5
African American Vernacular English
(AAVE) 21; autonomy and ideology
27–30; features of 22; grammar 25, 28;
identity politics 14–15; methodology
24; and social control 32–5; status of
11–12, 30–2; style-shifting 158
African Americans: culturally distinct 27
African languages: "curse of Babel" 93–4;
disinvention 145–6; domestic domains
96; in education 86–8; heritage from
41; interconnections 143–8;
misinvention of 135–42; mixed forms
143–4; new visions 97–9; orthography
115; political discussion and planning
97; power and terminology of 84–6;
"purity" 148; scientific and technical
terminology 86, 89, 93, 96–7;
standardization and harmonization
94–7; tri-lingual model of education
95–6; value in Southern Africa 91–3

African National Congress (ANC):
education policies 188; language policy
121–2, 123–5, 126–7
African Teachers Association of South
Africa (ATASA) 120
Afrikaans language 93, 96, 117, 132;
apartheid period 117–20; Black South
Africans object to 120; divergence from
Dutch 118; mixed forms 143, 146–7;
official documents 128–9; political
ideology 123–4
Alexander, Neville 95, 118
Alidou, Hassana 13; "Language policies
and language education in
Francophone Africa" **103–15**
Alim, H. Samy 7, 9, 12; "We are the
streets" **40–55**
Alzheimer's disease 6
Ambatchew, Michael 91
Amharic language 91
Anderson, Elijah 51
Angola 91, 94; Portuguese language
92
"ank" and "ang" 46
Arabic language 182; in Francophone
Africa 105
Asmara Declaration: *Against All Odds* xiii
Au, K. 192, 203
autonomy: and ideology 27–30

Baby Madison 51
Bakhtin, M.M. 181, 182, 193
Baldwin, James 60
Ball, Arnetha F. 7, 14, 15; "US and South
African teachers' developing
perspectives on language and literacy"
186–212
Bamgbose, Ayo 85, 87; African

221